The Right to Higher Education

The Right to Higher Education

A Political Theory

CHRISTOPHER MARTIN

OXFORD
UNIVERSITY PRESS

OXFORD
UNIVERSITY PRESS

Oxford University Press is a department of the University of Oxford. It furthers the University's objective of excellence in research, scholarship, and education by publishing worldwide. Oxford is a registered trade mark of Oxford University Press in the UK and certain other countries.

Published in the United States of America by Oxford University Press
198 Madison Avenue, New York, NY 10016, United States of America.

© Oxford University Press 2022

All rights reserved. No part of this publication may be reproduced, stored in a retrieval system, or transmitted, in any form or by any means, without the prior permission in writing of Oxford University Press, or as expressly permitted by law, by license, or under terms agreed with the appropriate reproduction rights organization. Inquiries concerning reproduction outside the scope of the above should be sent to the Rights Department, Oxford University Press, at the address above.

You must not circulate this work in any other form and you must impose this same condition on any acquirer.

Library of Congress Cataloging-in-Publication Data
Names: Martin, Christopher, author.
Title: The right to higher education : a political theory / Christopher Martin.
Description: New York : Oxford University Press, [2022] | Includes bibliographical references and index.
Identifiers: LCCN 2021036253 (print) | LCCN 2021036254 (ebook) | ISBN 9780197612910 (Hardback) | ISBN 9780197612927 (updf) | ISBN 9780197612941 (Online) | ISBN 9780197612934 (ePub)
Subjects: LCSH: Educational equalization. | Education, Higher. | Education, Higher—Aims and objectives. | College attendance. | Education and state. | Right to education. | Educational sociology.
Classification: LCC LC213 .M376 2021 (print) | LCC LC213 (ebook) | DDC 378—dc23
LC record available at https://lccn.loc.gov/2021036253
LC ebook record available at https://lccn.loc.gov/2021036254

DOI: 10.1093/oso/9780197612910.001.0001

1 3 5 7 9 8 6 4 2

Printed by Integrated Books International, United States of America

And oh, oh oh
Oh ain't it going well?
And oh, oh oh oh
But it's so hard to tell

It's like everything you never said
But always meant to say
It's like everything you never did
And did it anyway

But in between the morning and the evening light
It's how the days go by
In between the morning and the evening light
Oh don't the stars look nice
British Sea Power, "Like a Honeycomb"

A second exception to the doctrine that individuals are the best judges of their own interest, is when an individual attempts to decide irrevocably now, what will be best for his interest at some future and distant time. The presumption in favour of individual judgment is only legitimate, where the judgment is grounded on actual, and especially on present, personal experience; not where it is formed antecedently to experience, and not suffered to be reversed even after experience has condemned it. When persons have bound themselves by a contract, not simply to do some one thing, but to continue doing something for ever or for a prolonged period, without any power of revoking the engagement, the presumption which their perseverance in that course of conduct would otherwise raise in favour of its being advantageous to them, does not exist; and any such presumption which can be grounded on their having voluntarily entered into the contract, perhaps at an early age, and without any real knowledge of what they undertook, is commonly next to null.
J.S. Mill, *Principles of Political Economy*, 1871, Book V, Chapter XI

Contents

Permissions ix
Acknowledgments xi

Introduction: Changing the Conversation About
Higher Education 1
The Concept of Higher Education 5
Two Challenges to the Right to Education 7
The Normative Weight Problem 8
The Paternalistic Aims Problem 9
Overview of the Argument 10
Conclusion 13

1. Values and Aims of Higher Education 15
   The De Facto Value of Higher Education 18
   Rethinking the De Facto Value of Higher Education 27
   Conclusion 39

2. Citizenship as an Aim of Higher Education 41
   The Liberal Argument for Compulsory Civic Education 43
   The Liberal Argument for Higher Civic Education 47
   Higher Civic Education, Autonomy, and Convergence 52
   Higher Civic Education as Vocational Education 58
   Conclusion 67

3. Adulthood and the Right to Education 69
   Personal Autonomy and the Right to Basic Education 70
   The Political Conception of the Person and
     Adult Citizens 74
   Adulthood and the Value of Education 83
   Conclusion 89

4. The Right to Higher Education 91
   The Political Responsibilities of Institutions 92
   Higher Education and the Basic Structure 94

Liberty-Maximizing Justice 103
Liberty-Maximizing Justice and the "Fixed" Values of
   the University 106
Autonomy-Supporting Knowledge and Educational
   Institutions 114
Conclusion 121

5. **The Right to Higher Education and Political Authority** 125
   The Necessity (and Limits) of Political Authority Over
      Higher Education 126
   Anti-Perfectionism and Educational Authority 131
   Perfectionism and Educational Authority 135
   Liberty-Maximizing Educational Authority 142
   Applying Liberty-Maximizing Authority to
      Higher Education 149
   Conclusion 152

6. **The Right to Higher Education and the Problem of Unequal Benefits** 155
   Why the Distribution of Benefits and Burdens
      (Still) Matters 156
   The Socioeconomic Argument for Higher
      Education Funding 158
   The Liberty-Maximizing Argument for Higher
      Education Funding 163
   The Right to Higher Education and Unequal Benefits 171
   Conclusion 185

7. **What Should the Right to Higher Education Look Like?** 187
   The Argument Revisited 188
   Toward a Normative Stage Theory of Higher Education 192
   Social Forms, Expensive Tastes, and Ideal Institutions 205
   Conclusion 218

Notes 219
Works Cited 237
Index 259

Permissions

"Like a Honeycomb"
Lyrics by Yan Scott Wilkinson
Lyrics cited with permission BMG Rights Management (UK). Lyrics from "Like a Honeycomb" taken from the "Open Season" LP by British Sea Power released on Rough Trade Records.

Elements from Chapter One and Chapter Six were adapted from Martin, C. (2016). Should students have to borrow? *Impact, 2016*(23), 1–37.

Elements in Chapter Five were adapted from Martin, C. (2018). Political authority, personal autonomy and higher education. *Philosophical Inquiry in Education, 25*(2), 154–170.

Elements in Chapter Six were adapted from Martin, C. (2017). Should the public pay for higher education? Equality, liberty, and educational debt. *Theory and Research in Education, 15*(1), 38–52.

The author would like to thank these journals for permission to adapt these materials in the form that they are offered here.

Acknowledgments

This book has been the realization of a self-determined goal that I've been plugging away at for a long time, and I have been very fortunate to have benefited from a great deal of support along the way.

The philosophy of education is a valuable social practice in its own right, one defined by the generosity, kindness, and collegiality of the people that make it possible. Many thanks to the Canadian Philosophy of Education Society for their invitation to share material from the book as part of their Early Career Invited Lecture series, as well as to Michael Geiss for the opportunity to share an overview of the project at the University of Zurich. I also thank Judith Suissa and Tristan McCowan, both of whom organized opportunities for me to share early chapters at the London Institute of Education. Thanks to Lauren Bialystock and her "Applied Ethics in Higher Education" seminar students at the University of Toronto for their incisive engagement on issues of student debt, university admissions, and justice. And I also would like to thank audiences at conferences and talks hosted by the North American Association for Philosophy and Education, the Philosophy of Education Society of Great Britain, the Philosophy and Theory of Higher Education Society, the University of British Columbia, and Memorial University of Newfoundland.

I was supported by institutions and generous mentoring. The seeds of the book's argument were planted when I was given the opportunity to contribute to the Philosophy of Great Britain's IMPACT publication series on the topic of student debt. I benefited tremendously from the guidance of Michael Hand, who serves as editor of this series. The critical attention he brought to that project redounded on the book many times over. I also thank the Okanagan School of Education at the University of British Columbia for granting me a research leave to work on this project. I am also extremely grateful to both the Center for Ethics and Education at Wisconsin-Madison and the Spencer Foundation for research grants that enabled me to carry out the work. The Center's current Director, Harry Brighouse, was key to this project in a number of respects that are not easily condensed in an acknowledgment. He encouraged me to continue with the book at a crucial stage, not to mention providing incisive critical feedback on an earlier draft of the manuscript (along with Kailey Mullane). Charitable reading and critical feedback are a rare and precious thing, and both Harry and Kailey provided them in spades.

I was lucky to work with two fantastic research assistants: Andrew Pulvermacher and Anya Goldin. Anya provided editorial support on the earliest versions of the first three chapters and found a number of research papers that helped me think through the argument. In addition to his research support, Andrew was an indispensable interlocutor during our weekly meetings. His excellent questions led to many important additions to the book.

There are a number of other people who also provided feedback and encouragement at various stages of the work who deserve thanks. In no particular order: Sarah Stitzlein, David O'Brien, Jennifer Morton, Nicholas Tanchuk, Walter Okshevsky, Phillip Cook, and Ross Hickey. Thanks also to the band, British Sea Power, for the permission to use the band's lyrics as part of the book's epigraph as well as their manager, David Taylor, for facilitating that process.

Thanks also to my many friends who flourish in worlds far removed from academic life but who always showed an interest in higher education, its aims, and other topics related to the book's argument. Your interest and willingness to engage gifted me with the energy to keep plugging away at it.

Thanks to Lucy Randall and Hannah Doyle at Oxford University Press for the care and discernment they brought to the manuscript over the course of its development. It means a great deal to know that your work is in good and trusted hands.

Nothing that I do in this life that has any value could be at all possible without Vanessa Martin and her enduring support and patience. This is also for Charlie and Lauren Martin, both of whom are young (9 and 6) but wise in heart and who supported me in all the best ways, from informing me when they thought that the writing seemed to be going well (i.e., "you are working on it a lot"), to retelling me stories from *The Hobbit* while I cleared out printer jams, to asking questions like, "Dad, why do you have to use so many *words* to say something that's so simple?"

Thanks also to my father, John Martin, who has been dialoging with me on philosophical questions since as far back as I can remember.

And finally, to Mom. You could not be here to see this project to its end, but I always write in the hope that you can be proud of what I'm trying to say. This one's for you.

Introduction

Changing the Conversation About Higher Education

All citizens in a free and open society should have an unconditional right to higher education. Such an education should be costless for the individual and open to everyone regardless of talent. A readiness and willingness to learn should be the only qualification. It should offer opportunities that benefit citizens with different interests and goals in life. And it should aim, as its foundational moral purpose, to help citizens from all walks of life live better, freer lives. Anything less is a dereliction of the liberal state's obligation to its citizens.

Liberal societies are largely on board with the idea of compulsory education as a basic right. That there are important social and individual benefits to be gained from ensuring that everyone gets a decent basic education is a widely accepted view. We are well practiced at singing the praises of educational goods for children, in particular, enumerating the many ways in in which it will help them become better citizens, more productive workers, and all-around better people. We may disagree about the extent to which such an education should be managed by the state, what its curriculum should look like, and how well it should be resourced. But few people in liberal democratic societies believe that education is something that *should not* be provided to all citizens.

Curiously enough, this educational bonhomie quickly evaporates when we turn to the question of higher education. To be sure, we often point to the importance of higher education for society.

The Right to Higher Education. Christopher Martin, Oxford University Press. © Oxford University Press 2022. DOI: 10.1093/oso/9780197612910.003.0001

Economists emphasize its role in economic growth. College and university presidents talk up the contributions of higher education to democratic citizenship. But the conversation about education also changes in palpable ways. We see more talk about competition for university places, elite admissions, and SAT scores. Focus shifts to parsing out the differences between the benefits of education for the individual and the burdens of public financial support for such an education. Problems of status, stratification, and selectivity capture as much, if not more, of our attention than the value and quality of what these institutions aim to achieve.

There is, of course, quite a bit of rhetoric about the right to higher education, both in the general public and in some public policy circles. This talk is sometimes couched in debates about debt forgiveness, or widening participation, and other policy goals. But the claim that higher education is a right is often an unjustified assertion used to gain rhetorical ground in such disputes without any obvious sense in which there is, or really ought to be, a right to higher education. In fact, it is probably fair to say that those who think a lot about higher education do not believe that citizens should have a right to higher education. In order to see why, consider one very prominent debate: student loans. It's not unusual to hear people claim that student fees should be lowered because access to higher education is a right. This is an undeniably appealing position. It seems intuitively unfair that ambitious young people should have to take on large amounts of debt in order to get a decent education after high school. But what advocates of a debt-free higher education seem to miss is that not everyone is admitted, some higher education institutions are obscenely costlier and confer far greater socioeconomic benefits to some graduates than other institutions, and many citizens prefer not to attend at all. And yet, when we say that higher education should be free we really mean that *everyone* should pay, in the sense that the state should foot the bill with our public money. This means that in order for higher education to be free for the individual the state must require non-attendees to support, through taxation, the attendance of those who do. This *also* seems unfair.

My point is that the move from educational provision for children to educational provision for adults marks a strange transformation in the public conversation about its value and importance: from one about how it can improve the lives of all individuals, to one preoccupied with fairness, competition, merit, dessert, personal responsibility, and the sharing of benefits and burdens. And this is, unfortunately, an all too understandable transformation. Compulsory education is far from perfect. But it's at least animated by the idea that everyone can go and everyone can benefit.

We don't talk about higher education in this way at all. We are more at ease in saying that some people are sufficiently talented to benefit from a higher education while others are not. And we've built elaborate regimes of testing, financing, and admissions in order to rationalize this approach.

It's therefore understandable why some critics believe that higher education has become just one more way for the already advantaged to distance themselves from those who are not. Some have even suggested that higher education has played a direct causal role in the political divide emerging in democratic countries such as the United States, sorting citizens into those who go to university and those who do not (Bishop, 2009). These critics are on to something. And yet, my view is that this transformation in the conversation, even when it trains its attention to matters of justice and fairness, does more to reinforce existing inequalities in higher education than it does remedy them. And this is because a public preoccupied with the search for distributive perfection of the higher education system—mitigating the injustices of that system by making it more genuinely meritocratic, less discriminatory, more diverse—misses the forest for the trees. It is far too invested in tinkering with a system that fails to achieve what it really ought to achieve and, in so doing, underestimates the extent to which that system fails to make society better for everyone.

My argument is that a closer look at the value of education in a free and open society reveals that many of the distributive problems we see in higher education today can be attributed, fundamentally, to the failure to recognize higher education as an individual right. Egalitarian concerns about higher education—its undeniable stratifying effects, its valorization of elite success, its exclusion of those less fortunate—weigh so heavily on our conscience that it is hard to set aside these concerns long enough to fully consider this possibility.

I share many of these egalitarian concerns. However, I think we are better advised to think about the justice and fairness of higher education in terms of the positive potential it can have for any citizen's life instead of, say, pressing for greater inclusion just for those who are aiming for upward social mobility and elite institutions. I think that that latter approach, while morally laudable, is conceptually short-sighted. Instead of a just and fair higher education system designed specifically for the "best" of us, we need a vision of higher education for the rest of us (or, more accurately, all of us). We need a conception of higher education that is *also* for citizens who are not necessarily going to crush the SAT, who may not have fabulous reference letters by esteemed members of the scholarly community close at hand, and who may not have had the opportunity to supplement their personal statements with volunteer trips abroad. We must extend our educational bonhomie to adulthood and take a serious look at what a higher education intended for all citizens can and should look like.

In this book I take an approach that I think can help us think through this possibility. Instead of starting with the higher education systems that we have, I begin from a different place: *if* higher education were a right, what would it have to look like, both in terms of its aims and how it structures opportunities for citizens to benefit from these aims? *Then* we can ask if a system of higher education founded on such a right is a desirable and legitimate feature of a liberal society.

The advantage of this approach, I think, is that it allows us to temporarily put to the side some of the distributive worries that (rightly) inform debate and discussion about the higher education systems we have. To turn back to debates over student financing, for example: a focus on the fair distribution of socioeconomic benefits and burdens of a higher education appears to rule against full public funding for reasons I have briefly sketched out, earlier. But a focus on the fair distribution of socioeconomic benefits tends to get in the way of an even more egalitarian possibility: that higher education is something to which all citizens are entitled. That is to say, what makes full public funding of higher education unjust or unfair is not the unequal benefits that such a funding regime might bring about (where the less well-off pay to boost the socioeconomic advantages of the already well-off) but that less well-off citizens are being asked to support a system of education that they are, in many cases, told that they are not qualified to, or deserve to, partake in.

Approaching the problem in this way, I believe, reveals that higher education is dramatically out of step with the social vision of a liberal democratic society. And the corrective—while requiring some philosophical argumentation to work out—is really quite simple: we need to stop allocating higher education to some, and allocate it to all who choose to take it up. Instead of picking over the same old bones of resource scarcity, equality of opportunity, and merit, we should first focus our discussion on what higher education can do for all individual citizens, and work out the appropriate distributive convictions from there. Higher education, I argue, ought to be a right.

The Concept of Higher Education

One reason why it may seem counter-intuitive to think about higher education as a right is because of the many different meanings that we can ascribe to the term. Are we talking about the right to attend

Cambridge, for example? The problem with the term "higher education" is that it projects different, but often very specific, institutional images of what we are claiming that citizens have a right *to* depending on the audience.

These are images that need to be put to the side. There is a cautionary tale in what the great sociologist of higher education, Martin Trow, called "The Robbins Trap" (1989). Trow is referring to the U.K.'s landmark Robbins Report. This report charted the future expansion of British higher education. But the problem, Trow argues, is that this model of higher education expansion was based on a fairly narrow and elite institutional conception of its values and aims. It takes Oxford and Cambridge and aspires to make them universal. Such a picture insists on resource-intensive delivery and rigorous admissions in order prop up "elite quality." But this, we discover, puts a tight lid on expansion. As Trow puts it:

> The Robbins Report was a powerful conception . . . of how to expand Britain's elite higher education through liberal instruments and traditional processes, without having to surrender the basic values and assumptions on which its elite forms of higher education were and are based . . . And that is why Robbins was a trap, because it promised growth, and indeed delivered growth, without creating the structural or normative conditions for continued growth and development toward mass higher education. It carried the system right up to the ceiling of elite higher education . . . and that is where it has been stuck since. Indeed the system stopped growing just about the time when the older relationship between higher education and the state began to break down, and the system entered its present crisis of governance, autonomy and management. (p. 62)

I'll revisit Trow's ideas in more detail in chapter 7, where I show how his own account of higher education can benefit from the rights perspective that I defend. But the key lesson to draw from the

Robbin's Trap is that the right to higher education, if there is indeed such a right, cannot be inferred through an appeal to the values and aims of the traditional university. These values and aims may well be a necessary part of the picture, as I argue later, but it is certainly not all of it.

What this means for my argument is that, while I use the term "higher education," I do so in an institutionally agnostic fashion. I see the term "higher education" as a placeholder for whatever educational provisions we think should be typically reserved for citizens after their compulsory education is complete. The full picture of what a right to higher education should look like, in policy and practice, depends on its justification. Only then can we can start digging into the institutional details and identify the various ways in which our current institutional arrangements may fall short. In this spirit, it might be helpful for some readers to replace the term "higher education" for the less common "post-compulsory education" because it makes clearer that we are simply referring to something beyond the completion of compulsory/basic schooling.

Two Challenges to the Right to Education

I have suggested that our prevailing anxiety about the distributive unfairness of the higher education systems we have shifts needed attention away from a more fundamental reassessment of its values and aims. While some of this anxiety is surely motivated by broader concerns about wealth and income inequality, it would not be quite right to suggest that this is the *only* thing getting in the way. There are (at least) two conceptual difficulties in justifying the right to higher education, even *in principle*. And if we cannot make a principled argument for the right to higher education, the assertion of a "right to higher education" may indeed be a rhetorical move, only. Meeting these two challenges serves as a backdrop informing the major steps of my argument. More specifically, the right to higher education needs to contend with the what I call the *normative weight problem* and the *paternalistic aims problem*.

The Normative Weight Problem

One way to justify the claim that people have a right to something is to show that access to that thing is fundamental to their interests. It may be essential to their dignity, their human functioning, their welfare, and so on. The right to compulsory education works this way. We can say that all citizens need a basic level of education in order to participate fully in the economy, choose their own path in life, or have a strong voice in a democracy.

The normative weight problem comes to light when we try to extend this approach to higher education in order to justify it as a right. The more crucial we claim that higher educational goods are for citizens, the more plausible it is to judge that these goods should be allocated through the compulsory system where all citizens, with few exceptions, are obligated to attend. That is to say, the "weightier" the claim about the value of education, the less plausible it is to think that this value should be promoted through a higher education system as a matter of right.

Consider: if one were to say that citizens have a right to higher education because education is crucial for equal citizenship, why would we extend this responsibility to the higher education system where access is voluntary? If abilities related to effective citizenship are something that everyone has a pressing need to cultivate then we should make this a focus for a basic education, not a post-compulsory one. This is especially if we are committed to the ideal of *equal* citizenship. Otherwise, we would have a system where everyone gets citizenship education, and a select few get citizenship+. In short, any claim that the goods of higher education are so valuable that citizens should be entitled to them must explain why it would not be better to make these goods available to all through a compulsory education.

The normative weight problem says that any argument for the right to higher education "sinks" under the seriousness of its own claim, becoming an argument in support of a compulsory education, instead. I plot a route around this problem by arguing that citizens have interests that require support through a basic education, but that the end of a basic education does not mean that citizens no longer benefit from that interest being supported or facilitated by educational goods. Compulsory education sets the foundations for this interest; post-compulsory education ensures that all citizens can build something worthwhile on those foundations.

The Paternalistic Aims Problem

The justification of a right also requires that we show that the interests that this right protects is one shared between all citizens regardless of their individual differences. Another way of saying this is that the interests that support rights-claims are objective in the sense that they are shared by all citizens. And again, this kind of argument is highly plausible when we defend the right to basic education. For example, we can say that all citizens, regardless of their hopes for the future, should be literate, be able to earn a decent living, be free to choose their own future, and participate in democracy. These are (hopefully) non-controversial ideas.

The paternalistic aims problem comes in when we try to push this argument into the world of post-compulsory education. Paternalism makes sense when we are dealing with children. They do not always know what is in their best interests, and so one task of an education system is to decide *for children* what they need to know. Citizens in a post-compulsory system, however, are adults, and we tend to think that adults are in a position to make their own decisions about what is in their best interests.

And yet, a right to higher education should, as I have said, be founded on some objective values and aims. They are values and aims that citizens *should* desire from a higher education regardless of what any individual citizen happens to want from a higher education. The consequence is a conception of higher education that takes a paternalistic approach to their interests. It knows what is in any student's best interests better than the student knows. For example, if higher education is a right because it rescues students from their "false consciousness," students who receive a higher education should be educated in such a way that they are liberated from their false view of the world irrespective of what they want to get out of such an education.

The paternalistic aims problem says that any argument for the right to higher education can only succeed by insisting that adult citizens are not in a position to determine their own educational priorities. I address this problem by arguing that the reasons any citizen has for receiving a higher education are logically connected to the free pursuit of a good life. By this I mean that the aim of higher education—and of liberal institutions more generally—is to support the freely chosen goals of all citizens, regardless of their particular ideas about the good life. The extent to which any one citizen will require such support will vary depending on their aims and goals but the infrastructure of that life-long support ought to be in place, regardless. The right to education is a right that applies over a complete life and not just in one's younger years.

Overview of the Argument

I justify the right to higher education in what some call "liberal political" terms. By this I mean that the right to higher education is an essential feature of any political community that calls itself "liberal." In chapter 1, I set out my reasons for thinking that this is a line of argument worth undertaking. I show that the basic interests that contemporary higher education systems seem to serve—*consumer sovereignty* and *distributive fairness*—are either misconceived or altogether mistaken. This justifies the search for a better understanding of the interests that education in an adult's life should serve.

Chapter 2 takes a closer look at an educational interest advocated for by many as an improvement over the contemporary model of higher education: education for liberal democratic citizenship. This account is appealing because it can be plausibly linked to the role of education in ensuring that citizens can lead free and self-determined lives. This, because the knowledge and skills we need to be good citizens in a liberal democracy significantly overlap with what we need to live free and happy lives. However, I show that justifying the right to higher education on citizenship grounds runs afoul of the paternalistic aims problem, however desirable such an aim may be, because it inevitably imposes unjustifiable restrictions on the student's own educational goals.

Chapter 3 and 4 are the argumentative core of the book—where the right to higher education really begins to take shape.

Chapter 3 takes the lessons of the civic argument's failure and turns to personal autonomy as a fundamental aim of higher education. Here I endorse a conception of personal autonomy advanced by the philosopher Joseph Raz. Raz points out that personal autonomy is a desirable state to be in because of its role in helping us lead flourishing lives. I use his account in order to show that liberal citizens have an interest in access to education, not merely to put in place basic intellectual and characterological foundations for personal autonomy, but also to support the achievement of citizen's self-determined aims and goals in the long term, the realization of the latter being necessary for autonomous flourishing. In short, citizens have a right to educational goods over a complete life.

With this entitlement in place the question now becomes: why should we think that liberal institutions, such as those we normally think of as "higher education," have any business securing this right? This is the focus of chapter 4. Here I dive into some fundamental questions about the role of basic institutions in supporting the interests of liberal citizens, or what some political philosophers refer to as "the basic structure" of society. I argue that the basic structure of society, those key institutions that make society a liberal one, ought to work for *liberty-maximizing justice*. Liberty-maximizing justice, in its most basic formulation, is the idea that all citizens should be free to pursue a good and happy life and that constraints on that pursuit should not be due to morally irrelevant reasons, such as wealth. I then claim that higher education institutions should be considered part of that basic structure and, for this reason, they should be rightly tasked with responsibility for supporting the autonomy of citizens.

One problem with the institutional argument is that we normally think of higher education institutions, universities especially, of charting their own course, their own priorities and goals. But placing higher education within the basic structure subjects it to a fairly demanding form of political authority. Because higher education institutions must fulfill the requirements of liberty-maximizing justice, the liberal state is authorized to ensure that the higher education system is compliant with these requirements. This raises troubling questions about the nature and scope of political authority over higher education, especially since we are dealing with *liberal* political authority where the threshold for the justified use of state power is typically higher than it is in other political frameworks. How do we know, for example, that a liberal state imbued with such authority won't command citizens to pursue a specific program of study simply because it is in the interest of so-called liberty-maximizing justice? In chapter 5 I show how the exercise of political authority in the interests of liberty-maximizing justice is consistent with the personal autonomy of citizens.

In chapter 6 I revisit important questions about distributive fairness and equality in a world where higher education is a right. In particular, I address a legitimate worry that informs much of the contemporary debate over higher education: that full public funding for higher education would lead to a system in which the benefits and burdens of the system are unfairly distributed across civic society, especially between those who choose to receive higher education goods and those who do not (or cannot). I try to meet this concern by identifying three distributive conditions that I believe are necessary and sufficient for a citizen to make good on their right to higher education (openness, diversity, and full public funding). I argue that the closer the basic structure gets to fulfilling these three distributive conditions the more just the allocation of the benefits and burdens of a system of higher education will be.

This leads to chapter 7, which also serves as a conclusion to the book. Here I go into more detail about what the right to higher education can and should look like at the level of policy and practice. I do this by engaging in some key objections that were left mostly unaddressed in chapters 1 through 6. I show how this conception can relevantly apply to contemporary higher education policy and practice by engaging with Martin Trow's stage theory of higher education. I argue that a rights-based conception can serve as a standard or criterion by which citizens can judge the justice, fairness, and general desirability of the different directions that the growth and transformation of higher education may take in the future. I then go on to address two classic distributive objections that could apply to my account of higher education: (i) that higher education is not really a basic good so much as an expensive taste and (ii) that my account relies on an "ideal theory" conception of education that, in failing to fully appreciate how deeply unequal liberal societies are and can be, would in practice lead to an even more unequal society. I deal with these objections by demonstrating how higher education goods are importantly different from "tastes" or "preferences," and I also show how my argument, while pulling from methods in political philosophy that have come to be associated with ideal theory, does not depend on such idealizations.

Conclusion

I hope that my case for the right to higher education encourages a shift in public debate and discussion about the goods that education is supposed to serve in a free and open society, any flaws in the argument notwithstanding. The line of argument I pursue over these chapters is motivated by the belief that education can do far more to promote the well-being of citizens in our societies than the current arrangement of higher education signals to the public. We've become far too preoccupied with status, mobility, selection, merit, and educational rationing in higher education to the detriment of a serious understanding of what higher education is actually supposed to be for, fundamentally. Such a preoccupation has led to a miserly and unimaginative vision for higher education and one that, I am fairly sure, does not come at all close to what education in a liberal society should be.

Perhaps you share this belief, but you're nonetheless unpersuaded by the philosophical terms of reference that I use in trying to breathe some into it. Fair enough. I hope that you make your own case for the right to higher education and, in the very making, encourage the same shift in the conversation about that I've tried to encourage, here.

1
Values and Aims of Higher Education

Education plays an undeniably important role in preparing children for adult life, and this fact strongly influences society's beliefs and assumptions about its fundamental values and purposes. It also informs the importance that liberal democracies assign to a state-managed, publicly funded education system. For example, a basic education is widely understood to be a right owed to all citizens. Because children are not in a position to exercise this right for themselves, we make its provision free and compulsory. As we move closer to adulthood, however, formal education begins to shift away from something basic and preparatory to something optional. At this stage of life, the value of education depends on the particular goals that we, as (presumptively) mature individuals, have in view. For some, this will mean year upon year of further study at a university or some other post-secondary educational institution. For others, a high school diploma is enough. Many of us fall somewhere in the middle.

One implication of this shift is that when we think about the value of education in the lives of adults, we see it less a *need* so much as a *want*. It is a privilege, not a right.[1] Consequently, the role of the state in the provision of higher education is far more discretionary and circumspect than it is for a basic education. For example, many governments see subsidizing college affordability as a worthwhile way of bringing about a more productive industry and greater democratic engagement (BIS, 2011a). They use public sector funding mechanisms to encourage higher education admissions to strive for equity (Lang, 2005). But they also endorse policies that require students to take on greater responsibility for the financial costs of attending, in some cases going so far as to exempt student debt from bankruptcy protection (Austin, 2013) and introducing tax deductions designed to draw more private donations to selective and elite institutions (Eaton, 2018). This policy flexibility arises, in part, because the right to education is not typically seen to extend to higher education.[2] Instead, state provision of higher education is determined by the costs and benefits of voluntary consumption by citizens. The transformation of educational needs into wants, or desires, is the conceptual bedrock on which contemporary higher education policy and practice is built.

Is this how we should be thinking about higher education in liberal societies? It's tempting to see contemporary higher education as "second nature," or inevitable. However, what we know today as higher education is the product of a relatively recent post-WW2 expansion driven by the belief that further education could serve both as a valuable gateway to upward social mobility and as a contribution to the public good (Labaree, 2016; Trow, 2007). As the private costs of higher education have appeared to outpace its economic return, however, public intellectuals, scholars, and policy-makers have endeavored to disentangle the values and aims of higher education from the economic policies that once drove its rapid growth.[3] What has resulted from this general dissatisfaction with the status quo is a growing list of candidate aims for higher education: promoting economic justice, protecting basic liberties, cultivating civic virtues, and righting historical wrongs, to name but a few.

All of these proposed aims may speak to things that society could use more of. If you care about income inequality, and you think higher education can mitigate income inequality, it seems natural to conclude that combatting income inequality should be an aim of higher education. However, arguments of this kind are aimed at nudging the higher education systems we have inherited toward (allegedly) better uses. It is a remedial project, making the best of what we have, but it does not address what higher education in a free and equal society should really be about.

I am not claiming that higher education systems should ignore income inequality or other pressing social issues. My point is that arguments about the aims of higher education motivated by problems that have the attention of society in the moment can distract us from more fundamental questions about the value of education in the lives of adult citizens. Extreme income inequality is surely unjust. But from an educational point of view, a focus on income inequality may come at the expense of a more conceptual, and consequential, injustice. By this I mean that many of the injustices within, and propped up by, higher education might come down to the fact that we have an inadequate conception, or idea, of what higher education should be for.

We need a more precise understanding of the role that higher education should play in a just, free, and open society, and we need to develop a social vision for higher education from that understanding. This social vision should orient our efforts at change and reform.

But how do we get to this understanding? It requires that we answer three basic questions:

1. What value should education beyond a basic level have in the lives of free and equal citizens?
2. Is this value sufficiently important to warrant a role for the state in its provision?
3. If it is, what should this role look like at the institutional level?

While the remaining chapters of this book take up these questions, this chapter is focused on showing why contemporary assumptions about higher education and its value can represent what we might say is a *conceptual* form of injustice. By this I mean that much of the injustice of higher education can be attributed to the fact that it is misconceived in its values and purposes.

First, I show how the contemporary conception of higher education is built on foundational assumptions about the public and political interests that higher education is responsible for securing on behalf of citizens. These assumptions take the form of de facto educational interests that structure the provision of higher education. Second, I show why these foundational assumptions are likely to be misconceived or, at the very least, require a stronger justification. I also show how these misconceptions have come to hold undue sway over the way in which we often reason about justice in higher education.

The De Facto Value of Higher Education

Why do we think of basic education, and not higher education, as a universal entitlement? One obvious answer is that we value the former differently from the latter. We assign to basic education a different importance than to higher education. In what follows, I describe four major differences in the way that higher education is conventionally valued that set it apart from a basic education. This description serves as an initial basis for understanding the extent to which, and ways in which, our assumptions about higher education may require greater scrutiny.

First, a basic education is so important that we think it reasonable to make it compulsory for all children, and the education of children is a seen as a core parental responsibility. We see things this way because a basic education ought to provide knowledge and skills that every citizen needs in order to live well. This is also why parents and children are not usually expected to pay for its provision. The consumption of higher education goods, on the other hand, is voluntary. The state does not use its authority to compel citizens to receive a higher education, and because citizens freely choose to consume it, they accept responsibility for its financial (and other) costs.

Second, a basic education is thought to be essential to functioning in a society. A higher education, while surely beneficial in many ways, is not. When done well, compulsory schooling really is for children's own good. But the value of a higher education depends on the preferences of the person choosing it, and the preference for a higher education is in turn situated within a range of other preferences that may have more importance. Perhaps I prefer to earn a living on graduation from high school, and this preference is stronger than attending (even) more classes. Others might question the wisdom of my following through on that preference. But it wouldn't generate the same concern as if I dropped out of primary school.

Third, even though many citizens may prefer a higher education, the particular preference being satisfied will depend on the individual. For some people a higher education is about charting a path to a scholarly life. For other people it is a gateway to a lucrative profession. Some want to broaden their intellectual and social horizons. Some see it as a way to escape poverty. For many it is a combination of all of these and more besides. No singular want is served by the provision of higher education. A basic education, however, is just that, *basic*. It provides for something that citizens will need regardless of the preferences they happen to have (or will have).

Finally, the provision of a basic education has large payoffs for society, while the payoff of a higher education mainly goes to the person attending. Having basic skills, understanding the law and common morality, being literate—we can easily imagine that a society in which everyone has the opportunity to acquire these things will be collectively better off than one that does not. Higher education also contributes to a greater good. There are essential roles in society, for example, that require people willing to undertake years of study beyond a basic level. But a higher education is far more beneficial for the person who receives it, especially in terms of income and social esteem. The reason why we compel children to go to school is because it will benefit individual children *and* the society they will become a part of. The reason why I choose a higher education is because I believe that it will make *my* life better in some way.

These differences between a higher education and a basic education feed into the idea that they each represent a different *kind* of good, and this gives us some initial insight into why liberal states tend to have a different relationship to higher education than to basic education. A compulsory education is thought to be a good with "special" status. It is special in the sense that there is something about its value that makes allocating it to people on the basis of status and wealth intuitively objectionable. These are goods that have such singular place and importance for the individual that how much of it we get should not be determined by an ability to pay or even, in some instances, voluntary choice (Segall, 2007, p. 343). They should not be allocated like a commodity, but as equally as possible. Health care is another example of a good with special status. We value the public health care system because health care helps people get back to a relatively normal state of function when they get sick (Daniels, 2001). How much health care a person gets should have no bearing on how many resources they have in other parts of their lives. If someone is denied life-saving health care we are morally outraged regardless of how high or low his or her income. It is only when people's reasons for accessing health care go outside this common range of need that we usually expect them to pay, such as with most cases of cosmetic surgery (Segall, 2007).[4] We would worry if someone refused urgent medical care and, in some cases, even compel them to get it against their own wishes. Finally, health care has at least as much payoff for the community as the person seeking care, exemplified in the free provision of vaccines.

The conventional view is that higher education is not at all special when put alongside a basic education and health care. This explains, in part, why liberal states observe no principled, rights-based reasons for covering the cost of higher education provision or securing access for all citizens.[5] I say "principled" because some governments justify public subsidy for tuition on the grounds that they are necessary for generating positive externalities—aggregate social benefits unintended by the individual consumer, such as reduced crime and increased voter participation. But note the conditional nature of the policy: if enough students enrolled in higher education to generate externalities without a subsidy in place, they would no longer be justified. We might say that higher education is the cosmetic surgery of the educational world: undeniably enhancing, but nothing I could reasonably expect the state to pay for on my behalf as a matter of right.

Justifying the Value of Higher Education

In the last section I offered a descriptive account of higher education's value. The upshot is that higher education has less "specialness" relative to its compulsory counterpart. But do we have good reasons for seeing higher education in this way? In order to answer this question, we must turn to the candidate values that help to support or justify this picture of higher education. We are here talking about the *justification* of the values of higher education.

Justifying educational values can easily become a circular enterprise. Take, for example, the specialness attributed to a basic education. Maybe we attribute specialness to a basic education simply because basic education is set up *like* a special good, where we ensure that access to such an education is freely available to all. We're just used to things being this way. After all, once people come to see a particular good or resource as an entitlement it is very hard to convince them that they shouldn't. But we can raise similar questions about the "non-specialness" attributed to higher education. It could be that higher education really is a service. But it could also be that we see it this way just because it tends to be allocated *like* a service.

How do we break the cycle? Because we are talking about state provision of education in a particular political arrangement of society—a free and open one—its value ought to be justified in terms of what makes that political arrangement desirable for its members. Literacy is a good example. Every liberal citizen has an interest in being literate because it is a necessary precondition for participation in civic life and the economy. Public schools, insofar as they aim to promote literacy, arguably help to secure an important interest for liberal citizens. The specialness of a basic education is therefore derived from the role it plays in providing opportunities for cultivation and development necessary for life in such a society.

What of our beliefs about the value of higher education? Do adult citizens—citizens who have already benefited from a basic education—have educational interests? I believe there are at least two basic interests that we tend to fall back on when justifying higher education policy: consumer sovereignty and distributive fairness. These might not be the right, most desirable, or most important values on which higher education should or could be founded but, as we will see, they are nonetheless definitive.

Consumer Sovereignty

Higher education institutions act in a market. For example, they compete for students, donors, and for the status needed to attract those students and donors. Liberal democratic states intervene in this market for different reasons, sometimes to increase efficiency, and sometimes to promote equality. Yet, ultimately, the wants and preferences of students drive the shape and scope of the system.[6] In this way, higher education is responsive to what is sometimes referred to as the principle of consumer sovereignty (Heath, 2005; White, 1990). *Consumer sovereignty* derives from the view that citizens should be empowered to demand those goods they want instead of delegating that power to another authority, such as the state (see Heath, 2005, pp. 207–208). To say that consumer sovereignty extends to higher education is to mean that people's access to higher education goods should be in the main free from political authority. Education is but one of many resources or opportunities that citizens are free to avail of, and markets help to ensure that they can use their (current and future) economic power to demand the specific educational goods and services that they want.

There is one final point that I want to make about consumer sovereignty that will take on much greater significance for the argument, later. Consumer sovereignty is a thin, or partial, version of a more comprehensive ideal: personal autonomy. Personal autonomy refers to one's ability to make self-determined choices. The personally autonomous person is the author of their own life. The idea that a person should be free to demand the goods and services that they judge will best support how they want their life to go is derived from, or can be justified through, the ideal of personal autonomy. But we should be careful not to assume that sovereignty and autonomy are one and the same. For example, consumer sovereignty might suggest that a student's personal autonomy is being fully recognized so long as they are free to buy educational goods and services. But what if all the educational goods and services are bad, or different only in the most superficial of terms, or too costly? My point is that consumer sovereignty may be used to justify a certain way of thinking about the provision of higher education. But if it is true that (i) consumer sovereignty is justified by the ideal of personal autonomy and (ii) consumer sovereignty is itself a kind of diminished or incomplete accounting of the education that personal autonomy requires, it is plausible to think that this way of thinking about the provision of higher education is also thin or incomplete in some important respects. When someone says that a certain higher education policy proposal is "good for the consumer" they are in fact depending on this more comprehensive ideal, even if their own policy proposal neglects this comprehensive ideal in favor of its consumerist version.

Distributive Fairness

One might argue that consumer sovereignty fully explains the value of higher education and the limited role of the state in its provision.

After all, consumer sovereignty entails its own norms and principles of fairness. In the higher education context, for example, consumer sovereignty should mean that higher education systems not only cater to the educational goals of individual students but also respect consumer protections accorded to any participant in a free market, such as laws against fraud or policies requiring colleges to disclose accurate information about the goods and services they provide. It should also strive to minimize state interference in citizen's decision-making as much as is reasonably possible.

Yet, leaving things here would be a mistake. Why? It could be the case that so long as consumer's demands are being satisfied and no market norms are being violated, the higher education system is doing a good job of protecting the public and political interests of citizens.

This thinking might make sense when applied to the management of relatively low-stakes commodities such as furniture and flat-screen TVs. However, higher education goods do far more than satisfy discrete wants and desires; rather, they make available highly prized (and scarce) socioeconomic opportunities. These opportunities have powerful effects on the relative equality of citizens economically, in their capacity to pursue their private aims, and on their ability to effectively engage in the public and political matters.

First, it can improve the objective welfare and resources individuals come to have. Access to higher education goods makes a real difference in citizens' life chances with respect to both market (income and earnings) and non-market (health, relationships, and political participation) outcomes (BIS, 2013).

Second, because higher education makes a difference in the welfare and resources citizens come to have, it also makes an objective difference in how citizens stand in relation to each other in terms of resources and welfare. It does this by distributing the benefits and burdens of higher education goods across the entire polity regardless of who actually receives them. It can take resources away from the public in order to make higher education less costly for those who wish to attend, or it can reduce public expenditure and let the private cost rise. It can make it easier for already well-off citizens to access higher education goods, or it can try to level the playing field (Fullinwider & Lichtenberg, 2004).

Higher education is a good whose consumption, unlike flat screen TVs or fine dining, has powerful socioeconomic consequences for individual citizens and for relative equality between citizens. These harms may not be freely chosen, nor intended, by any one consumer. All liberal citizens have an interest in how these consequences are managed even when they do not directly access educational goods and services themselves. This justifies certain forms of state interference in its provision. We can say, then, that a second interest informing the value of higher education is our interest in society being a just and stable one. Let is call this interest *distributive fairness*.

De Facto Educational Interests in the Higher Education System

It is fair to ask why I focus on these two interests at the expense of other candidates. For example, civic engagement seems to be an important theme in the conversation about higher education. And we would be hard pressed to deny that citizens have an interest in receiving some kind of civic education. I agree, and because of its promise I consider this possibility in some detail in chapter 2. But for now, it is worth emphasizing that my aim is to describe what I take to be the most prominent and general interests of the higher education system, not the more philosophically or politically attractive ones.

That said, civic engagement is surely an educational aim nested *within* these larger interests. It might have potential as an educational aim that higher education systems ought to make a priority.

But it would not be accurate to claim that this aim defines the system and how it functions, currently. Civic engagement is but *one* among many educational aims competing for attention within a system of higher education. For example, notice that while many higher education institutions talk up their contribution to the civic education of their students, liberal states do not typically compel higher education students to receive an explicit civic educational curriculum.[7] This is because civic educational aims are subordinate to a more fundamental value implicit in higher education provision: that it is voluntary/chosen. This effectively constrains how far higher education institutions can go in pursuit of such an aim. There is certainly a market for students interested in civic engagement and, in response, formal and informal education paths in the system available for them to pursue such interests. And, as I point out in chapter 2, many scholars and educational leaders have suggested civic education as an aim that *should* define higher education systems. But it would be odd to claim that civic education is a fundamental aim writ large, at least as higher education is conventionally understood and practiced from a system-wide point of view.

I believe that the twin interests of consumer sovereignty and distributive fairness inform many of our beliefs about how higher education should be allocated as a public and political good. This should come as little surprise. All educational systems have an individual dimension (the educational aims that shape the experience of the student in that system) and a distributive dimension (how opportunities to access those aims ought to be structured) (Brighouse, 2009). In the case of higher education, this individual dimension takes the form of consumer sovereignty. This interest, as I described earlier, reflects the idea that it is the individual student that is best positioned to decide what their educational goals are. The distributive dimension takes the form of what I have called distributive fairness. Graduates stand to benefit in ways that may set them apart from other citizens who may not have chosen (or are unable to choose) such an education. Yet, society has an interest in ensuring that the benefits and costs of a higher education are allocated on the basis of some distributive ideal.

Of course, this all paints an admittedly broad picture of the value of higher education. But I make no claim that my description accounts for the specific higher education policies of every liberal democratic state. Citizens can, and do, dispute the general trends of higher education policy. For example, some have argued that governments undervalue the public benefits of higher education and are therefore not justified in shifting the distributive burden of higher education's cost onto the consumers who invest considerable time, effort and personal resources that have payoffs for everyone. Others have claimed that higher education is a right and not a privilege, though justifications for this claim have remained elusive.[8]

My key point is that consumer sovereignty and distributive fairness are highly influential interpretations of what the individual and distributive dimensions of higher education should look like.[9] But while they serve to justify and shape the system, they are themselves in need of justification. That is to say, these educational interests are *de facto*, not *de jure*. In the next section I will explain why these educational interests warrant closer justificatory scrutiny.

Rethinking the De Facto Value of Higher Education

I have so far argued that higher education is assumed to be less "special" than a basic education or health care. I then showed how this assumption is supported by a particular interpretation of the public and political interests that a system of higher education is aimed at securing on behalf of citizens. In the next section I will offer some reasons why we should revisit this interpretation.

Conceptual Reasons

Schooling is thought to play an important role in enabling future citizens to participate in economic life. But political philosophers have shown that, such economic benefits notwithstanding, the individual right to a basic education is logically connected to what it means to be free and equal. What do I mean by "logically connected"? I mean that this right is not contingent or variable. It does not depend on the preferences that particular citizens happen to have. It does not depend on economic or political outcomes. It is connected, as Schouten puts it, to "the idealized conception of political personhood that lies at the heart of liberal theories. In this politically liberal framework, this notion of citizenship . . . is not meant to describe actual citizens. It is, rather, a tool for systematizing the constraints on legitimate exercises of political power that such a framework is committed to imposing" (2018, pp. 1080–1081).[10]

On this view, the rights and guarantees that we think the state should exercise its authority in order to protect are fundamentally grounded not in, say, a majoritarian voting scheme or popular social or economic policies, but in the basic interests that *any individual* would have were they to enter into a liberal society, ideally conceived. Most basic among these is an education for personal autonomy—the capacity to make self-determined choices about the good life.[11]

There are important insights to take from this analysis. I've spoken of the differences between the provision of basic and higher education as if they were a matter of degree. The state is highly interventionist about basic education, relatively hands-off about higher education. A basic education is a very special good, a higher education less so.

However, the difference is something more than a matter of degree. A basic education is not just "special"; rather, it informs those social institutions that define liberal society. The political philosopher John Rawls called these institutions "the basic structure" of society.[12] The provision of an autonomy-promoting education supported by a well-funded system of public schooling is, on a basic structure view, a distinctly liberal institution responsible for the interest in liberty that any individual has simply by virtue of being a citizen. A society without an institution that helped citizens realize this interest would not be a fully liberal one.

Important to note is that this institutional role holds independent of any status quo assumptions about what schools do and why. Access to a basic education is key to the protection of the individual rights and liberties of citizens. A politically just conception of public education should therefore strive to ensure that this right is sufficiently protected for all citizens. It is as interested in the justice of rights as it is in the justice of socioeconomic distribution.

What is the relevance of this analysis for higher education? Political philosophy can tell us a cogent story about the values and aims of basic education in a liberal society. This story has, in turn, enriched our understanding of the place and importance of public schooling in such a society. It can also inform trenchant social criticism when schools fall short of these values and aims.

Do we have as cogent a story to tell about higher education? I think the answer is "no," and I think the reason why can be traced back to some deeply held, but unexamined, assumptions about the interests that it is supposed to serve. These assumptions introduce a lot of ambiguity about the kind of institution higher education is supposed to be.

For example, we can say that higher education systems can be found *in* liberal democracies. But can we also say that they are *part of* liberal democracy? The difference is subtle, but significant. That higher education systems can be found in liberal democracies is a contingent fact. Taken alone, this fact means that higher education is like any other association or organization that finds itself in a liberal society, such as churches or volunteer organizations. They are valuable, but not something that the state should have a heavy hand in managing. This way of understanding higher education fits well with the view that, for the individual citizen, higher education is a consumer good or service like any other. We have no right to such goods or services.

But when we say that higher education systems are *part of* liberal democracy, we have something more substantive in mind. Higher education is here seen to be part of the basic structure. And on this view, higher education has a non-contingent relationship with liberal society. By this I mean that higher education systems have a key and distinctive role to play in the lives of all liberal citizens. This line of thinking fits well with the view that higher education matters for the overall fairness and equality of society.

In reality, it looks as if higher education is both inside *and* outside of the basic structure. Individual institutions are seen as free to compete against one another in line with a free market economy, but the larger system is often managed by the authority of the state (the United Kingdom's higher education policy is a good example of this). This institutional ambiguity has real consequences. There is much debate in Canadian jurisprudence, for example, over the extent to which the Canadian Charter of Rights and Freedoms applies to universities. Specifically, how far should universities go to protecting citizen's liberty-based right to freedom of expression? Provincial Supreme Courts have diverged on this question, in part due to conflicting judgments over the university being part of government, including the activities undertaken by the university that could be plausibly seen as a legitimate aim of government (McKay-Panos, 2016). We might say that higher education has a "quasi-structural" status.

Of course, it could be the case that this ambiguous state is simply an accurate reflection of the complex nature of higher education. There are simply a number of competing interests in play, and a little ambiguity can go a long way in terms of allowing higher educations to be nimble enough to address these competing interests. But what if this view is too complacent? The analysis of a basic, preparatory education has revealed that liberal citizens have a clear public and political interest in receiving an autonomy-promoting education as children. The interests of adults have been given comparatively little attention. Without a parallel analysis of similar depth and scope, our understanding of the place of higher education in a liberal society risks falling far short of what it ought to (and can) be.

Before moving on, I want to offer an extended example of how these ambiguities might impact on our philosophical conceptions of justice and fairness in higher education. I believe that consumer sovereignty and distributive fairness have become embedded assumptions in public debate and discussion about the justice, fairness, and value of higher education. To be clear, there may be nothing inherently wrong in thinking that citizens who desire a higher education should have choices. And it seems highly intuitive that we should allocate higher education goods according to some fairness criterion. However, something significant happens when these two interests carry over into our reasoning about the political justice of higher education. More specifically, they combine to form what I call an *asymmetric* conception of political justice. These interests inform ideals of fairness that motivate many of the arguments that scholars draw on when they critique the provision of higher education from justice point of view.

A turn back to the specialness of basic education can help to explain what I mean by an asymmetric conception of political justice. Recall that liberal political philosophers typically hold that, for individual citizens, access to a basic public education is fundamental to participation in liberal society. It involves much more than the mere protection of a child's nascent liberty, rather, it means providing the resources and opportunities necessary for the cultivation of a capacity for freedom. The state therefore must exercise its political authority to ensure that all future citizens can access these resources and opportunities regardless of who they are, leading to the establishment of a public education system. But the state's responsibility does not end here. It is also responsible for the fair distribution of *the benefits and burdens* of a publicly funded system of education. For example, when wealthy citizens opt out of a public education in order to gain competitive advantages for their children through private schooling, the liberal state should take reasonable measures to mitigate this unfair advantage. If parents are opting out because the quality of a public education is low, the state has reason to exercise its authority in order to increase the quality of the public system so as to lessen the incentive to opt out. This is all to say that political justice (and the political authority required to realize it) apply *both* to the individual right to basic education *and* to the fair distribution of the benefits and burdens of such a system. Liberty and equality are both public interests. Our conception of justice in compulsory education therefore applies symmetrically: it works to secure fair outcomes both in the distributive sphere *and* in terms of our individual interest in liberty.

Justice in higher education is not symmetrical in this way. Conceptually speaking, it leaves the individual value of a higher education exactly as consumer sovereignty says it should: autonomy narrowly understood as the freedom to consume (educational) and other goods and services. Put differently, this conception of justice is *agnostic* about the individual value of higher education. Agnostic because individual citizens should be free to choose. Agnostic because the reasons citizens have for desiring a higher education is theirs' alone to decide, not the state.

Consequently, scholars see the distributive consequences of higher education as a primary concern. Consumer sovereignty helps us to understand why. For individual citizens—from the point of view of those citizens, that is—the value, desirability, and general importance of accessing a higher education comes down to the particular plan for life that the individual citizen has in view. Higher education goods are valuable but *non-essential* to the pursuit of that life. Some citizens will desire a higher education but will lack the merit necessary for accessing the system. Other citizens will qualify for admission but have no desire for more schooling. Neither scenario should be morally troubling. As important as such goods may be for some, and as much as an impact they may have on the economic life of the citizens who access them, at the end of the day the goods of a higher education are not *by themselves* fundamental for liberal citizenship. They are not fundamental in the same way as they are for children.

The general importance of a higher education must therefore be based on the second basic interest: the distributive consequences of access for a just and fair political community. Consider some basic examples that reflect this reasoning. First, many citizens desire a higher education because it is an opportunity that is almost certain to help their lives go better. But even if a student does not choose a higher education for reasons of social mobility, they will be very likely to experience such mobility by virtue of their higher education, all the same. Therefore, all such opportunities should be allocated fairly, on non-arbitrary grounds. We don't want individuals having a better chance at accessing such goods because of some unearned or unchosen advantage. Ideally, you should not be able to buy (or bribe!) your way into an elite university. Accordingly, we constrain private freedom in the interest of equality and fairness. You have to qualify—have merit—in order to get into a university. Second, if the benefits of a higher education mainly advance the private interests of the individuals attending—making them richer, increasing their social esteem—it follows that these individuals should assume a greater share of the costs of attending than the public.[13] This is because on at least some reasonable conceptions of distributive fairness it would be harmful to take away resources from some citizens simply in order to subsidize the advantages of other citizens or, better yet, this distribution should redound to the least well-off in society.[14]

When I say that scholarly conceptions of justice in higher education are asymmetric, then, I mean it in the sense that such conceptions treat the consequences of higher education for socioeconomic fairness as having primary political importance, but not so much individual liberty. And we can once more draw a parallel to the specialness of compulsory education in order to understand this asymmetry. An education for personal autonomy gets a lot of normative "attention" at the compulsory level. Scholars debate what an education for autonomy should look like, and why it is owed to children, and how far the state may go in promoting it, and so on. But we see little to no such analysis when we turn to the education of individual adult citizens.[15] It is almost as if the fact of individual choice takes the aims of higher education—its content—as a matter of justice independent of its distributive consequences entirely off of the board.

The asymmetric conception of political justice in higher education is indeed misconceived. In short, I think that when scholars debate the justice and fairness of higher education, they emphasize the distributive interests of citizens at the expense of their consumer sovereignty interests. But they undervalue the latter because consumer sovereignty is a misconceived, or narrow, interpretation of personal autonomy. And the consequence of this misinterpretation leads to further misconceptions about what the distributive commitments of higher education really ought to be.

Of course, this is all a yet-to-be-defended claim on my part. In chapter 3 I will argue that we should replace consumer sovereignty, or the "weak" idea of personal autonomy, with a more expansive conception. And I'll also be arguing that a conception of political justice for higher education that takes person autonomy seriously will be more "balanced," more symmetrical, in the sense that it will be more consistent with the social vision of a liberal democratic. This is not only a scholarly point. I think that it really matters, practically, if the educational interests that structure higher education are misconceived. In the next section, I explain why.

Moral Reasons

We have scholarly reasons for pursuing a better understanding of the value of education in adulthood. It promises an account of educational justice that is more balanced across compulsory and post-compulsory systems. But we also have moral reasons. Our understanding of citizen's interests impact on what we think makes for just and unjust, moral and immoral, fair and unfair, treatment. If we are not clear on these interests, we risk supporting a higher education system that treats citizens poorly. In order to see how, consider the following thought experiment:

Imagine a narrow bridge spanning a fast-running river. The bridge has been newly built and the contractors need to make their money back. Your job is to collect an expensive toll from people who want to cross. You see me running toward the bridge. You stop me and demand that I pay. Luckily, I have the money and because I am in too much of a hurry to complain, I drop the necessary amount into your hand and keep going.

By your lights, your actions are reasonable and fair. I really wanted to cross the river. And instead of turning back (which I could have freely chosen to do) I paid your toll. My strong desire to cross—and the fee I paid—is something that I should take responsibility for.

It turns out, however, that I needed to cross the river in order to access some life-saving medicine waiting for me on the other side, and the medicine's effectiveness was about to expire. Would you still believe that the toll is a reasonable policy? You could argue that my case is an unusual one and that, generally speaking, people don't have such a desperate need to cross bridges. The toll is reasonable but for these unusual circumstances, you counter, and we can always waive the fee for cases such as mine. Satisfied, you continue to charge a high fee to anyone that crosses.

But what if you find out that the contractors knew that crossing at this particular point in the river is a life-saving matter for *anyone*? It turns out that I am just one of an entire village of people on one side of the river who are continuously exposed to a toxin that needs to be neutralized as a matter of life and death, and the factory that produces the neutralizing agent is on the other side. Most would agree that the expensive toll is now far less defensible.

This fictional example tracks something real. What counts as fair and just treatment turns on people's needs and interests. Misjudging those needs and interests can lead to unjust policies and unfair treatment.

We should think of higher education systems as being a bit like the toll bridge. Yes, this analogy simplifies the many complex political and economic features of contemporary higher education systems. But getting bogged down in these complex features can obscure the moral dimensions of these systems. Both the bridge and higher education systems are similar in a very basic way: both are a type of infrastructure—not themselves ends, but a way to get to something valuable. It therefore matters, morally, that we are clear on what that valuable thing is—its importance in people's lives—as well as the position that we put people into when we introduce barriers into that infrastructure.

One could argue that the toll bridge is a misleading analogy because it exaggerates the moral stakes. For example, in the bridge case we did not know the (very desperate) reasons that villagers had for crossing. But in higher education we have reliable information about the reasons that citizens have for seeking it out. We know, for example, that many higher education students have economic motives.[16] So, we can't say that higher education systems are like naïve bridge operators, failing to treat students justly because they don't sufficiently understand the needs and interests in play.

It is certainly true that public debate about who should bear the costs of funding higher education—private citizen or state—has worked from the belief that a higher education is an economic investment in which most of the benefits go to the person attending. This belief has structured the higher education debate, such as determining how much of those benefits students should be responsible for and how much the public should bear the burdens of its provision. If accessing higher education is in the main a private preference, and most citizens prefer a higher education because employers are willing to pay those who graduate a lot more money, it may be reasonable to ask students to pay more and the public less.

This counterargument, however, elides an important difference between toll bridges and educational institutions. The actual reasons citizens have for choosing higher education are not necessarily authoritative in adjudicating questions about its justice or fairness.[17] These reasons are shaped by the larger political context within which people choose and act.[18] For example, the fact that employers are willing to pay university graduates more than non-graduates introduces a powerful incentive that influences why many citizens choose a higher education. It changes the balance of reasons that a person must consider when deciding if they should seek a higher education or not. The appropriateness of this incentive depends on how well it is aligned with what the values and aims of a higher education ought to be.

In fact, we can revisit the toll bridge example in order to see how incentives have no default moral authority in determining, and may even work to obscure, our basic public and political interests.

Imagine that the villagers need to get to the other side of the river for life-saving medicine, but the toxin makes them very forgetful. As a result, people often wait until it is too late to cross. The bridge owners have a change of heart and introduce a powerful incentive in order to prevent such tragedies: anyone who crosses gets *paid* a large sum of money.

We can easily predict what will happen next. People will start flocking to the bridge even if they didn't need, or want, to cross before the incentive was introduced. And we can further imagine that so many people will try to cross that the toll keeper will have to introduce a queuing system in order to prevent too many people from rushing the bridge at the same time. The toll keeper could line up those people in order of financial need, or hold a competition in order to see who would put their bridge payment to the best use.

From the perspective of an onlooker, it seems as if the point and purpose of the bridge is to provide an opportunity for people who want to make more money. They see lots of people flocking to the bridge, crossing, getting paid and then crossing back in order to line up again. But the onlooker also notices that there is high demand for this opportunity. The bridge is narrow and lots of people are waiting for their turn to cross. It would be natural, then, for the onlooker to focus their moral attention on the queuing system. Are the strongest permitted to push their way to the front? Are people who have already been paid to cross given less priority? Is it first come, first cross? If the onlooker assumes that the point and purpose of the bridge is to allocate a lucrative financial opportunity it makes total sense for them to focus their moral attention on how that opportunity is made available as opposed to the legitimacy, necessity, or value of that opportunity.

Now imagine that the onlooker discovers that the main purpose of the bridge is to help people who need life-saving medicine get to the other side. The payment is just an incentive to make sure that those who need to access that medicine actually take the time out of their day to make the crossing when they are likely to forget to do so, otherwise. The incentive to cross—more money—now looks far less appropriate. Perverse, even. For one thing, it crowds out people who really need to cross by also drawing in people who just want money. For another, those who really need to cross will have to follow a queuing process whose criteria may have no bearing on the merits. A lot of us lining up at the bridge need money. And this leads us to demand that the toll operator line us up according to financial need. This makes sense if we have no idea that the bridge is there to provide access to medicine. The terms on which access to the bridge is being structured, even though we are attending carefully to what we think merits fair access, does not match well with the purpose of the bridge.

Higher education is not a bridge to life-saving medicine. But many citizens see it as an important path to, among other things, upward social mobility.[19] I don't want to discount the value of this path. However, focusing on the justice and fairness of higher education as a valuable socioeconomic opportunity risks arbitrarily excluding other interests that matter to liberal democratic citizens and that educational goods are uniquely placed to serve, and these interests may motivate different requirements of justice and fairness.

I allow that one's reasoning about access to higher education, when it is framed as a valuable opportunity, can be internally coherent and justifiable. My point is that the very designation of higher education *as* a valuable opportunity may be an injustice for citizens with different goals in view. We think, for example, that access to valuable opportunities should come down to some (contestable) notion of merit or fair competition. But there are citizens in our society who possess talents and have goals in life that neither qualify them for, nor leave them likely to desire, such opportunities. And so, it may be that higher education *is* like the toll bridge, making people que up and compete for access for reasons that do not fully reflect its fundamental purpose. It may be an infrastructure built on an inadequate conceptualization of its fundamental aims and purposes, not (only) its distributive fairness.

Conclusion

Our assumptions about the values and purposes that a system of higher education should serve in a free and open society are just that—assumptions. And the tighter we hold onto these assumptions as we reason about the justice and fairness of higher education, the less likely that these other purposes become salient to us as we debate higher education policy and practice.

I have not yet offered my own argument for what those other values and purposes should be. I've only for made a plea for a more precise argument about them. It might be the case that so long as our higher education institutions allocate opportunities fairly, and the benefits and burdens of their provision by the state are allocated fairly, our interests are being fully served. On the other hand, it might be the case that access to educational goods are important for reasons that appeal to what it means to be a free and equal citizen in an open society. The latter is the position that I that will argue in the chapters that follow.

2
Citizenship as an Aim of Higher Education

In chapter 1 I argued that higher education policy and practice is structured by two basic interests: consumer sovereignty and distributive fairness. I also argued that these two interests, at least as they are conventionally understood, may serve as a poor foundation for the justification of higher education and its aims.

In this chapter I consider a promising alternative. The idea that the state should support civic norms and virtues has a strong influence on public discourse about the value of public schooling. But as liberal states have begun to reconsider their financial support for higher education, and in many cases have reduced that support, the civic contribution of higher education has been increasingly called on in order to justify renewed public investment as well. One need only look to the strategic plans and marketing materials of almost any contemporary university to see reference upon reference to "global citizenship," "civic engagement," or some variation on the civic education theme.

However, emphasis on the civic mission of higher education is more than mere marketing and public relations. There is a growing body of literature that has argued for the civic educational outcomes as a reason for the public's continued investment in higher education. Martha Nussbaum (2002; 2010), for example, has argued for the role of higher education in preparing graduates for civic life in general, and for the contribution of the liberal arts to that preparation in particular.[1] Other have focused on the contribution of higher education to civic virtue (Annette, 2005) or to public deliberation and public reason (Englund, 2002; White, 2016). Finally, this line of reasoning has received empirical support from the economics of education: elementary, secondary, and postsecondary educational attainment generates positive externalities in terms of civic engagement (Brand, 2010; Dee, 2004).

We have at least two basic reasons for taking citizenship seriously as an aim of higher education. First, an education for liberal citizenship is often justified on the grounds that all citizens have a basic interest in a democratically stable society, one where people know what it means to respect laws, value difference, and settle conflict through public reason and debate as opposed to violence. If higher education can effectively contribute to these outcomes, it is plausible to propose that democratic stability is one of the basic interests that a higher education should be responsible for protecting. Second, the promotion of a student's autonomy is often seen to be an essential feature of an education for liberal citizenship. But recall that in the last chapter I pointed out that while autonomy plays an important role in reasoning about the political justice (and justification) of compulsory or basic education, this value tends to drop out of the picture in reasoning about higher education entirely, or is narrowly interpreted in terms of consumer sovereignty. A civic educational argument for higher education might show us why and how autonomy can come back into that public picture. This may in turn justify higher education as a constitutive part of liberal political community.

In this chapter I assess the merits of civic education as an aim of higher education. First, I explain how a legitimate and justifiable liberal civic education for children must (and can) strike a balance between the goods of political stability and individual freedom. Second, I make the case for extending civic educational goals to higher education. In the third and fourth sections I argue that while civic educational aims look like a promising foundation for the justification of higher education, a closer look reveals that it can't strike a balance between stability and freedom. The upshot is that while it makes sense to cherish the indirect benefits of higher education for the civic capacities of graduates, these benefits ought not be understood as the overarching aim that justifies state involvement in its management and provision. Such involvement, I argue, would come at too high a price for the personal autonomy of citizens.

The Liberal Argument for Compulsory Civic Education

In order for a liberal democracy to function well its citizens need to know, understand, and care about the norms, values, and virtues that define it. A school system keyed to the preparation of future citizens therefore seems eminently justifiable. But the argument for a compulsory education system focused on liberal citizenship must negotiate a tricky balance between two basic interests: individual freedom and the stability of the state. This balancing requirement will also have implications for the justification of a system of higher education founded on civic aims and purposes. Therefore, before moving on to examine the prospects of a conception of higher education founded on such an aim, we should understand why these two interests require balancing in the context of a compulsory education.

Let's start with individual freedom. In the last chapter I outlined how the development of personal autonomy is an educational aim often appealed to in order to justify the state provision of public education as a basic entitlement. Autonomy is required, so this argument goes, for any liberal citizen to pursue a good and happy life. But consider that some liberals reject the idea that autonomy is neutral between various ideas about the good life.[2] By this they mean that autonomy is not the all purpose value that we might think it is. To value autonomy, they might say, is to value *a certain kind* of life—an autonomous one. And if this is true, state support for an education in personally autonomous living reflects a biased perspective on the kinds of lives worth living (and supporting). Such judgments, some liberals will claim, fall outside the scope of political justice and authority. For example, John Rawls famously argued that his account of political liberalism entailed only a minimum civic education as opposed to an education for autonomy (2001; see also Costa, 2004).

If Rawls and like-minded critics are right, an autonomy-based argument for educational entitlements empowers the liberal state to make illegitimate decisions about the kinds of good lives worthy of protection on grounds of justice.[3] These decisions will benefit only those citizens who value individualism, self-directedness, and choice while harming those that value community, belonging, and commitment.[4]

Let's assume for the sake of the argument that the neutrality objection is right. Autonomy is just one of a number of values that can orient a good life in an open society, and a state that uses its authority to promote autonomy should be rightly charged with playing favorites.[5] Does this take the state out of the business of education and autonomy-promotion altogether? Not necessarily. Some liberals who buy the neutrality objection have nonetheless tried to rescue autonomy as an educational goal. This is where a civic education comes into the picture.

The first step is to reframe civic education as a public good as opposed to an individual benefit. This can be done by claiming that the education of liberal citizens is indispensable for a healthy and stable democracy. In a diverse society, citizens need to be able to reflect on the fallibility of their own commitments and ideals, as well as exercise civic virtues such as toleration for the commitments and ideals of their fellow citizens, if they are to live together in a peaceable and cooperative way. Every citizen regardless of their conception of the good has an interest in political stability. Without stability, they could not pursue the good in the first place. And so it follows that everyone regardless of their views on the good life (and, more importantly, their views on the importance of autonomy within a good life) could support a compulsory liberal civic education.

This opens the way to explaining the educational value of autonomy in terms that bypass the neutrality constraint. An education for liberal citizenship, in order to be successful, requires students to acquire knowledge, skills, and dispositions (e.g., virtues of tolerance, reflectiveness, and critical thinking) quite similar to, if not indistinguishable from, those proffered by defenders of personal autonomy. This is sometimes referred to as the "convergence thesis" of liberal civic education (Davis and Neufeld, 2007).

The convergence thesis proposes that while a liberal civic education advances citizens' *collective* interest in a stable liberal democratic order, it unavoidably requires *individual* citizens realizing minimal conditions of autonomy.[6] The state is therefore free to indirectly promote minimal conditions of autonomy among citizens on the way to a stability-supporting civic education. This is because the state is not making autonomy the intended aim of compulsory education. It is not claiming that personally autonomous lives have greater intrinsic value than non-autonomous ones. Conditions of autonomy are a mere means to the further end of a diverse, civically educated public that can engage with one another in ways do not threaten democratic law and order.

The convergence thesis does more than rescue the educational value of autonomy from liberal neutrality. It also seeks to resolve a serious conflict over the purpose of education in the liberal state: some believe that its purpose is to cultivate our capacity for individual freedom, while others argue that its purpose is to maintain democratic order (Galston, 1989). Why not both purposes? The problem is that the two aims are ethically divergent. One promotes personal autonomy, the other conformity to civic principles and norms. Each purpose paints a different picture of the relationship between liberal citizens and educational provision, and these pictures do not overlap. The autonomy aim says that the state has an obligation to promote skills and dispositions that enable citizens to advance their own interests. The civic aim says that citizens have a duty to acquire skills and dispositions that will benefit the long-term health of the state.

These divergent ways of framing the educational relationship between citizens and state matters because the idea that the liberal state ought to pursue an educational aim presupposes the *legitimate authority* for it to do so. And each relationship poses its own distinct problems for political authority.

For example, some liberals are worried that even if autonomy contributes to human flourishing for many citizens within a liberal society, this does not by itself justify the imposition, by the state, of an autonomy-promoting education on everyone (De Wijze, 1999). Not all reasonable citizens—certain religious minorities for example—would freely consent to the use of such authority. For example, a compulsory education for autonomy could lead future members of that religious tradition to question their commitments to that tradition, undermining its long-term viability. We should therefore drop autonomy and focus on an education for loyalty to liberal norms such as civility and rule of law. Education for a just and stable society is legitimate, but not an education for autonomy.

But other liberals counter that even if we have an equal interest in a stable liberal polity, the use of state power in order to condition children to conform to liberal civic norms undermines their capacity to freely consent to the political arrangements of the society into which they are born (Brighouse, 1998). Effective citizenship may be essential to a functioning liberal society, but gaining that stability though the indoctrination of future citizens goes against the very point and purpose of an open society. Civic education for freedom is legitimate, but not a civic education for stability.

The problem of liberal legitimacy explains, in part, the appeal of the convergence thesis of civic education. An education for democratic order and an education for liberty conflict in principle. Shoot for autonomy and you lose legitimacy by imposing an ideal of the good life on citizens who do not share in that same ideal. Shoot for stability and you lose legitimacy by indoctrinating citizens and compromising their autonomy.

However, these two aims can be tied together through practical convergence. In a nutshell, the liberal political order cannot persist without its citizens receiving a civic education that promotes minimal conditions for autonomy. All citizens, regardless of their conception of the good, share an interest in political stability. Therefore, the disruption to some citizen's views of the good life arising from such an education is a lamentable *but unintended* side effect.[7] These minimal conditions of autonomy at the same time guarantee that citizens endorse liberal political norms consensually through the use of their own critical capacities. Autonomy is therefore legitimately promoted by state-controlled education (on indirect grounds) while at the same time securing political legitimacy in general.

The Liberal Argument for Higher Civic Education

I take the practical convergence account, or convergence thesis, to be the least controversial argument that we have for the state's role in the provision of a compulsory civic education for children. But what does a practically convergent civic education look like in the higher education context? Can we extend this argument to educational provision beyond the compulsory level? Before diving right into this question, we should first reconsider the relationship between citizens and educational provision envisaged by a civic argument for compulsory education.

While the knowledge, skills, and dispositions promoted indirectly through a liberal civic education are plausibly similar to those promoted more directly through an education for personal autonomy (they have practical convergence) they are dissimilar in terms of their intended aims (they have ethical divergence). An education for autonomy is owed to each individual qua citizen. That is to say, the liberal state has an obligation to each citizen for education provision. But according to the civic argument the state doesn't owe individual citizens anything; rather, it needs something *from* citizens: their capacity and willingness to engage in a tolerant and reflective way with their fellow citizens in the interests of political stability.

Civic education, then, is not strictly for the benefit of the individual. It is an effort to bring about a valuable public good. And as Gina Schouten rightly notes, this means that while a citizenry must be educated civically in order to bring about political stability, a practically convergent civic education does not have to be experienced by *all* citizens:

> Plausibly, the justificatory community of the liberal democratic state can be preserved so long as we educate ... only *some* to rationally engage with other's private unshared reasons. Because rationally engaging with other's values and ideas is the vehicle for autonomy education, the public-centered argument seems to provide only a "herd immunity" case for autonomy education. The public good is realizable so long as *enough* students are educated for autonomy. (2018, p. 1086–1087)[8]

Because the state only needs so much of its citizenry to be civically educated in order to secure political stability, there is a natural limit on are how far the liberal state really needs to go in pursuit of its promotion.[9] For example, the state may be justified in introducing a civic education curriculum with autonomy-promoting underpinnings as part of a state-funded school system. It may introduce incentives in order to encourage sufficient enrollment in such a system. But it does not have the political authority to demand that all citizens receive a practically convergent civic education. A minority of citizens can opt out if they think that compulsory education is detrimental or harmful without posing a threat to democratic law and order.

Initially, this line of thinking actually looks to set out some favorable grounds for liberal citizenship as a basic aim of higher education. The emphasis on the non-coercive, voluntary nature of educational provision maps on to the situation of adults more easily than it does children. Adults are free to choose or abstain from higher education. This fact is often taken as a reason for seeing higher education in private, commodity terms. Why should citizens who do not choose, or are denied entry into, a higher education system bear the burden of funding? But a public goods argument for civic education steers us away from this conclusion. By shifting the benefits of public provision away from the individual and toward the political community, the state has reason to structure higher education in order to promote political stability. And this means they have grounds to intervene by introducing policies that ensure a critical mass of adult citizens consume higher education goods. For example, one effective way of incentivizing consumption is to make higher education less costly, or even free. There may be better policy levers. Regardless, the argument for civic education, when applied to adults, points to a role for higher education politically important enough to justify its provision by the state.

There are some real problems with this argument, however. First, recall that political stability is a public good that requires *enough* citizens to undergo a civic education. The idea was that this threshold level of civic competence (however we define it) is supposed to be achieved in the school system. Yet, if the school system is successful in realizing this goal—if it produces enough civically competent citizens—there is no further rationale for the state to allocate additional resources to produce political stability through a higher education. In fact, these additional investments would involve the allocation of resources to citizens who have already received a basic civic education in the school system, making it wasteful.

But let's say that an additional investment is not a waste and that there are good reasons for the state to continue to support civic education through the higher education system. For example, perhaps the higher education system aims to promote civic *excellence* as a kind of collective achievement. In this case, a mandatory civic curriculum for higher education students has the aim of identifying and cultivating those with a talent for civic engagement. These citizens will have a disproportionate, positive influence in the political sphere relative to other citizens.[10]

More problems lie ahead, however. In order to get a return on that investment, these talented higher education students would have to experience a civic education robust enough to raise their civic competence above and beyond what they have already achieved through a basic education. In order to achieve this, the state would have to compel adult citizens who want a higher education to undergo even more civic education regardless of what they themselves want to learn. But keep in mind that these citizens are in pursuit of their own, self-determined educational goals. Imposing further compulsory civic studies on them would introduce opportunity costs of time and effort that detract from these educational goals. It would be very difficult for the state to justify the imposition of such costs, especially when citizens who choose to pursue goals or aims unrelated to a higher education do not have to bear a similar burden. What is it about a higher education, as opposed to other paths in life, that would justify such a burden? Luckily, the public goods nature of political stability actually equips a defender of higher civic education with a good answer to this question.

The first step is to show that everyone in society has an obligation to undergo a civic education on grounds of fair play. The principle of fair play states that those who benefit from a cooperative scheme designed to promote a good have an obligation to contribute to that same scheme (Cullity, 1995; Hart, 1955; Klosko, 1987; 1990; Rasmusen, 2004). For example, if everyone in my neighborhood is shoveling snow that happens to be blocking a shared exit, and I typically use that exit, I should probably grab my shovel and join in the digging.

Fair play applies to political stability. Why? Stability is not just any kind of good. All citizens have a compelling interest in it. It is not just a "nice thing to have." It is a good equally necessary for an acceptable life for all citizens—what Klosko calls a "presumptive public good." Presumptive public goods should be provided to all citizens as a matter of justice. Everyone benefits from a stable political community, and so everyone has an obligation to contribute to it. This obligation is in force even in those circumstances where enough people have already undergone a civic education.[11] Therefore, the state has a legitimate reason to compel all citizens to receive a compulsory civic education. No opt outs allowed.

The second step is to show why this argument applies to higher education as well as basic education. This can be done by pointing out that higher education graduates will experience greater individual benefits in comparison to those who only get the compulsory version. Nothing wrong with this, by itself. However, many of these benefits will arise from graduate entry into jobs and offices that have an outsized impact on the general stability of society. Think of jobs in the judiciary, public policy, academia, technology, and health. Political stability requires that citizens in important legal, political, and corporate positions such as these—the kinds usually only open to those who receive a higher education—have a well-developed sense of tolerance for lives that are not the same as their own. It is therefore a matter of fair play that citizens in these positions match the private benefits they receive with civic excellence and public service in return.[12] The liberal state therefore has the authority to set a civic educational curriculum for adults and compel any who choose a higher education to undertake that curriculum. Let us call this particular argument *the higher civic education* justification.

Higher Civic Education, Autonomy, and Convergence

The higher civic education justification envisages a liberal state that supports higher education because of the role it can play in ensuring that graduates have received the education that they need in order to make a positive contribution to the social fabric of a liberal democracy. These exceptional citizens uphold principles of justice, reflect critically on their own commitments, and model civic norms such as tolerance to other citizens. But to what extent does this account hold up under scrutiny?

Recall that the argument for civic education is also an argument for the legitimate (if indirect) promotion of autonomy by the state. Its original appeal comes from the idea that it can rescue an autonomy-promoting education from the constraints of liberal neutrality.

But something interesting happens when we apply this argument to the situation of adults. Compelling adults (be they "elite" or otherwise) to undergo a civic education is not only costly in terms of the time that those citizens would otherwise spend in the pursuit of their own education goals, but it also undermines the very conditions of autonomy that make the convergence thesis appealing in the first place. Here is why: if any adult citizen who freely undertakes a higher education incurs a political obligation (or duty) to undergo further civic education, it follows that the state must therefore have the authority to direct these citizens to undertake a civic education *irrespective of their own reasons for attending*. Yet, being autonomous—and being treated as an autonomous being—means being free to critically reflect and question values, beliefs, and commitments. It also involves independence in terms of what one sees as worthy of seeking out in life. And it seems reasonable to extend these norms of treatment into the higher education domain. Adult citizens should be free to critically think about—and even reject—those aspects of the education they receive, especially education aimed at shaping their character or instilling beliefs. They should also be free to determine for themselves the value of that education within their pursuit of a good life, as best fits their life plans.

For those who believe that the fundamental public and political role of higher education is a redistributive one, this objection is not going to hold much water. It jars with what, in the last chapter, I called an *asymmetric conception* of political justice for higher education. Shaping the attitudes, preferences, and outlook of would-be elite citizens—making them "more egalitarian," for example—is an effective way to bring about a more just society. Furthermore, equality is part and parcel of political stability. It is widely thought that when societies become radically unequal, they become unstable.[13]

However, even if one takes distributive justice to be a central feature of a well-ordered liberal society there are moral limits on how far the state should go in shaping citizen's outlook in order to bring about a more egalitarian distribution. Indoctrination is one such limit. And it is this same limit, recall, that motivated the practical convergence thesis in the first place. The attractiveness of the thesis lay in the claim that the state can promote political stability (of which we can include the inculcation of dispositions that will support a just liberal society) alongside autonomy. The question, then, is whether or not practical convergence is conceptually possible for higher education as it is for a basic education.

Frankly, I think it is hard to imagine the terms under which a compulsory civic education and autonomy promotion can converge for adults.[14] For example, consider the problem of how a civic education for adults should handle controversial political issues—issues such as abortion, economic justice, and the limits of freedom of expression—that citizens are bound to have strong views on. These are issues on which citizens may reasonably differ, and so we want citizens to exercise respectful tolerance of those that disagree.

Now imagine a civic educator who introduces these issues in class discussion in order to help higher education students develop their civic capacities. It turns out that these students had competent teachers and have already acquired the necessary civic virtues through their basic (compulsory civic) education. Consequently, while they disagree with their fellow students on some basic matters they do so respectfully. They give reasons for their viewpoint, and give due regard to the reasons given by their classmates. How should the civic educator respond? They could respond by doing nothing more at all. The fact that the students are able to respectfully disagree and give due regard for other points of view suggests that their civic educational preparation is already complete, and competed well.

This may be an understandable response, but it amounts to conceding that a compulsory civic education for higher education students is not needed in the first place. And we can expect this to be a frequent concession in a system where everyone who gets a higher education will have already received a civic education in the compulsory system.

Here one might object that I have set out an implausible set of circumstances. Even if we had a well-funded, well-executed civic education program for every K–12 school, we can anticipate that there will be some (many!) students who could benefit from even *more* civic education. For example, the civic educator could focus their efforts on students who are unreasonable about controversial issues in the classroom. Or those that seem willfully ignorant about the advantages they have received earlier in life. This approach is appealing because we would arguably be increasing the civic competence of students who may have failed to sufficiently achieve such competence at a more basic stage of their education. Higher civic education would function as a kind of "quality assurance process" for citizens moving into important jobs and offices that have an outsized impact on political stability.

It seems to me that this response is entirely appropriate in a non-ideal world, where institutions never function perfectly.[15] But note that the argument we are in pursuit of is that civic education should be a central public and political aim of higher education. It is a *justification* of higher education—a statement of the basic interests that the institution aims to serve and the warrants state support. That is to say, such an aim should structure what higher education institutions ought to be striving for in a liberal society. It should define its purpose within the larger political community.

To be sure, one indirect benefit of higher education is that it will "catch" students who have been ill-prepared to make their way through to more advanced forms of study, be they of a civic, vocational, theoretical, or other variety. For example, when students join a civil engineering program in order to learn, say, how to design a building, it is expected that these students already have a certain level of preparatory knowledge, understanding, and skill. But we also know that not all students are going to be as equally prepared. We should therefore build in a remedial education that gets them up to speed.

But it would be quite another thing to claim that a remedial education should be the ultimate goal. This would mean abandoning the distinctive point and purpose of the engineering program: learning how to design buildings. A remedial education is pointed in the direction of the (mis)education that came before it and, for this reason, makes little sense as the basis for the foundational justification of post-secondary institutions. Similarly, saying that we should make civic education a key aim of higher education on the grounds that not all students have received an adequate civic education at the compulsory level is similarly backwards looking.

If a basic education aims to instill civic virtues in the entire polity, continuing to pursue this aim at the higher education level (albeit limited to a selected segment of the population) calls for an explanation of how this further pursuit adds value in a manner that justifies that pursuit. This justification must be weightier than "remediation" or "quality control" or "more of the same." Otherwise, such an institution would have no independent standing. Its reason for existing would solely be to fix the problems of the imperfect institution (i.e., compulsory schooling) that comes before it. It would be an institution that exists for strictly post hoc reasons. And in this sense, it would really be a mere extension of the existing K–12 system.

So, do we have reasons for directing a higher civic education at adult citizens who have *already* received a basic education sufficient for securing political stability? One answer might be that such an education can condition students to shift their viewpoints in the same general ideological direction so that they are more likely to agree on a host of (normally controversial and divisive) issues. We could make them all social democrats, for example. The reasoning behind this approach would be that, as graduates, they will contribute to a stronger and hence even *more* stable political consensus. The average citizen may be free to disagree and harbor outlier ideological views, but elite graduates should share a strong consensus on a variety of public issues so that they can coordinate their actions effectively and get important things done for the rest of us.

The problem with this solution is that conditioning or indoctrinating citizens to adopt a particular political point of view means giving up on autonomy promotion, so this approach fails in terms of practice convergence. It promotes stability at the expense of individual liberty, but practical convergence is supposed to give us both.

Another solution is to go completely in the other direction and avoid engaging students on controversial political matters altogether. The would-be civic educator could focus on the development of intellectual habits believed to be constitutive of autonomy—reason-assessment and epistemic charity, for example—in the hopes that this will have a positive effect on their ability to handle political disagreement later in life, post-graduation. Students, for example, could bide their time reviewing informal logical fallacies and studying the nature and scope of cognitive bias. They could reflect on their reasons for choosing in spheres of life that are not explicitly political. This is surely "value added" because, if such an educational program were successful, graduates would be more skilled at critical thought.

Note, however, that this involves removing all the relevant civic content, making it a civic education in name only. What remains is not a civic education "practically" the same as an autonomy-promoting education, but an education that simply aims at the development of intellectual capacities required for autonomy (even if the civic educator *claims* to be doing otherwise).

But why should this matter, so long as it leads to better citizens as a consequence? Remember that the argument is that we are justified in compelling adult citizens who want a higher education to undergo further civic education in order to bring about great political stability. But citizens who see autonomy as a controversial ideal of character would have good reason to claim that forcing other adult citizens to undergo an education of this kind, even if you put the label "civic education" on it, goes far beyond what is warranted by liberal neutrality. They might buy the argument that civic education cannot but involve the reinforcement of some minimal conditions of autonomy, but an education squarely focused on the development of intellectual capacities strongly associated with autonomy in the hopes that it *might* help those students work through political controversy looks more like a philosophical sleight of hand.[16] Further, these citizens could object that the minimal conditions of autonomy realized as part of a basic compulsory civic education are sufficient for good citizenship regardless of one's future job or office. To claim otherwise is to suggest that citizens coming from cultural traditions that do not prize autonomy are unqualified for elite civic or economic roles. Therefore, this approach also fails in terms of practical convergence.

At this point one could object that the conditions for success that I have set out for a worthwhile, non-redundant higher civic education rests on the assumption that it ought to be practically convergent in the same way for adults as it is for children. By "just as practically convergent" I mean that a civic education for adults should, just as it is for children, be consistent with the *promotion* of autonomy. This assumption unnecessarily hamstrings our ability to extend the civic argument to higher education. After all, as I have already granted, adults are already presumed to have attained minimal conditions for autonomy in principle. Therefore, higher education institutions do not have to achieve practical convergence between the promotion of political stability and the *promotion* of their autonomy. They only need to make sure that civic education is consistent with *respect* for the autonomy of students. And this considerably lowers bar for practical convergence.

Does it lower the bar enough, however? A compulsory civic higher education imposes a burden on adult citizens against their own will. One might therefore argue that even if we drop autonomy *promotion* as a condition for practical convergence, such an imposition arguably *disrespects* citizens' autonomy. It therefore fails to achieve practical convergence on even this more relaxed version.

Higher Civic Education as Vocational Education

However, there is still room for the defender of a higher civic education to maneuver on this point. Recall that the original reason for imposing a civic education on higher education students is that they tend to have an outsized impact on the political culture of society by virtue of the jobs and offices that they tend to occupy. It is therefore possible to claim that a basic purpose of higher education is, in fact, preparation for a special civic vocation, or role, for which citizens ought to be qualified irrespective of whatever particular job or office they come to hold on graduation. To seek out a higher education is to consent to the preparation necessary for being so qualified, and we have no problem compelling people to become qualified before they are able to carry out a vocation. After all, when people choose to enter specific professions they consent to learning about the norms, standards, and values that define that field or profession. They are not free to pick and choose among these norms and standards. And yet we do not think of this as an attack on their autonomy. It would be hard to have sympathy for a dentistry student who balks at having to do a course in dental anatomy on autonomy grounds.

We can apply the same kind of reasoning to higher education. If higher education graduates play a special civic role by virtue of the esteemed social positions that they are likely to occupy and, further, they freely chose to receive that higher education, they are morally obligated to obtain the civic knowledge, skills, and dispositions that define that special civic role.[17] On this account, we indeed have convergence between further compulsory civic preparation and respect for autonomy. This is because respect for a person's autonomy does mean that we must refrain from requiring others to live up to the obligations that apply to them. These obligations must simply be freely entered into. So long as higher education institutions are clear to students about their civic educational aims and the requirements that come along with it, such institutions are on solid autonomy-respecting ground. Higher civic education conforms to the practical convergence thesis.

This argument, however, overreaches. It seems right that any professional program in which graduates are going to play an important role in society ought to—and often does—contain compulsory civic educational, moral educational, and other ethical curricular components. Framing graduates as citizens who are *in general* aspiring to a special civic role exploits this intuition by making us think that the same line of reasoning applies. Just as it is justifiable to compel students who have chosen to pursue a particular vocation, so it is justifiable to compel students who have chosen to pursue the "vocation" of active citizenship.

The problem is that framing graduates in this way elides important differences between the general student and students in particular programs, in terms of the nature and the scope of the compulsion involved. First, a compulsory curriculum, in the case of those aspiring to a particular profession, is absolutely necessary for safeguarding *specific* standards that come with being qualified for a profession. These specific standards are designed to protect the public interest. This especially because professionals often hold power over others, and so we want to leave very little room for dissent and ambiguity about what counts as professional and ethical conduct. Second, they specify standards *logically connected* to the work of the profession. A professional ethics curriculum for lawyers will look different than one for teachers. Finally, these logically connected standards also enable professionals to carry out their roles well. They are therefore aligned with, or may even be a constitutive feature of, the vocation through which graduates have *freely chosen to flourish*. Teaching primary school, for example, requires certain ideals of character such as care and sensitivity. People who are attracted to primary school teaching as a profession are unlikely to see a deep conflict between learning about what it means to care for younger students and flourishing in the role of teacher. If they do, they are likely better off in pursuit of a different profession.

In the case of the professions there is a clear compatibility between the justification of the compulsion, the interests of society, and the student's own autonomously determined interests. These requirements are logically connected to what it means to succeed in that professional role. Consequently, any paternalism involved will serve the student's own self-determined goals even if they may not fully appreciate this paternalistic treatment as they work their way through the curriculum.

A sweeping compulsory civic education for higher education students is not like this at all. A compulsory civic education, in the form of imposed preparation for a special civic role, is justified on the grounds that students need to be directed toward the specific standards of civic excellence or civic flourishing. But we cannot assume a similar alignment between such standards and the student's own goals. For example, you might think that society ought to be more heavily redistributive, but I happen to think that economic growth raises all boats. We may each disagree with the policy preferences of the other, but both views are reasonable. And we both share in the desire to contribute to society. This might mean joining a left-leaning think tank for you, and the private sector for me. We can therefore imagine each of us relying on different norms, values, skills, and knowledge in order to make good on that desire.

This is all to say that the "standards" of good liberal citizenship are not like professional standards. Because they are liberal, they have a good bit of freedom built into them. Far more than professional standards, in fact. Students choose a higher education for many reasons, and even if we allow that some of those reasons should connect to an other-regarding interest in contributing to society, their own developing sense of what this contribution should look like will *reasonably* diverge, and should be free to so diverge, from any conception of civic excellence more specific than the most general liberal values and norms concerning respect for the law and for others, for reason-giving, and for the democratic process—values and norms that will have already been inculcated, we might add, through a basic education. As Michael Huemer points out, for example, the political ethos of individual citizens can be wide and diverse while still abiding by civic standards of reasonableness and tolerance often associated with political liberalism:

> [A]narchist thinkers do not, as a rule, appear particularly less rational, informed, or reasonable than partisans of other political views. They do not, for example, refuse to offer reasons for their views, refuse to consider objections, or refuse to take into account the interests of others. (p. 43)

My point is that the compulsion involved in imposing a civic education for higher education students across the board is quite unlike the compulsion involved in an education for specific professions. First, the former involves imposing standards that have no logical relationship to a student's self-determined aims and goals. Second, because of this fact a civic education, if it is to surpass what would have already been achieved at the school level, must condition students into accepting a *specific conception* of civic virtue and accept it regardless of the student's own developing sense of civic flourishing. That is to say, the civic vocation argument not only fails to respect autonomy, rather, it is autonomy *undermining*. Worse still, this autonomy-undermining solution is unnecessary: we could probably get the same public benefits as a higher civic education without the (illegitimate) paternalism simply by making sure that civic aims are incorporated (in their own, relevant way) within professional programs.[18]

One might here object that many students really do aspire to be part of a civic, economic, or cultural elite. Further, these students will be stand in relation to the public in a manner similar to professionals: they will come to hold a lot of power over other citizens. It would be irresponsible to fail to provide such students with an education that makes them more conscientious about the powers and the advantages they have and how to use them in a responsible way.

I agree. But nothing follows from my agreement with this line of thinking that necessarily justifies civic education as a fundamental purpose of higher education. It is worth reminding ourselves that many, if not most, of the educational paths open to students simply don't lead to either elite positions or significant advantages unless we construe "elite" to mean "anyone who graduates from a post-compulsory institution" and "significant advantage" to mean something like "upward mobility relative to non-graduates." It would be more plausible to claim that such an education should target elite institutions (e.g., Harvard, Oxford) where pathways to the elite and disproportionately advantaged are well-trod. In a stratified and non-ideal world that has Harvards and Oxfords in it, a civic education of this sort makes sense as a remedy for unfair advantages. Although, we should here only target specific courses of study that are reliably shown to lead graduates into specific elite positions. And such specifically targeted curricula should also, given what I have already said about civic norms and reasonable disagreement, leave room for different conceptions of what good liberal citizenship can look like.

Nonetheless, the fact that elite higher education is a small part of the system does not really get to the heart of the objection: even in ideal circumstances, the fact remains that graduates *in general* will receive some advantages relative to other citizens simply by virtue of a higher education. There is nothing illegitimately coercive about requiring these students to undertake a civic education as a condition of admission into the system.[19] Given the uneven distribution of these advantages, graduates should learn how to give back for the benefit of the least well-off. The graduate's vocation, we might say, does not refer to any kind of special civic identity so much as an obligation to wield their advantages for the betterment of others.

This admirable assertion loses sight of what the argument for a compulsory civic education for adults is really all about. This idea is that we are justified in imposing a (i) compulsory *civic* education on all students because civic education is (ii) a fundamental aim of *higher education*. Talk about graduate benefits and non-graduate burdens does little to support this idea.

First, this assertion assumes that the fact of graduate advantage justifies civic education as a leading aim of higher education. But imagine an educational pathway that almost never leads to an advantaged position. If civic education is a key aim of higher education, it follows that this path should not be subject to curricular goals that address the ways in which that person ought to be more conscientious and other-regarding. It would effectively mean that this pathway is no longer a proper part of a higher education.

This because educational aims serve to justify what should properly be the business of educational institutions, and what should not. And according to the "giving back" assertion, only those paths that confer clear advantages to graduates belong in the system to begin with.

This seems to put the advantaged cart before the educational horse. The carpentry student, for example, may well benefit from knowledge and understanding about the health and other dangerous implications of (figuratively) cutting corners. Their customers will be better off if the carpenter knows and understands the how and why of safety regulations for different materials and so on. And understanding the structural inequalities in property development and home ownership can inspire then to contribute for the benefit of the least well-off through organizations such as Habitat for Humanity.

My point is that linking the necessity of such an education to "eliteness" and "advantage" could unintentionally reinforce the disempowering idea that citizens in esteemed positions in society have a more significant role to play in civic life. It would establish a kind of "institutional hidden curriculum" that messages to the public that the only citizens who can be consequential actors in the service of a more just and fair society are those who have most of the institutional power. One way to convince a person that they have no power is to tell them that they shoulder less responsibility than others.

Second, one can promote the interests of less well-off non-graduates without imposing autonomy-threatening civic aims on higher education students, and without raising civic outcomes to the status of a central aim of a higher education. The idea that either is necessary for the redress of unequal benefits between the graduate and the non-graduate trades on a lot of ambiguity about what a higher civic education actually entails.

Consider: the reason why we would still want the carpentry student to receive some kind of conscientious or other-regarding education as part of their training is because this is a necessary feature of any initiation into a particular social practice, be that an occupation, profession, discipline, or so on. What inclines us to think otherwise is the assumption that this education can only be achieved through a "civic" form advanced by its defenders: an emphasis on public reason, perhaps reigning in one's appetite for more political advantage and opportunity, reflectiveness about basic political principles, and so on. My point here is that the self-determined goals that a student has in view, as evinced by their particular educational pathway, should drive the other-regarding curriculum that they are required to experience. In some cases, this curriculum will be explicitly "civic" in the specialist sense of the term. A citizen aspiring to practice the law is one obvious example. But this is but one instance of a more general range of ethically minded educational goals that ought to be part and parcel of almost any post-compulsory educational pathway. To call this "civic" seems to stretch the meaning of the term too far. Civic aims are *but one kind* of educational aim we can marshal in the interests of mitigating unfair advantages.

Therefore, in order for the assertion that graduates should learn how to serve others to have purchase on the justification of a civic conception of higher education, we require further precision about the educational pathways that are likely to lead students into elite spaces and that would warrant a genuinely civic education as opposed to a more generic, other-regarding kind. But such precision must at the same time concede my earlier claim: that the kind of education an adult student may be legitimately compelled to receive should have a logical connection to the pathway they are taking. For example, nurses should be familiar with the diversity of cultural norms and meanings that citizens from different backgrounds ascribe to health and well-being. They should have a deep understanding of the many social determinants that lead to inequalities in the health care system. This is clearly autonomy facilitating. It will empower the nurse to do their job, and do it well, even if they do not recognize it at the time of their training. But is this really a "civic education"? If so, it would look very different from the "civic education" that a political studies student, or medical student, or physical education student, receives.

To be sure, when we claim that any education that requires students to think about others, the (dis)advantages that individuals may have experienced, or other ethical dimensions of the work they aspire to do as "civic education," a higher education cannot but be civic. But now the concept of a civic education simply means that for any educational path there are potential ethical and political issues worthy of exploring within that pathway. But this just *is* education.

In other words, to claim that all students entering into the higher education system ought to receive a compulsory civic education is just another way of saying that anyone who chooses a higher education consents to an education! To refer to this as a "civic" education is therefore misleading. It suggests that this is a separate education that we need to bring in from the outside in order to compensate for the intellectual or moral blindness of "non-civic education." This is an oddly transactional view of the matter: we will let you be a doctor so long as in return you *also* consent to also learning about how you can better serve marginalized communities. But it is not clear why it should be framed in this way. Such learning is easily defensible as a necessary—immanent, to put it more accurately—part of what it is to be a good and virtuous physician. Think about how peculiar it would be to say something like, "He was the very model of good physician. Not that great at helping patients that were poor or impoverished, mind you, but just watch the magic he could work at his expensive private practice!"

Where does this leave a civic conception of higher education? At the compulsory level, practical convergence means that we can promote personal autonomy on the way to a civic education. But when we reach the post-compulsory stage, practical convergence must work in the *other* direction. By this I simply mean that we can promote all the skills we need in order to ensure that graduates will conduct their lives in a respectful, politically stabilizing, and prosocial manner on their way to realizing their own, self-determined educational goals. And these skills will in many cases look indistinguishable, in practice, from what a civic education might call for. In fact, it will include these and more, besides, because it will be responsive to the distinctive roles that various educational pathways will typically nudge graduates toward.

The claim that reflective, ethical, and other so-called civic aims should be an important part of what makes different pathways educationally worthwhile is quite different from the claim that civic education is *the* aim of higher education. The latter suggests that the justification of higher education as an institution is grounded in its civic educational function, that is, its ability to promote our interest in both individual freedoms and political stability. It is the institution's *raison d'etre*. But it is exactly *this* claim which I have argued does not stand up to scrutiny, not the idea that citizens should learn to be more conscientious and other-regarding as part of whatever education they choose to take part in. To be sure, liberal societies need civic education. But civic educational *purposes* belong to the compulsory stage of education where all young citizens ought to receive them as equal citizens. And so an argument in search of the public and political role of higher education in a liberal society must look to other aims and purposes.

Conclusion

In this chapter I assessed the prospects of citizenship as an aim that could justify a public and political role for higher education. Such an education must address a tension between two interests that such a conception of higher education would be responsible for protecting: the autonomy of citizens and the political stability of society. The promise of the practical convergence account of civic education was that it could show how the provision of higher education can respect both of these interests.

The attempt to make good on this promise encountered a number of difficulties. Practical convergence looks to be unattainable in the case of adult students, favoring either autonomy or political stability in a way that runs afoul of legitimate liberal worries about indoctrination. And even when we ease up on the conditions required for practical convergence by claiming that citizens freely consent to a higher civic education, the convergence thesis seems to hold only when we draw a false equivalence between preparation for professional life and preparation for civic life, or by stretching the concept of "civic" education past the point at which the term has any precise meaning that distinguishes it from education more generally. We should therefore conclude that while it makes sense to cherish the indirect benefits of higher education for citizens' civic capacities, liberal citizenship ought not be understood as an overarching aim that justifies state involvement in its management and provision. This leaves us free to consider the argument that autonomy alone should be a key public and political aim of higher education.

3
Adulthood and the Right to Education

Over the next two chapters I will argue that the personal autonomy of citizens is an interest for which higher education should be primarily responsible and that this interest is sufficiently important that higher education should be understood a right. In this chapter, I argue that holding personal autonomy as a political ideal entails a right to education over a full life, not just childhood. In chapter 4 I argue that higher education is the institution that ought to be primarily responsible for ensuring that this right is claimable by any adult citizen. From there I turn to the implications of this right for the political authority of the liberal state (chapter 5), distributive justice (chapter 6), and policy/practice (chapter 7).

In the first section, I review the terms under which autonomy is basic to liberal citizenship and I explain how this justifies an individual right to a basic compulsory education in childhood. In the second section, I argue that the tendency to see this right as applying to childhood only is due to an unduly narrow view of autonomy as a political ideal. Finally, I defend an expanded view of autonomy that justifies a role for education in a good life *in media res*. I argue that this role is sufficiently important enough to warrant extending citizens' educational rights to include post-compulsory provision.

Personal Autonomy and the Right to Basic Education

A fundamental idea motivating the social vision of higher education that I defend is that liberal citizenship means equal access to education over a life. One implication of this idea is that citizens have an individual *and equal* interest in access to post-compulsory education. By this I mean that this interest does not merely reflect the preferences that some citizens might happen to have in receiving education beyond a more basic level. Rather, citizens have an interest in post-compulsory education as a primary good available to all simply by virtue of being a liberal citizen.

Before I go into the justification of this interest in further detail, it's worth reviewing how this account differs from the usual path to justifying the public and political value of higher education. Typically speaking, we justify public support for higher education by pointing to public goods generated by the higher education system such as political stability (as in the last chapter). On this view, citizens indirectly benefit from the spillover effects of higher education even if they do not access higher education goods themselves.

This approach is understandable. If we accept the premise that higher education is an individual benefit, the fact that some people prefer not to attend makes it difficult to explain why it would be just or fair to require non-attendees to take on any of the burden of funding the system.

An argument for post-compulsory education grounded in the claim that it is in the equal individual interest of all citizens rejects this approach. It sees the availability of higher education as something to be extended to all liberal citizens *even if* some citizens decide not to avail of it at all. It therefore bypasses the need to point to public goods as a fundamental justification for public support.[1]

Public goods are surely a feather in the cap of a publicly funded system of higher education. For example, on a public goods account it makes sense to lower the economic barriers to higher education because the more people access the system, the more law-abidingness and civic engagement we get in return. And this outcome benefits everyone by making for a more robust and stable democratic community. But on the account that I defend, these public goods are not the *fundamental* reason why the state should make higher education accessible to citizens, funded by that state. It should be accessible on the grounds that access to the system is something that every individual citizen can in principle directly benefit from. That is to say, it ought to be accessible as a universal entitlement similar to health care or compulsory education.

It is not too difficult to see that a conception of higher education justified (fundamentally) in terms of the individual interest that citizens have in education throughout a life would look different from one justified (fundamentally) in terms of public goods. In the latter, the state wants more citizens to access the system only up until that point at which greater access is sufficient enough to generate the desired positive externalities for the rest of society. But once this critical mass of society is accessing the system, further increases won't add much to, say, political stability or other public goods. The state can then permissibly ease off of its efforts at increasing access. But in the former case, the state must ensure that each and every citizen can exercise their right to further education irrespective of the effect of access on the (over)production of public goods.

But now one should ask: what grounds do we have for ever thinking that access to post-compulsory education is an equal interest for citizens to begin with? After all, that fact that something is beneficial for me and many others does not entail a right to that thing. I have two young children, and it is clear that making higher education free would make life much easier for me, financially speaking, in the event they decide to access the system. Many parents in the same position as myself would agree. Should society therefore make higher education free? It is true that many people would directly benefit if higher education were costless for the individual. And it may also be true that many others will benefit indirectly from such a policy. Less money spent on servicing student loans means more money for buying a first home (and more money for realtors and property developers, as well as the many people who work in adjacent industries). But this does not demonstrate that access to a higher education is an interest shared by each individual citizen in principle, and nor does it show that access is sufficiently important for higher education to be allocated as an entitlement. All it shows is that some citizens would benefit individually from a free higher education, and there may be enough of a social return to the society that helps make it free to justify a public subsidy.

What we are looking for are interests shared equally by individual citizens *irrespective of their actual preferences*. How can we discover these interests? One method, prominent among liberally minded conceptions of political morality, is to ask what *any* free and equal citizen would need in order or to live well regardless of their particular ideas or preferences about what a good life would consist in.[2] This is sometimes referred to as an argument from a *political conception of the person.*

On this approach, determining what is in every citizen's interest involves figuring out what any person would need in order to lead the best life they can without prejudging what a good life ought to look like in its particulars.[3] The aim here is to reason about what is just or fair without lapsing into self-interest, motivated reasoning, or other biases. For example, to claim that a university education should be free because devotion to academic disciplines and the pursuit of knowledge for its own sake is a good way for anyone to live would fail as an argument from a political conception of the person. This is because such a claim is plainly based on a particular, non-generalizable view of what a good and happy life must consist in. It is simply implausible to think that every citizen wishes to spend their life in this way.

Claims about universal entitlements are therefore restricted to what any individual citizen requires simply in order to be a citizen of a liberal society. In the Rawlsian framework, for example, such interests are called *primary goods*, a specification of the needs of all citizens when questions of justice arise (Rawls, 2009, pp. 54–55; Rawls, 2006 pp. 188–189).[4] This formulation transcends Rawls' liberalism, however. George Klosko, for example, refers to entitlements as *presumptive public goods* (1987). These are goods necessary—*needed*—for an acceptable life for all citizens. The philosopher Jurgen Habermas calls them *generalizable interests* (1990).

In sum, for something to pass as a basic interest or entitlement it must be:

i) in the *equal* interest;
ii) of each *individual* citizen;
iii) regardless of their *particular* conception of the good.

I should note that failure to satisfy these criteria does not *prima facie* disqualify a popular preference from having legitimate purchase on educational policy or practice; rather, it calls for a different justification.

Here is what I mean: imagine a society in which a majority of citizens want a free higher education. The fact of majority preference for free higher education does not make it an entitlement. But citizens are free to advocate for this preference. One way is to vote in a majority party that supports free higher education as a public policy. So long as the policy does not undermine basic liberal principles of legitimacy and justice, we could accept it as a reasonable outcome of the democratic process. The policy is legitimate for the particular democratic community, a justification grounded in a majoritarian principle of democracy.

However, this is not the same as the justification of an enshrined basic right or entitlement endogenous to liberal societies in general.

Our imagined society's policy of free higher education is surely legitimate. But it is also contingent. By this I mean that the next government would be well within its rights to roll back the policy if the preferences of the majority of citizens changed. An argument for free higher education justified in terms of a political conception of the person, however, would try to show that access to higher education satisfies, or secures something, essential to liberal citizenship. As such, it could not be (justly) rolled back with a change of government.

Justification by way of political conception of the person makes it possible to see why citizens have specifically educational entitlements by virtue of their status as free and equal. All children have an interest in acquiring, through an education, minimal conditions for autonomy. These conditions empower citizens to make informed choices about how they want to live and who they wish to be, regardless of the particular conception of the good they end up adopting. And because personal autonomy is, on this view, a political ideal shared by all, a liberal state that secures such an interest through a publicly funded system of education isn't playing favorites between citizens with different conceptions of the good life.[5] In fact, a society that did not provide for such an education would be at risk of undermining citizens' equal interest in personal autonomy: some citizens will inherit social, cultural, economic, and other resources bases as a matter of luck that will make it easier for them to cultivate minimal conditions of autonomy than it will for unlucky citizens.[6] The state therefore has a reason to provide such resources to all.

The Political Conception of the Person and Adult Citizens

In the last section, I showed how an individual entitlement, or right of citizenship, identifies something basic to life in a liberal society.

A right to education holds irrespective of the particular policy choices that actual liberal societies make. I also outlined the terms under which education is an individual entitlement in the form of an education for minimal conditions of autonomy. But why should we think that adults have any further educational entitlements once these minimal conditions have been justly met?

The answer involves making explicit a logical move in the argument for educational entitlements that is often overlooked. Citizens are entitled to a basic education because they have an interest in autonomy as a condition of liberal citizenship. There are, of course, a number of practical and empirical reasons for thinking that realizing this interest requires a basic education for all children (see, for example, Colburn, 2010, p. 96). However, we can and should distinguish between the *logical conditions* necessary and sufficient for autonomy, on the one hand, and the *educational conditions* that have to be satisfied in order to fulfill these logical conditions, on the other. It is the relationship between these two sets of conditions that I want to examine more closely.

If one assumes that the development of certain internal conditions—say, cognitive and affective capacities such as reflectiveness and self-control that, once developed, remain firmly in place for the remainder of a citizen's life barring physical or mental decline—are necessary and sufficient for a personally autonomous life understood as a political ideal, it follows that citizens should be entitled to a basic education aimed at cultivating these conditions. But no more than this. Any further education is at the discretion of the autonomous individual themselves, for which they are responsible, and wholly dependent on the preferences that they choose to act upon.

In practical terms, the public and political emphasis on the right to public education seems to mirror this view. Children, lacking the requisite conditions, are non-autonomous and therefore entitled to an education; adults, now in possession of the requisite conditions, are autonomous and therefore no longer entitled.

Now, if someone wanted to show that educational entitlements should not be restricted to a basic education it would make sense to challenge the assumption holding the entitlement back: that the development of these cognitive and affective conditions are individually necessary and jointly sufficient for autonomy. But note that there are actually *two* assumptions in play. One assumption is about the *amount* of education empirically necessary and sufficient in order to ensure that people develop these internal cognitive and affective conditions to a degree what would put them into a permanent autonomous state. The other assumption is about the *logical conditions* necessary and sufficient for a person to be in an autonomous state. This is a subtle distinction. Let's consider each of these assumptions, in turn.

First, one could agree that some range of affective and cognitive (or other) conditions are necessary and sufficient for autonomy but reject that claim that a one-off educational development of these conditions is sufficient for personal autonomy over a full life. Perhaps we can say such a one-off is merely necessary—it gets us to autonomy—but that further educational interventions need to take place in order to ensure that citizens remain in an autonomous state. For example, we could argue that autonomy is like endurance training. Endurance athletes are to exercise as autonomous citizens are to education. That is, citizens must be continually engaged in a process of formal education over their entire lives if they are to maintain the cognitive and affective fitness for minimal autonomy.

If true, this would succeed in extending the entitlement to education beyond the traditional K–12 timespan. Personal autonomy is basic to liberal citizenship, and so we'd have a compelling reason to conclude that access to education should be a lifelong necessity, not merely childhood specific. Of course, this is unlikely to be the case. The idea that people need to be managed by an educational institutional over their complete life in order for autonomous living is surely a contradictory one. It would mean that we really aren't autonomous in any meaningful sense; we require perpetual institutional support.

My larger point is that challenging the sufficiency of the current K–12 allocation of education for achieving an autonomous state of mind is simply to claim that we need *more of the same* education. In practical terms, this might mean that a compulsory education should follow us much further into our lives. Maybe we would need a K–18 education in order to reflect the longer timespan citizens need in order to permanently develop the internal conditions for autonomy. But note that adjustments to the duration of the basic education to which citizens are entitled have no bearing on citizens' educational entitlements *after* these conditions have been achieved. It tells us nothing about any entitlement to education beyond the adequate fulfillment of these conditions.

Second, one could challenge the assumption that internal conditions of autonomy are themselves sufficient for autonomy. This approach is more promising. In order to understand how such a challenge might go, consider debate over the political justice of health care provision. In *Just Heath Care* (1985), Norman Daniels has appealed to the principle of equality of opportunity in order to justify the value of health care. On his view, health care is, in essence, an entitlement that helps secure our right to equal opportunity. Equality of opportunity is the political ideal, and health care for all is what gets us to that ideal.

But Daniels argues that this all rests on an unjustifiably narrow take on the meaning and scope of "opportunity" in a free society (i.e., jobs and offices). On the contrary, he claims, what counts as a meaningful opportunity changes along with the circumstances of a person's stage of life. For example, many senior citizens shift their focus to opportunities linked to the completion of (and enjoyment of) major life projects. Time spent with family or volunteering in the community are good examples of this. Disease and chronic illness can interfere with such pursuits. Accordingly, health care should be allocated on the grounds that it is indispensable to the fair pursuit of valuable opportunities *over a life*.[7] Here we are not talking about how much health care we need in order to pursue opportunities, but the logical conditions that make something *count* as an opportunity worth supporting through access to health care.

Consider the following example. The relationship between health care and opportunity for an early-career professional athlete will be very different than it is for a retired athlete. The professional athlete puts a degree of stress on their body that leads to the occasional hospital visit. The retired athlete is no longer competing in professional events, but they enjoy a casual run and joining in amateur races with grandchildren. This difference does not justify a right to health care for the active professional athlete and not the retired one. Accordingly, the design of basic institutions should follow from a broad interpretation of the meaning of opportunity, allowing us to see why the right to health care extends over one's entire plan of life (Daniels, 1985, pp. 103–105). A lifespan view of the meaning of opportunity entails, logically speaking, much more than valuable jobs and offices for a political conception of the person. One significant consequence is that health care institutions have a more robust public and political role to play than earlier theories of justice have tended to assume.

What holds for health care may not hold in quite the same way for education. My point is that our conception of what opportunity means as a political ideal informs principled, not merely empirical, judgments about the nature and scope of citizens' entitlements. And so too our conception of what personal autonomy means as a worthy political ideal. In fact, Daniels' broader insight into the relationship between the meaning of basic political ideals and political justice points to a way forward in the argument for educational entitlements: just as we can expand the meaning of *opportunity* in order to explain why health care ought to be an entitlement irrespective of a citizen's stage of life, so too can we expand the meaning of *autonomy* in order to explain why education represents a more robust and wide-ranging entitlement than a more constrained view of autonomy might otherwise suggest to us.

Why is such an expanded view warranted? My view is that the public and political value of autonomy as an educational aim is shortchanged by the assumption that autonomy is strictly an internal capacity—a certain set of cognitive and affective conditions—unrelated to the broader social environment in which an individual pursues the good. If you are committed (rightly, on my view) to the view that education is an entitlement on the grounds that it is necessary for securing the autonomy of all citizens, but you assume (wrongly, on my view) that autonomy is one and the same as an individual's particular state of mind, then educational entitlements will only be justified up until that point at which the individual has achieved that state of mind. (Note that this treatment of personal autonomy is similar to the consumer sovereignty interpretation that I outlined in chapter 1.)

But just as opportunity means more than merely jobs and offices when we take a lifespan view, autonomy means more than merely internal conditions when we account for the demands that autonomy places on citizens beyond childhood. Here is why:

The idea that autonomy is more than a set of minimal conditions related to thinking, judging, and choosing is Joseph Raz's.[8] He describes autonomy as being more like a project, or achievement:

> An autonomous person is part author of his own life.... The autonomous person's life is marked not only by what it is but also by what it might have been and by the way it became what it is. A person is autonomous only if he has a variety of acceptable options available to him to choose from and his life became what it is through his choice of some of these options. (1986, p. 204)

On this view, a capacity for autonomy—to be able to achieve self-determined goals—has "partly to do with the state of the individual concerned (that he is of sound mind, capable of rational thought and action, etc.) and partly to do with the circumstances of his life (especially that he has a sufficient range of significant options available to him *at different stages of his life*)" (Raz, 1986, p. 204, emphasis mine). Both conditions must obtain for a self-determined life.

First, if a person does not have the moral and cognitive ability to identify and pursue goals worth seeking, they cannot be said to be acting autonomously.[9] Second, even if they have the capacity to choose, it may be that few worthwhile choices are on offer. If so, we would not say the person is living a meaningfully self-determined life. Imagine, for example, a bright young student whose family has told him that he must pursue a profession. He is given the choice of law, medicine, or engineering but is strictly forbidden from contemplating anything outside of this narrow range. The student has a restricted range of significant options. He can choose a profession, but he can only *be* a professional. The young student is not in a good position to be the author of his own life.

It's the second condition that deserves further attention and will, as I argue in the next section, help to make the case for an entitlement to education over a life. There are three aspects of this condition worth elaborating.

First, the range of options that a person can choose from constitutes the environment in which individuals flourish. This environment exists independent of a person's state of mind. It represents the totality of social forms, or practices, through which people can flourish and bring meaning to their lives. The idea here is that people's opportunities to lead a good life are linked to, and shaped by, various ways of living that are available in their society. Steven Wall puts it in the following terms:

> [T]he social forms of a society determine (to a large extent) the nature and range of the relationships, projects and options available to its members. This is true for a number of reasons. First, many projects and options are brought into existence by particular social forms. One cannot play football unless a social form

has emerged that defines this pursuit. Second, pursuits that exist in different societies acquire a different significance in the lives of those who take them up depending on the nature of the social forms that predominate in their society. Leading a Christian life has a different significance for those who live in religious societies than it does for those who live in secular ones. Third, the opportunities for experimentation are sharply circumscribed by social forms. People often invent new pursuits and new ways of acting; but these are, for the most part, variations on existing social forms. (1998, p. 165)

Second, while most any stable society will support a range of social forms, societies defined by openness and individual freedom will tend toward social forms that rely on openness and individual freedom in order to function. This is sometimes called the *social forms argument* for autonomy (Colburn, 2010, pp. 47–48; Raz, 1986, pp. 390–395; McCabe, 2001). The social forms argument claims that the range of options available to members of a liberal society tend to be ones that require an individual to possess a sufficiently developed capacity for autonomy in order to access and flourish through them.[10] Prevailing norms around social forms such as marriage/civil unions and occupations, for example, work on the expectation that we independently arrive at decisions within these and other spheres.

Third, because a range of meaningful options sets out the environment through which an individual can flourish, and in a free and open society this environment is predicated on such individuals being in possession of a relatively high degree of independence, autonomy (in the broader sense currently under consideration) is the dominant form that the good life takes in such societies.

Consider the difference in flourishing through a social form, such as musicianship, when it is freely chosen and when it is unchosen. In most cases, learning a musical instrument is not a self-determined goal for very young children. This does not mean that children cannot flourish through their mastery of a musical instrument. Parents often have their child's flourishing in view when they conscript their children into music lessons. The experience of mastering a complex task, acquiring a work ethic, and learning how to value music for its own sake are all well-cited reasons. If lucky, these hopes come into fruition. But there comes a point in time when the child, moving into adulthood, is expected to make their own decision about whether to continue in their musical training. This decision is logically connected to their flourishing as an adult. The talented child who is pressured into becoming a professional musician may, of course, derive benefits from that life in the form of an income and worldly success. But it would be an odd thing to say that they are the author of their own lives—that they are flourishing by virtue of the exercise of capacities related to their status as a free and equal person.

Of course, there are many people who resolve to persevere in a path that is not a good fit for them. But insofar as they resolve to persevere in that life, they have made that life their own, in a self-determined or independent sense. They have, on reflection, chosen to make perseverance a goal as opposed to, say, opting for another goal or set of goals. (Note also that there is a clear difference between resolving to persevere in a difficult life when one has no other options, and resolving to persevere in a life when one has options.) Autonomous flourishing is the result of a life that we strive to achieve, more or less, through our own efforts. That is to say, it structures how we pursue the good life in an open society defined by a plurality of social forms and practices.

On the expanded view that I'm aiming to defend, then, securing the political ideal of personal autonomy involves at least two necessary conditions. The first condition is the development of individual capacities related to independence and self-determination such as reflective choosing, judging, and acting. I have referred to these as cognitive and affective, or *internal*, conditions. Autonomy can involve a number of more specific capacities, of course, but what they will have in common is that they are internal to the individual.

But these internal conditions, however we describe them, has relevance for a good life only insofar as they can be linked to a second condition: a meaningful range of social forms that have themselves come to be defined by independence and self-determination. This second condition requires access to an environment populated with such social forms through which a person can flourish as part of a good life. In the next section, I turn to the question of how this expanded view of autonomy bears on the right to education.

Adulthood and the Value of Education

What are the consequences of autonomy for the educational entitlements of liberal citizens, on this expanded view? One place to start is with the *kind* of education required to secure the conditions of an expanded conception of personal autonomy, and see how this differs from that standard view of educational entitlements.

I believe that the two conditions of autonomy—the state of the individual and the environment within which the individual determines their own aims and goals—roughly parallels a distinction between what we can call the *instilling* and the *supporting* focus of an autonomy-promoting education. Instilling educational efforts are directed at altering or bettering the state of the individual. Educating for autonomy can involve instilling, firmly, minimal conditions of rationality and reflection that a person needs in order weigh and choose among options. These are the internal cognitive and affective conditions that I referred to in the previous section of this chapter.

However, education can also *support* the autonomous pursuit of a good life by opening up options in the environment that would not otherwise have been accessible to the individual, even when that individual is in full possession of the conditions associated with an autonomous state of mind.

I use the terms "support" or "supporting" because such an education aims to increase a person's capacity for autonomy by making a certain range of social forms more accessible to the individual, as opposed to aiming to cultivate the general virtues and values that structure that individual's state of mind. This is a conceptual distinction. Empirically speaking, instilling and supporting can occur at the same time. As I learn more about, say, the philosophy of law, I may become more skilled at assessing reasons in a more general sense (an instilling development) even as legal *practice* becomes more accessible to me as a social form (a supporting development). The distinction aims to capture a difference in emphasis for an autonomy-promoting education between childhood and adulthood.

In order to get a handle on the relevance of this distinction for educational entitlements, consider someone who in their retirement years wishes to incorporate competitive athletics into their life. They reside in an athletically focused city with plenty of sports leagues, relevant facilities, and a climate that supports both winter and summer events. We might initially think that this individual has satisfied both of Raz's conditions. They are of a state of mind that enables them to set out on a new direction in life, and they find themselves in circumstances that can support that direction. But imagine further that this person is unlucky. They have little in the way of raw athletic talent or physical conditioning, nor did they encounter many opportunities to acquire an understanding of the norms and values of competitive athletics such as training, goal setting, teamwork, and mental fitness. There is a sense in which the available options are not *really* available to them. By this I mean that while the retiree has successfully deliberated on and chosen among their available options (they have not been coerced into making their choice, nor are they setting out to achieve ends or goals that have no plausible existence in their environment), they are unlikely to succeed in accessing and flourishing within their chosen option: competitive athletics. They are very unlikely to realize their particular chosen end, in practice.

Of course, there are some straightforward ways to address this problem. First, the retiree could hire a personal trainer or coach who could teach them some basic skills or cultivate a mental attitude conducive to athletic success. Second, athletic organizations are usually keen to bring in new members and usually host entry-level events specifically aimed at helping novice members develop the skills and conditioning they need in order to participate more fully. These organizations intuitively understand that a gap in knowledge, understanding, and skill can be a barrier to access and full participation.

This example tells us something important about the relationship between personal autonomy and education. Education in an open society is not only required in order to prepare citizens for the fact of options in an abstract and general sense, but it also enables those citizens to access and flourish *within a particular social form*.[11] That is to say, education has an important *supporting role* to play in realizing the conditions of personal autonomy.

We can use this example in order to make explicit three features of the supporting contribution of education to personal autonomy.

First, an autonomy-supporting education must increase knowledge, skills, and understanding in a way that helps the individual realize a self-determined goal. In order to realize what they have set out to achieve, our athletically minded retiree will have to acquire the right habits of endurance training, as well as understand the principles that underpin a sustainable athletic life so that they can make good judgments in spheres such as rest, recovery, and nutrition.

A second feature is that the self-directed goals an autonomy-supporting education aims to help the individual realize must be socially significant, meaningful, or worthwhile. Athletics represents a wide-recognized path to flourishing. But recall the social forms argument: if nobody was interested in athletics other than our retiree—if there was no athletic community to join—we would be hard pressed to say that a sports education has autonomy-supporting value because it does not link the individual to any particular option or options.

Third, the social forms in a liberal society are typically going to be diverse and open. One important implication is that an autonomy-supporting education has value regardless of any particular adult citizen's stage of life. Being the author of our own lives is an authorship that runs, ideally, from the earliest days of a mature life until the very end. Our would-be athlete has decided that they want to be more active later in life. But we can think of other examples. People who are well established in their careers often resolve to contribute back to society. Sometimes we realize that a chosen path in life is not quite what we thought it would be, and so we look for opportunities to try again. Key, here, is the idea that education has autonomy-supporting value for citizens regardless of how far along they are in their pursuit of a good life. All that is required is that they find themselves in a situation that demands that they make a self-determined choice and that there are significant options available for them to choose between.

Contrasting the role of education in childhood with that of adulthood can go some way to demonstrating the value of education across life. For children, education involves an initiation into conditions necessary for the autonomous pursuit of a good life. And while these dispositions and capacities are certainly developed with a view to the pursuit of a wide range of social forms available in the particular society in question, they are nonetheless relatively general and required for anyone to effectively carry out that pursuit. Education at this stage of life is largely (though not entirely) instilling in the sense that it is directed at the state of the individual independent of any particular option or social form. Furthermore, while these general dispositions and capacities are unchosen by the learner, they are nonetheless *autonomy* instilling because they are necessary for the autonomous pursuit of a good life.

The generality and paternalistic delivery of education progressively lessen as the child approaches an autonomous state of mind. Anyone who wishes to flourish in a free society must acquire, no matter how mundane or minimal, some degree of knowledge, understanding, and skills after their basic education is complete. Education conceived in such broad terms becomes largely (though not entirely) supporting in the sense that it is directed at enabling the individual to access and flourish though a social form or range of social forms. Further, adults have to make their own judgments about the role of knowledge and understanding in their lives, and shape this role in particular directions depending on the goals they have in view. This expectation is written into the very social forms available to citizens in a free society, from the free choice of occupation to the responsibility we hold for our own character to the modern concept of leisure time. Therefore, because there is a logical connection between the value of education and self-determination in adulthood, such an education is not merely supporting, but *autonomy* supporting.

Linking the supporting focus of education to a political ideal such as personal autonomy potentially redounds on our understanding of fair access to post-compulsory education in two ways.

First, if we think that personal autonomy is a sufficiently important political ideal that it justifies a right to a basic compulsory education, and education facilitates adult citizens in their effort to lead personally autonomous lives by making their chosen options accessible to them, it lends some plausibility to the claim that citizens ought to have a further right to the education they need in order to access those options. That is to say, it sets out some conceptual ground for the claim that the liberal entitlement to education should be extended to adults over a life.

Second, if access to education over a life is justified on the grounds that it is necessary for realizing the political ideal of personal autonomy, and realizing this ideal means linking citizens to a significant range of options, the *reasons* justifying the provision of post-compulsory education by the state have to be broader than socioeconomic opportunities and the fair distribution of benefits and burdens.

In non-ideal liberal societies, moral attention is almost exclusively focused on the ideal of higher education as an equal opportunity gateway to upward mobility for ambitious young people. To be sure, a decent job is a key part of many citizen's autonomous pursuit of the good life, and a decent job is something that people usually benefit most from early on in life. But according to the analysis I am offering, it would be a mistake to see personal autonomy and economic security as one and the same.

Consider once again the case of health care. The fact that many young citizens need to be healthy in order to pursue valuable jobs and offices should not mean that those who do not value health care for the same reasons—the infirm, for example—ought not to be entitled to health care resources, nor does this fact fully explain the value of health care over a life. Similarly, the fact that many high school graduates desire high-status jobs and require a higher qualification in order to compete for them should not mean that these who value education for different reasons—they have different social forms in view—ought not to be entitled to educational resources. For example, many Canadian universities, including the University of British Columbia, the University of Calgary, and York University, have a policy of waiving admissions criteria, registration, and tuition fees for senior citizens. Yet, this policy does not fit into a conception of political justice for higher education that sees access exclusively as a problem of fair socioeconomic opportunity. Such a policy would be wasteful on this logic because senior citizens are unlikely to use these education resources to propel themselves upwards in a competitive economy. These resources should be redirected to young students. But on the terms that I have been setting out, access to jobs and offices represent just *one way* in which education can support the autonomous lives of citizens. And on this view, education supports citizens in their self-determined pursuit of the good life by helping their lives go in the directions they think best fit who they are, who they wish to be, or who they find themselves becoming. What this good life consists in can certainly include, but does not require, employment as a self-directed goal.

Conclusion

In this chapter, I have argued that citizens have an individual interest in personal autonomy which requires the satisfaction of two sets of conditions: internal conditions and environmental conditions. I then showed how these two sets of conditions roughly parallel a distinction between two emphases that an autonomy-promoting education can take: autonomy instilling and autonomy supporting. I argued that the environmental condition is especially relevant to adult citizens in their pursuit of a good life and, because such a condition is a necessary condition of personal autonomy, we have grounds for seeing access to an autonomy-supporting education as an entitlement that extends over the lifespan of adult citizens. This opens a way of thinking about the public and political role of higher education as an institution. Like basic education, perhaps it is the case that higher education is an institution which ought to secure a citizen's interest in leading a personally autonomous life. And also like a basic education, it is something that citizens have a right to.

But there is one important question left unresolved by the analysis undertaken in this chapter. It may be true that that adults need access to knowledge, understanding, and skills in order access a range of worthwhile options, but why should we think that they require specific institutions in order to guarantee such access?

For example, any liberal citizen, having achieved minimal conditions for autonomy through a basic education, is free to learn whatever it is they need in order to access significant options without the support of formal institutions. Our would-be athlete can read books on personal training, check out the many YouTube channels devoted to endurance sports, can watch other people playing sports and emulate their style through practice drills, and so on. Similarly, someone who decides to devote themselves to a field of study, such as philosophy, is free to do so by reading all the philosophy books in their local library. Such a person would be well prepared to engage in philosophical debate with others.

Addressing this question involves saying more about the role of social institutions as they relate to values such as freedom, education, and the good life. In the next chapter, then, I will show why the liberal state ought to take measures to secure adult citizens' right to education through a system of higher education.

4
The Right to Higher Education

The last chapter concluded that an adult citizen's interest in personal autonomy justifies access to education over a life. This conclusion was based on two claims: that (i) the exercise of personal autonomy is essential to any liberal citizen's flourishing, and that (ii) education has a distinctive role to play in supporting such autonomy by enabling adult citizens to access an environment populated by valuable social forms and practices. Adult citizens have a right to education on these terms.

Now the argument turns to the question of whether or not this right has any bearing on higher education as an institution. Why this question? Some of our entitlements are political, but pre-institutional. They reflect needs or interests that apply to all citizens irrespective of the institutions that actually exist within a particular liberal society. I have argued that the right to education over a life reflects a need of this kind. It is justified in terms of a liberal political conception of the person and represents a claim about what any citizen would need in a free and open society.

But how should this entitlement inform the values and aims that define institutions of higher education? It's important to keep in mind that there is no necessary, or logical, relationship between an adult's right to education beyond a basic level and the aims of *higher* education. It could be that higher education should be exclusively focused on the pursuit of particular goods such as scholarly knowledge and understanding. The wider mandate implied by an autonomy-supporting education could detract from these more specific aims. It's possible that the aims of an autonomy-supporting education and the aims of higher education are incompatible.

The Right to Higher Education. Christopher Martin, Oxford University Press. © Oxford University Press 2022. DOI: 10.1093/oso/9780197612910.003.0005

There is, however, a way forward. Institutions contribute to the production of needed goods. Seumas Miller (2010) has pointed out it is the *need* that justifies the institution, not the other way around (p. 57).[1] We should therefore ask if the need for an autonomy-supporting education provides justifying reasons for higher education as an institution.

I think it does, and the focus of this chapter is identifying these reasons. First, I argue that the primary political responsibilities of social institutions in a liberal society are derived from a more basic obligation to promote citizens' ability to freely (and successfully) pursue the good life. These political responsibilities arise from what I call *liberty-maximizing* requirements of justice. Second, I argue that liberty-maximizing justice warrants the inclusion of higher education as a liberal social institution whose overarching purpose is the provision of an autonomy-supporting education to all citizens. Finally, I specify why an autonomy-supporting education requires a *specific class of institutions* for its provision and why direct access to public knowledge—through the Internet and public libraries, for example—is insufficient for this purpose.

The Political Responsibilities of Institutions

Every institution, organization, or association has aims or purposes. But not all institutions are created equal.

On the one hand, we have institutions that provide services, goods, or benefits exclusively for a particular group or community. For example, theater companies aim to provide opportunities for people who want to join in the production and consumption of theater arts. But these goods are expressly for a particular kind of person: theater lovers. In this case the institution has a fairly restricted *telos*, or purpose.

On the other hand, we have institutions that provide services, goods, or benefits for the enjoyment of everyone and which anyone in the community may claim in principle. Miller (2010) refers to the latter as *normative* institutions. Miller argues that an institution is normative when it produces collective goods: goods objectively valuable to, and available to, all (pp. 56–66). His examples of normative institutions include universities, professions, and the police. These institutions are normative by virtue of the fact that they produce goods that are of undeniable importance for all citizens (note the similarities between Miller's collective goods, Rawls' primary goods, Klosko's presumptive public goods, and Habermas' generalizable interests as discussed in chapters 2 and 3).

Could it not be said that a theater company produces a collective good, namely, creative art? Creative art may be objectively valuable, but institutions of the kind that Miller is concerned with take the provision of valuable goods for *all* to be their purpose. In order to understand the difference between a normative institution and the more generic kind, consider a homeless shelter and a hotel. If you need shelter, you can rent a hotel. But you will be turned away if you don't have the money. Yet, everyone *needs* basic shelter. Homeless shelters aim to meet this need. Homeless shelters and hotels may share a similar purpose (the provision of shelter), but the shelter's purpose has an added moral dimension by virtue of the *collective good* that it strives to serve—shelter for all.[2]

The collective goods Miller believes that social institutions ought to be responsible for range widely. They include basic material needs such as food and security, as well as more expansive goods such as the dissemination of knowledge and international cooperation. They encompass universal moral obligations and constraints, such as human rights.

However, among these normative institutions we can include those that are responsible for the provision of goods specific to the needs of a liberal society and its citizens. Is it plausible to claim that an autonomy-supporting education is one of these goods? If so, does this justify higher education as the institution responsible for its provision?

The answers to these questions are not obvious. Liberal citizens may benefit from an autonomy-supporting education *in principle*, but this education may not be of the kind that justifies or requires an institution to be morally responsible for providing it. We can think of at least two reasons why this might be so.

First, it might be that an autonomy-supporting education does not fall within the goods that liberal social institutions are responsible for realizing in general. For example, it could be that socioeconomic equality is the primary concern of the institutions of a liberal society (Julius, 2003; Ronzoni, 2008). But an autonomy-supporting education, as I have defined it, is not justified in terms of its contribution to socioeconomic equality. Therefore, autonomy-supporting education does not warrant a basic social institution responsible for its provision.

Second, it may be the case that an autonomy-supporting education can be sufficiently produced without the need for a specific institution responsible for its provision. Social institutions are responsible for the provision of goods that are not only valuable but *scarce*. But autonomy-supporting educational goods may be plentiful and cheap by virtue of the (un)coordinated activity of a number of other institutions. For example, knowledge—which we can assume would play a significant role in an autonomy-supporting education—is a plentiful public good. We have the Internet and public libraries that almost any citizen can access at little or no cost. If most of the valuable social forms and practices in an open society are already well-supported by freely available knowledge, what we have is more than sufficient for citizens to access those social forms.

Higher Education and the Basic Structure

The first way in which autonomy support can fail to justify higher education is that it simply isn't something that the social institutions of a liberal society ought to be responsible for providing. Addressing this possibility requires saying more about the grounds that justify liberal institutions, or that justify a change in our assumptions about the main responsibilities of the institutions that we already have.

John Rawls sets out a useful starting point for identifying such grounds. He claims that institutions have political responsibilities to liberal citizens when those institutions have a pervasive influence on how we see ourselves and what we want out of life (Rawls, 2005, p. 68). These institutions are part of the basic structure of society—institutions that are so consequential for citizens that everyone has an equal interest in ensuring that those institutions observe principles of justice and fairness.

We can use the basic structure as a guiding concept and ask if supporting the autonomy of citizens is something that the basic structure should be responsible for and, if so, whether not education has a specific role to play in that support. The most straightforward way to get at this question is to look to existing accounts of higher education in the basic structure and work from there. The problem is that political liberals have had very little to say on this matter. To my knowledge, the most careful assessment is David O'Brien's (forthcoming). His account sheds needed light on if, as well as *how*, the basic structure bears on higher education and the interests of citizens.

The Concept of "Higher Education" Revisited

Before going on to explain O'Brien's position and how it relates to my own, we should make an important clarification. I have up until this point been using the term "higher education" in an institutionally indeterminate way. Do I mean colleges? Universities? Vocational schools? There is a sense in which I mean all of them and none of them. In order to understand why, think of the argument in this book as an extended thought experiment: imagine a liberal society that had no formal education after a basic education.

What kind of educational institutions, if any, would liberal citizens benefit from having *after* such an education was complete? Are the benefits that these institutions provide essential or merely discretionary? What aims should they be committed to? What role would the state have in managing them?

I have two related reasons for approaching the concept of higher education in this way. First, at a conceptual level it allows for the possibility of a principled role for education in the lives of adult citizens that diverges from, or greatly expands on, how actual liberal societies have conceived of this role. In fact, this is what I have argued in chapter 3. Fundamentally, education should be about helping adults in their autonomous pursuit of a good life. The pursuit of socioeconomic opportunity, for example, is but one among many possible goals that a liberal citizen might have that could be better served by education. I have also argued that this autonomy-supporting role is of such importance that its provision is something that all citizens have a claim to as a matter of right.

Second, at a more institutional level it steers us away from resting arguments about the role of education in the lives of adult citizens on de facto educational values and aims embedded in the many post-compulsory educational institutions that we already have. After all, we have an institutional regime that embodies entrenched ideas about what a post-compulsory education looks like, including who can attend and how it can be funded. We can certainly apply ideas about justice and fairness in order to arrive at insights into how these existing institutions can do a better job of promoting a just, fair, and free society. However, the critical potential of these ideas is greatly limited when we take these institutions as given because it leaves these assumed values and aims largely untouched.

Imagine a society in which all food is served through drive-thus. Fast food is the only option. No other form of provision exists. Citizens in this society accept by convention that this is simply what food is like and how it is allocated. They debate the distribution of such food, such as how long people have to wait in the drive-thru, the fairness of requiring people to pay for such food, and how much they should pay. But it does not occur to any of the citizens of this world that food has a value and purpose other than convenience and a quick dopamine hit. It brings families together. It expresses cultural ideals. It can improve our health. By taking fast food establishments as an institutional given, however, the citizens in this world are so focused on improving its efficiency and fairness that they have missed out on much of what makes food valuable (and missed out on the development of alternative institutional arrangements that better reflect this value, such as fine dining, community kitchens, meals at home, picnics in the park, and so on). Replace "fast food" with education and "drive-thru" with higher education institutions, and you get the picture.

I've taken the opportunity to revisit the rationale behind my use of the term "higher education" at this point because we are moving into to a stage of the argument where it looks as if I am now contradicting this stated approach. It looks to be this way because when O'Brien is talking about higher education what he really means is actual universities in the world we inhabit in the early 21st century: three- to four-year institutions that have a clear teaching and research function. And here lies the ostensible contradiction: why should we be concerned with actual universities? According to the terms of my own thought experiment I should proceed as if universities do not exist and only through the course of the argument determine if they *ought* to.

Why look to O'Brien's account, then? The main reason is that his analysis is focused on the place of the university in the basic structure. And while the university is just one kind of higher education institution, not itself an ideal or general type, his analysis may point the way to some generalizable insights helpful to my own argument. But there is another reason. O'Brien takes the view that the university has values and purposes that are not merely conventional, rather, they *should be* part of the basic structure. A liberal society would be far less liberal without universities. I agree. But the consequence is that my thought experiment cannot proceed as if the university and its values do not exist. Such values not only exist, rather, they *ought* to exist. My argument therefore has to show why the values and purposes of the university are compatible with the right to higher education. This presents its own problems for the role of higher education in the basic structure, as we will also soon see.

The University in the Basic Structure

It seems intuitive, claims O'Brien, to assume that universities warrant inclusion in the basic structure. They play an undeniable role in distributing opportunities, benefits, and burdens throughout society. The kind of policy directives that O'Brien believes that could be rightfully required of a university system compliant with justice and fairness would include the ending of elite legacy admissions, or having professor encourage well-off students into other-regarding professions such as social work.[3] These directives would be justified on the grounds that they would help to promote greater socioeconomic equality in the larger society.

We can call this approach to institutions in the basic structure *justice-maximizing authority*. Justice-maximizing authority simply refers to the idea that the state may legitimately act through institutions in order to promote a just and fair society. The range of institutions to which justice-maximizing authority applies are limited to those in the basic structure: the judiciary, basic education, and the family to name but a few. For example, on this view it is legitimate for the state to compel public schools to ensure that poor children get enough resources to mitigate the disadvantages that they may experience due to their economic background. Institutions that fall *outside* the basic structure are exempt from political authority of this kind. Churches, for example, may have to respect the basic rights and liberties of citizens, but they may not be compelled to distribute their charitable giving in accordance with any particular egalitarian (or other) distributive principle.

O'Brien argues that applying justice-maximizing authority to universities is too hasty even if forcing elite colleges to promote equality has intuitive appeal. He points to the family as an instructive example. In the Rawlsian political framework the family is part of the basic structure. This makes sense given that the family has a pervasive influence on the life chances of almost every liberal citizen. Some of these influences are positive. However, the family also contributes to inequality. Parent's partiality toward their own children leads wealthy families to provide advantages that less well-off families cannot afford.[4] Rawls claims that the problem of parental partiality does not justify outlawing partiality or abolishing the family. The important role that the family plays in the good lives of individual citizens and the reproduction of society means that there are limits on what the state can reasonably do in order to counteract family-generated inequalities (2005, p. 467).

O'Brien believes that the case of the family points to a more general principle about the relationship between the institutions of the basic structure and their political responsibilities: norms of political justice ought not to be applied in such a way that the distinctive contributions that those institutions make to the good lives of citizens are undermined. Such institutions enjoy a kind of "special-status" in relation to the political authority of the state. O'Brien states this in the following terms: there are limits on the political interventions that the state may impose on any social institution that is both central to realizing many reasonable people's life plans and that performs a politically essential function (p. 19).

One important implication of this principle, argues O'Brien, is that some of the institutions in the basic structure should be exempt from a justice-maximizing application of principles of justice:

> special status ... within political liberalism amounts to the ruling out of a "justice-maximizing" attitude toward the basic structure.

Institutions like the family, taken in isolation, would tend to cause the values expressed by the [political] principles to be worse realized. A "justice-maximizing" attitude would therefore license direct intervention on the offending institutions. Political liberalism does not license such direct intervention. Institutions like the family are instead to be taken as fixed and worked around. (p. 15)

Does this constraint on authority apply to the university? O'Brien seems to think so. He claims that within the university there are a range of socially valuable jobs and offices that are central to the good life of many citizens. For example, the university is home to social forms and practices such as the pursuit of knowledge and scholarly excellence. These ways of life would be undermined by certain applications of justice-maximizing authority. O'Brien also points to a second reason why justice-maximizing authority should be constrained: higher education contributes to public knowledge essential to the maintenance and development of modern society (p. 22).

Accordingly, many reforms that would be intuitively appealing from the standpoint of justice are inappropriate. For example, universities may not be compelled to alter their admissions requirements in the interest of socioeconomic equality when doing so will be detrimental to the production of public knowledge.[5] Universities may not be treated as a *mere means* to other political ends because they are political ends in themselves. They have a special status by virtue of their essential, and therefore fixed, political function. We might say, using Miller's terminology, that the norms of political justice may not be applied in such a way that they undermine the purpose, or *telos*, that makes an institution normative.

How does this account inform the justification of autonomy support as a responsibility of the basic structure? Unfortunately, O'Brien's analysis actually generates two reasons ruling *against* the view that higher education (in the more general sense in which I use the term) has a political responsibility to support the autonomy of adult citizens.

First, on O'Brien's reading of political liberalism the basic structure is fundamentally oriented to the fair distribution of socioeconomic benefits and burdens. However, an autonomy-supporting education is concerned with the personal autonomy of individual citizens. It has a different normative *telos*. Accordingly, no institution could be held politically responsible for the provision of an autonomy-supporting education because the promotion of autonomy does not fall within the range of political responsibilities that a basic structure could be held.

But what if it turns out that an autonomy-supporting education could be shown to contribute to the overall socioeconomic quality of society? Perhaps supporting access to different social forms has an incidental, but nonetheless generally positive, effect on income distribution. While this might justify the provision of an autonomy-supporting education, it would not justify autonomy support *as a right or entitlement*. We are simply justifying whatever educational means are most effective in realizing socioeconomic equality, which in this case just happens to be an education of the autonomy-supporting kind. This justification is contingent on a number of external factors, and rights should not be contingent in this way. For example, it would be entirely just for institutions in the basic structure to shift away from the provision of an autonomy-supporting education if other educational approaches were shown to contribute to equality more effectively. If we discovered, for example, that a strict focus on vocational education was a more effective means of extending upward social mobility to the least well-off, educational institutions in the basic structure would be within their rights to make vocational education a priority—in fact, such institutions would have an obligation to make it so by virtue of the basic structure's overriding commitment to material equality. This, even if it led to other educational pathways being underfunded. The fact that an autonomy-supporting education can contribute to overall equality does not justify an institution that takes an autonomy-supporting education *as its moral purpose*.

O'Brien's account also generates a second reason to think that autonomy support fails to justify higher education as a normative social institution. His conclusion is that universities should not be held to justice-maximizing responsibilities even though they *are* part of the basic structure. Consequently, his account does not merely show that universities should be exempt from some instances of state authority exercised in the service of fair distribution, rather, it shows that universities should be exempt from *any* application of justice that poses a threat to its fixed and essential social function.

What this means is that even if the provision of autonomy-supporting education falls under the general aims of the basic structure, one could object to requiring *universities* to take responsibility for such provision. And this presents a serious problem for my argument. Here is why: I agree with O'Brien that universities are part of the basic structure. And according to O'Brien, universities should *not* be subject to a maximizing approach to justice. For example, one could argue that an autonomy-supporting education would require the provision of a wide range of knowledge, understanding, and skills, thereby "watering down" the fixed values and aims of the university such as the pursuit of scholarly knowledge. But the university should hold the line and focus on training talented citizens who can further, say, the science of human sport and performance, not on helping citizens of average talent participate in competitive athletics as part of their vision of a good life.

On this view, the university is incompatible with the right to higher education. And our inability to include the university in that right greatly undermines its plausibility. It would mean relegating a huge swath of institutions that we generally accept, rightly, as belonging to higher education to the sidelines. If I had a good argument in support of the idea that the values and purposes of the university are merely de facto and poorly justified this would not be so much of a problem. But I don't, and my thought experiment cannot dismiss the existence of something that I acknowledge to be essential for any liberal society and that we can plainly recognize as "higher education," if higher education is anything.

To summarize: autonomy support may fail to align with the political responsibilities of the basic structure for two related reasons: (i) autonomy support fails to align with the political responsibilities of the basic structure in general, and (ii) autonomy support is incompatible with the fixed values and aims of university as an actual, real institution. I will deal with both of these objections before going on to tackle the question of whether or not an autonomy-supporting education is already sufficiently produced in modern societies.

Liberty-Maximizing Justice

The concept of the basic structure has come to be far more than a question of Rawlsian exegesis, informing more general debates about liberal institutions, political principles, and political authority. One such debate is over the nature of the influence required for an institution to count as part of the basic structure. It looks to be the case that, for many, "pervasive influence" is too vague a term to allow for meaningful distinctions between institutions that belong in the basic structure and those that do not. This is an important issue because, as we will see, the reasons *why* an institution so belongs will bear on the political responsibilities that apply to it.

Consider, for example, that some have argued that Rawls' version of the basic structure is *too narrow* in its focus on the pervasive influence of institutions, and that political justice should apply to the ordinary choices and preferences of individuals (Cohen, 1997; Murphy, 2017; Syme, 2018). This, because individual choices have collective effects on the justice and fairness of society. Of course, citizens should think about the side effects and consequences of their choices for other citizens.[6] But this seems to discount the disproportionate influence that institutions have on citizens' lives.

Others, meanwhile, have argued that Rawls' use of the term "pervasive influence" is *too broad* and that only those institutions that influence through legal coercion should be included (Blake, 2001). But this seems too narrow for our purposes. It would seem to exclude a number of non-coercive social institutions that play a highly important role in a citizen's life chances including, but certainly not limited to, the family, health care, and public education.

Where should we stand on this question? Promising is Louis-Phillipe Hodgson's *controlling influence* account. He has argued that institutions belong to the basic structure when they "set rules and constraints through which the person has to act to exercise her capacity for a conception of the good" (2012, p. 306).[7] On this account, the main concern of justice within the basic structure is with the role of institutions in structuring a citizen's pursuit of the good life (2012, p. 306).[8]

On a controlling influence account, political authority can be exercised in order to maximize the *collective* liberty of equal citizens. As Ferdman puts it, "[o]ne has to act through the rules generated by the basic structure if one has to have projects at all. Importantly, the basic structure's primary focus is not on the distribution of benefits and burdens as such but rather on a person's ability to set and pursue ends for herself" (2019, pp. 877–878). If controlling influence is what justifies the inclusion of institutions in the basic structure, these institutions have a political responsibility to take each citizen's capacity to set and pursue ends as a fundamental concern.[9]

In order to distinguish this fundamental concern from an account of the basic structure that takes egalitarian distribution to be fundamental, we can say that the controlling influence of the basic structure must be conditioned by *liberty-maximizing* requirements of justice. That is to say, the basic structure ought to be justice-maximizing *with respect to a citizen's pursuit of the good life*. As

Hodgson puts it, for example, "the system must not let morally irrelevant factors play an undue role in determining a person's success in pursuing her conception of the good" (2012, p. 318).

How is this different from requirements of justice that take equality of resources to be a priority? To start with, controlling influence does not mean that distributive fairness is irrelevant to how institutions within the basic structure ought to function. But distribution becomes relevant by virtue of its impact on the pursuit of the good between free and equal citizens. Consider taxation for public goods such as defense and health care. This tax burden places an undeniable material constraint on a citizen's capacity to set and achieve their ends. This constraint is justified because it enables all citizens to pursue the good in important ways—defense protects citizens from conflicts that would set back other goals and projects, while health care gets us back on our feet when we are sick. It justly maximizes the liberty of citizens. But it would be difficult to justify the tax policy if the constraint were more keenly felt by the poor (if it applied regressive taxation, for example). Therefore, on a controlling influence view, it could be argued that poor citizens ought to be taxed less for the reason that it places an unequal burden on these citizens *in terms of their ability to pursue the good*.

But there is also a more fundamental commitment to individual freedom that does not depend on relative equality. Consider the example of a school system that cultivated minimal conditions of autonomy in some children, but not others. This would involve a morally arbitrary constraint on the freedom of the latter relative to the former. But this is not unjust simply for the reason that it would lead to a difference in relative freedom between citizens. Personal autonomy is basic to the pursuit of the good for any liberal citizen. Consequently, it would be unjust to refrain from providing such an education to some children on the grounds that doing so would lead to all children being relatively equal in terms of their (in)capacity to pursue the good.[10] On a liberty-maximizing view of the basic structure, rules and constraints are presumptively unjust when they undermine an individual's capacity to pursue the good in an absolute sense. Under a liberty-maximizing requirement of justice, equality is a reason to increase the freedom of some, not reduce the freedom of others.

A liberty-maximizing basic structure addresses the first sense in which the right to an autonomy-supporting education may fail to justify an institutional response. Institutions in the basic structure have a political responsibility to enable free and equal citizens to set and pursue ends. This includes ensuring that their successfulness in that pursuit is not constrained by "morally irrelevant factors." This brings autonomy support into the picture. Many of the valued social forms and practices through which citizens aim to flourish over the course of a self-directed life may be inaccessible for some simply by virtue of the fact that they had not been given the opportunity to enter into and flourish within such social forms. Or they may be inaccessible in the sense that one does not have the time, leisure, or material resources to take advantage of opportunities that are available in principle. Accordingly, it is plausible to see the mitigation of morally irrelevant factors of this kind as a liberty-maximizing requirement of justice (i.e., autonomy support). The particular institutions, or institutional aims, appropriate for this kind of autonomy support is a separate question, which I deal with in the next section. My point at this stage of the argument is simply to show that autonomy support falls within the basic structure's range of political responsibilities at a very general level.

Liberty-Maximizing Justice and the "Fixed" Values of the University

Would a liberty-maximizing political requirement to support the autonomy of citizens undermine more traditional values and aims of the university? Before answering this question, we need to say more about why we should think that autonomy support is something for which a system of higher education in a liberty-maximizing basic structure ought to aim.

The Case for Higher Education in the Basic Structure

Higher education belongs to the liberal institutions of a basic structure on the grounds that it has a controlling influence on the exercise of citizens' capacities in their pursuit of the good. Its inclusion in the basic structure subjects it to liberty-maximizing requirements of justice. One of these requirements is the political responsibility to provide an autonomy-supporting education to all liberal citizens, making higher education a normative institution in Miller's (2010) sense of the term. Here is why:

Recall that, from a liberty-maximizing view, the social institutions of a liberal society are politically responsible for citizens' prospects for living life as free and equal because they establish a powerful network of rules and constraints that citizens must follow in order to exercise their capacity to pursue the good (Hodgson, 2012, p. 313). These rules and constraints must be justified to citizens because they may have a better or worse, arbitrary or less arbitrary, fair or unfair, impact on that pursuit. But it is not enough to claim that these institutions should maximize the collective liberty of equal citizens in the abstract. Goods, rules, and constraints advance freedom in different ways.

If educational institutions belong to the basic structure, it is because they exert a controlling influence of a distinctive kind. They produce goods through which liberal citizens can *develop their capacity* to pursue the good by instilling general conditions for autonomy. Recall, for example, that political philosophers point to the influence that schools have on children's basic autonomy as a justification of state authority over compulsory provision of basic education. This distinctive controlling influence also entails the inclusion of higher education in the basic structure.

Why? Because the controlling influence of the basic structure extends far beyond that starting conditions of a person's life; rather, it refers to the way in which institutions impact on a person's pursuit of the good *in media res*—from birth until death. It applies to educational institutions that deal with mature citizens, as well, because they also set rules and constraints relating to how citizens acquire *and maintain* a capacity to live freely. We can therefore say that higher education counts as part of the basic structure: it establishes rules and constraints over a citizen's access to (or exclusion from) the knowledge and understanding they need in order to pursue certain kinds of lives. It is therefore subject to liberty-maximizing requirements of justice.

What does this mean for *higher* education? Educational institutions in the basic structure are not merely obligated to justly structure the rules and constraints that apply to the achievement of minimal "starting" conditions of autonomy citizens; rather, they are also responsible for rules and constraints that bear on our capacity to exercise these conditions in the service of a self-directed life. An autonomy-supporting education ought not to be denied to citizens on morally irrelevant grounds. Consequently, the availability of an autonomy-supporting education to all mature citizens regardless of talent or wealth should be counted among the political responsibilities of higher education within the basic structure.

For example, some citizens are excluded from higher education because they do not have the financial resources to access the system (or, they have the resources but the private costs are so high that the investment is too risky to choose). This is widely recognized as unjust because it leads to unequal opportunities to access well-paying jobs and offices. But on a liberty-maximizing account, inequality of opportunity is not the fundamental reason why exclusion from higher education is unjust (though this *is* unjust). It is fundamentally unjust because a lack of resources places an arbitrary constraint on the citizen's individual freedom qua freedom. If, for example, a person did not desire valuable opportunities—if, say, they wished only to learn because learning is an important feature of their conception of the good—such exclusion would be unjust, nonetheless.

In order to see what a controlling influence account adds to our understanding of justice and fairness, consider another example. Imagine that my self-determined goal is to become a physician, and all the institutions in my society are medical schools. I am denied a higher education simply because I lack the talent or ability to qualify for admission. But my failure to qualify cannot be attributed to any material disadvantage I might have experienced. Access to medical school places are open to all citizens under fully realized conditions of equality of opportunity.

What is unjust about this situation? It is not *prima facie* unfair that a social form demands a certain level of ability. Being a competent physician requires some level of talent that not everyone has, and the public has an interest in competent physicians. The system is unjust because the social forms and practices that this imagined higher education system supports (physicianship) is structured in such a way that citizens who lack a certain kind of talent or ability are unable to access autonomy-supporting goods *at all*. The system arbitrarily restricts autonomy support to citizens of a specific kind of talent or ability.

For a conception of higher education that is part of the basic structure and subject to liberty-maximizing justice, autonomy support is the collective good at which a system of higher education ought to aim: something objectively good for, and available to, all. In other words, in the basic structure the fundamental aim of higher education is not civic engagement, or the development of mind, or upward social mobility. Rather it is an *autonomy-supporting conception* of higher education.

What do I mean by an autonomy-supporting conception of higher education? A *conception* of higher education is an answer to the question, "what should education for adults in a just and fair liberal society look like, in principle?"[11] An autonomy-supporting conception of higher education is the answer to this question: one that treats personal autonomy as the most fundamental, overarching purpose of educational provision. This conception is what the right to higher education consists in.

I claim that this conception best aligns with the social vision of a liberal society among all of the major alternative conceptions. What about these alternative conceptions? Some argue that civic engagement, or upward social mobility, or the development of mind are fundamental. Am I denying that these are valuable educational goals? Not at all. On my account, these alternative conceptions are better understood as aims that are educationally valuable, if they are educationally valuable at all, by virtue of their contribution to a citizen's autonomous pursuit of the good. For example, a system of higher education should provide a pathway that helps citizens achieve upward social mobility for the reason that upward social mobility is part of the life plan of these citizens. Jobs and offices are social forms that people need to be able to access. But it should also provide pathways for reasons having to do with social forms that depend on the development of mind, democratic engagement, and so on. Social mobility, development of mind, and aims like it are parts of a more expansive good—autonomy support—that a system of higher education ought to serve.

One last point before moving on. The right to higher education, as a conception, is highly general. It does not entail a particular pedagogy (but it would clearly rule out teacher practices that undermine autonomy). It does not warrant a specific curriculum. It does not dictate a particular institutional blueprint. (Although see chapter 5, where I set out criteria for how a liberal state may exercise its authority in order to ensure that an autonomy-promoting system of higher education stays true to its purpose, and chapter 7, where I detail how the right to higher education might apply to existing arrangements). Rather, it functions as a political standard that liberal citizens may appeal to in holding the state to account for the fair provision of educational goods and services. To be sure, we must apply this standard to different contexts and national systems. And, as I will show, it recommends a particular regime of funding and a particular relationship between educational institutions and the liberal state. However, what we ultimately mean by an autonomy-supporting conception is a fundamental purpose or *raison d'etre* of higher education writ large, one to which judgments about institutional design, state provision, and political authority must conform as part of their justification. That is to say, it is the conceptual foundation that makes the right to higher education what it is.

Autonomy-Supporting Higher Education and the Fixed Values of the University

Now that we have established autonomy support as a fundamental aim of higher education within the basic structure, we are now free to turn to the question of fixed values: is the inclusion of higher education within the basic structure an unreasonable threat to the aims of the university as they are traditionally understood? Does this mean that the university should be granted special status, as O'Brien puts it, which should leave it essentially untouched by liberty-maximizing requirements of justice?

Recall that when we say that an institution has "fixed" aims, we mean that the institution in question has a certain *telos* or purpose. Were we to significantly change that *telos* or purpose it would no longer *be* that institution. Changing the fixed values and aims of an institution is not *prima facie* wrong. But for normative institutions— institutions responsible for producing an essential collective good—a change in value and aims *is* a wrong because it would undermine something that has value for everyone. Consequently, it is reasonable to place a limit on liberty-maximizing political authority when it would otherwise undermine the fixed values and aims of a normative institution.

For example, some citizens are attracted to university life—and flourish through their participation in it—because of its commitment to the free pursuit and growth of knowledge for its own sake. It therefore serves as an important path to their autonomous flourishing. One worry might be that an autonomy-supporting conception of higher education would warrant opening up the university to all citizens regardless of ability or interest in knowledge, a move that would cost the university both as a distinctive way of life and as an important producer of knowledge. It would undermine the ostensibly "fixed" values and aims of the university.

However, an autonomy-supporting conception of higher education is not one and the same as the university as a fixed institution with special status. Why? A conception of higher education that was one and the same as the university could not be justified to liberal citizens on liberty-maximizing grounds. Such a "university-centric" conception only would support access to an arbitrarily privileged range of social forms and practices—the pursuit of scholarly knowledge and understanding as a way of life, for example. A system of higher education based on this conception would place constraints and rules on the exercise of autonomy that apply to some citizens' self-determined goals and not others *without good reason*. Some further argument would have to be made for why an autonomy-supporting education ought to be offered to citizens who are aiming for this particular social form, but not others.

To be sure, a basic structure conception of higher education would not be able to support access to every social form, and in the next section of this chapter I set out some conditions for the kind of knowledge, understanding, and skill that such a conception of higher education should be concerned with providing. However, a liberty-maximizing conception of higher education must be one that, in the interest of ensuring that all citizens can exercise their capacity for autonomous flourishing, links citizens to a much broader range of social forms and practices than a university-dominant system of higher education would.[12]

What does this mean for the university? The university can be understood as *one kind* of autonomy-supporting institution. Scholarly knowledge, understanding, and intellectual skills can open up social forms and practices to citizens that pursue the good outside of the university. However, the university is *also* a valuable social form in its own right. The university supports a scholarly way of life and as such belongs to the range of valuable options that a liberal society should make available to free and equal citizens.[13] One important consequence is that while the university belongs to the basic structure, it ought to be subject to liberty-maximizing *protections* necessary for ensuring that this way of life persists as a viable option for citizens. These protections may involve limits on the authority of the state to obligate universities to satisfy other liberty-maximizing requirements of justice, such as opening up the university to any citizen regardless of ability or interest in learning.

One might from here conclude that the university's special status makes it effectively free from such requirements. But this isn't the case. First, we should understand that protecting the fixed values of the university follows *from* requirements of justice. If a social form requires protection on the grounds that it is essential to an autonomy-supporting environment such protections are in fact requirements of liberty-maximizing justice.[14] The university life seems to warrant such protection, both because it generates public knowledge and understanding that citizens in general can avail of in support of their pursuit of the good and because the university is itself home to a scholarly way of life—a social from in its own right.

Second, citizens' ought not to be prevented from accessing and participating in scholarly life for morally irrelevant reasons. The state is therefore justified in obliging the university to adopt measures that will help citizens to access and flourish through scholarly practices. It would be easy to imagine, for example, that universities could be required, on liberty-maximizing grounds, to allocate resources for the delivery of entry-level courses that support access in communities that have been traditionally excluded from university spaces. These measures would help to mitigate some of the morally arbitrary constraints that keep citizens from those communities out (geographical distance, for example). This, and measures like it, are warranted so long as they do not undermine the university as a distinctive social form or unduly hamper its knowledge-producing function.[15] The right to higher education does not pose an inherent threat to the fixed values and aims of the university.

Autonomy-Supporting Knowledge and Educational Institutions

In the last section, I showed how autonomy support falls within the collective goods that liberal social institutions ought to be responsible for, motivating a conception of higher education that takes the provision of an autonomy-supporting education as a requirement of justice. This takes us to the second major objection. It may be true that adult citizens require access to knowledge, understanding, and skills for the reason that it enables them to access social forms and practices that contribute to their autonomous flourishing. It may also be the case that an autonomy-supporting education calls for knowledge, understanding, and skills wider in scope than those that are traditionally associated with higher education. But why do we need an institution to supply this knowledge at all?

Consider that liberal citizens are free to learn without formal institutions. Our would-be athlete can watch people playing sports or training on YouTube. And we already have institutions, such as libraries, that make access to knowledge free for the individual. Someone devoted to the study of philosophy can read all the philosophy books in their local library and be well-prepared to engage in philosophical discussion. The Internet, libraries, and free online courses all contribute to the wider pool of knowledge, understanding, and skill that citizens can freely avail of in order to support their self-determined goals. Let us call this *the autodidact's objection*.

The autodidact's objection points to something right: higher education institutions in the basic structure should only be required to support access to social forms and practices which it would be unreasonable to expect citizens to access on their own. Such an expectation would place an unjust constraint on that citizen's pursuit of the good. But how do we know when such an expectation *is* unreasonable?

From an educational point of view, access to social forms and practices present a challenge to citizens in the sense that they put demands on their *capacities*. A characteristic example would be intellectually demanding social forms—those for which the acquisition of advanced knowledge, understanding, and technical skill are a constitutive feature of the activity. Examples of such intellectually demanding social forms include academic research and other types of so-called gold collar labor.

Would the fact that a social form is objectively demanding suffice as a criterion for judging when a social form warrants institutional support? It would certainly be unreasonable to expect citizens to independently develop the capacities necessary for successful participation in objectively demanding social forms. However, this would only serve to justify institutional support for an arbitrarily narrow range of activities. This is because the criterion makes it seem as if we can draw a line between "demanding" and "non-demanding" social forms independent of what the agent takes to be valuable about knowledge, understanding, and skill in the context of a good life. But this isn't the case. What makes a social form demanding is as much a product of the aims or goals of the individual as it is the form itself. Take art, for example. There is a difference between demands on our capacities necessary for taking up art as an occasional way to kill time versus taking up art as a profession. There are also many gradations between these two extremes. Within any particular social form, there are varying levels of seriousness and achievement.

By failing to recognize this relationship it becomes tempting, in the desire to arrive at an objective standard, to presume that the only social forms that it would be reasonable to support are the most demanding *versions* of any given social form. But this presumption is not well justified. In our kind of society, at least, the most demanding version of a social form is usually one linked to labor, especially labor of a relatively high social status. Acquiring artistic skill requires hard work; acquiring it well enough to make a living as a professional artist requires obsessive devotion. Consequently, we are tempted to identify an autonomy-supporting education with valuable employment and other "objective" markers of worldly success. Certainly, successful participation in the labor market matters for the good life of free and equal citizens, and it is also true that education plays an important role in enabling such participation in advanced economies. However, just as an education for autonomy involves the cultivation of conditions far broader than what is merely required for economic participation (independent thinking, familiarity of a wide range of different ways of living, and so on), so too does an autonomy-*supporting* education entail access to social forms and practices for reasons that run broader than labor-market access.[16] Autonomy as labor-market success sets out rules and constraints about access to education that support an arbitrarily narrow range of self-directed goals, especially those that prize career and professional success. It works from the presumption that the requirements of the labor market, not citizens, should determine what warrants educational support. And while employment is certainly not a bad goal, this presumption risks crowding out access for citizens who have altogether different goals in view.

Access to social forms and practices present a challenge for citizens when those social forms require a demanding level of knowledge, understanding, or skill *in virtue of the significance that the individual assigns to successful participation in that social form in the context of a self-determined life.* The greater the significance that a citizen assigns to a social form within a self-determined life, the higher the stakes are for their flourishing; the greater the stakes for their flourishing, the greater the importance of knowledge, understanding, and skill relevant to their successful participation in that social form.

Consider the difference in what successful participation in a social form means for someone who is merely dabbling, and someone who sees that same social form as a self-determined goal that structures their view of the good life. For example, the dabbler in athletics can try their hand at running or hockey and fail to get much out of it—or fail to be particularly accomplished at it—without that failure impacting on their autonomous flourishing. This is because athletics is not a self-determined goal for the dabbler. Social forms take on the character of goals in the pursuit of a good life when they impart a conscious and deliberate investment of our time, effort, material resources, and emotions. As Raz puts it, self-determined goals "guide [the agent's] actions towards them, they color his perception of his environment and of the world at large, and they play a large part in his emotional responses and his imaginative musings" (p. 291). The dabbler in athletics can get by without a robust autonomy-supporting education behind it because athletics play no significant role in their flourishing as a free and equal citizen. This person only needs the knowledge, understanding, and skill required in order to participate in a "dabbling" sense. This may involve very little in the way of instruction, mentoring, coaching, direction, critical feedback—those educational activities that tend to involve more than the transmission of propositional knowledge and which we associate with being initiated into a practice with some view to succeeding in it.

The citizen who has decided to make athletics key to their pursuit of the good is in a different practical situation. Much of who they are and wish to be is staked on their capacity to access and flourish through that social form. Access to an educational process can ensure that they acquire the knowledge, understanding, and skills—including an initiation into the norms and values that define an athletic community—that makes them less likely to fail to the detriment of their autonomous flourishing. For such citizens it is not enough to dabble. They need to know how to do it, and do it well.

The idea that citizens only need libraries and the Internet to secure support for autonomous flourishing introduces a peculiar dichotomy where any social form that is not embedded in the labor market is mere "dabbling" of a low-stakes kind and wholly undeserving of educational support. On the contrary, the grounds on which we make judgments about institutional support should be the importance of knowledge, understanding, and skill in the context of a citizen's pursuit of a good life.

What, now, of the autodidact's objection? The autodidact is no challenge to the importance of formal educational institutions in supporting the autonomy of liberal citizens. The fact that some citizens can access a social form without institutional support does not entail that it would be reasonable to expect *all* citizens to independently access a social form. A social form may be relatively undemanding from the point of view of a citizen lucky enough to be imbued with certain natural talents or inherited social networks, but demanding in the relevant sense for another.

Consider what the autodidact is able to achieve on their own. The autodidact has in their private possession the leisure and personal resources necessary for figuring things out for themselves. They are naturally imbued with the cognitive and non-cognitive talents necessary to master a social form or practice without pedagogical help and support. They are able to initiate themselves into the norms and values that define a practice, discipline, community, or other social form without a community supporting that initiation. The autodidact is equipped (by brute luck) in such a way that they are essentially insulated from the high risk to one's autonomous flourishing that would accompany the requirement that all citizens be fully self-reliant in their pursuits.

To be sure, if every liberal citizen were an autodidact, then it might be plausible to claim that autonomy support does justify formal institutions. It is certainly possible that there are some citizens like this. But I do not think that we have good grounds for assuming that citizens are very apt to be like the autodidact. To do so would link adult citizens' success in the pursuit of a good life to morally arbitrary factors such as inherited power, wealth, and talent. To expect citizens to be autodidacts is unreasonable.

Another example: let's assume that political engagement is part of an adequate range of valuable social practices in an open society. Now consider a mature citizen who develops a strong sense of civic duty about democratic reform. They begin to notice how certain policies and practices—the rules of the game, as it were—were making life arbitrarily more difficult for her and her community. They want to do something about it. This sense of duty develops, incrementally, long after their formal K–12 schooling. Note also that this citizen does not see the stakes of their political engagement in careerist terms—they work in a field entirely unrelated to politics—but it has nonetheless begun to take on a degree of meaning to their life that was not there before. Their fight for reform—to make life better for the members of their own community—has taken on the character of a self-determined goal of the Razian kind: it is something key to their autonomous flourishing. However, this same citizen may lack much of the knowledge and skill necessary for successful engagement in political reform efforts compared to citizens who have social connections and other resources that make access to politics relatively less effortful and demanding.

The fact that some citizens are not born into an environment where the knowledge, understanding, and skills necessary for a valuable social practice such as political engagement are close at hand should not be a morally relevant reason in preventing them from making such engagement part of their self-directed life. The basic structure therefore warrants supportive access to this social form by making an appropriate autonomy-supporting education available to citizens. This could involve theoretical forms of knowledge and understanding, more practical skills, or some mix of both.

Of course, one might object that if this citizen really wants to engage in the political sphere, they should make a career out of it. They should seek out educational programming that promises to serve as a gateway to that kind of career. And, assuming they qualify for admission, that program will likely increase their earning potential. They therefore ought to be responsible for the costs of that programming. But, from a liberty-maximizing point of view, making access to a valuable social form contingent on a person's willingness to adopt that social from as a pervasive goal (as a new career, for example) places a morally arbitrary constraint on that citizen's freedom. Free and equal citizens should be empowered to flourish through social forms and practices without having to treat that social form as a means to some other end.

This leads us to the question of "payback" and "return on investment." Public funding for higher education is partly justified on the grounds that graduates will acquire skills that will contribute to economic growth. The social returns of the graduate's "learning and earning" is a kind of payback to the community. But what of the citizen who learns about politics but fails to pursue a political career contribute? This is an important question because a liberty-maximizing account of the basic structure is still subject to general considerations about the fair distribution of benefits and burdens to the extent that this distribution might place an arbitrary constraint on the freedom of some citizens. And we could argue that requiring *me* to pay for *your* access to higher education without getting something back in return is an unfair constraint on my freedom. I address this objection in greater detail in chapter 6, where I show how a liberty-maximizing conception of higher education can inform current debates about public funding and student debt. I also address a more specific version of this objection—the idea that higher education is a kind of expensive taste that others should not be required to subsidize—in chapter 7. But we can offer two preliminary replies.

First, on the terms of the argument I have offered, the availability of an autonomy-supporting education is basic to a liberal political conception of the person. It is allocated like a primary or presumptive good, not a valuable opportunity. So long as the provision of such goods are genuinely autonomy-supporting and any citizen can access them, they are justly funded by the public. Second, an autonomy-supporting education has real social returns for society in the form of personal autonomy *as a collective good*.[17] An autonomy-supporting education contributes to the broader environment that is a constitutive feature of a liberal society. When citizens are able to freely participate in valuable social forms, they stand to make an important contribution to that broader environment. Not only does their participation help to ensure that a particular social form remains a live option for other citizens in the future, but also the diverse reasons that citizens have for engaging in that social form will help to ensure that such a form can continue to contribute to the autonomous flourishing of a diverse citizenry. Consider that if citizens can only participate in a given social form as a means to professional success the very things that make that social form valuable can be undermined. For example, a social form can become overpopulated with individualistic, competitive, or careerist motivations. The professionalization of politics is as good example as any. Unreasonable constraints on individual efforts at autonomous flourishing constrain the autonomous flourishing of everyone.

Conclusion

In this chapter, I justified the moral foundations of higher education as a basic social institution of a liberal society—one that serves as an institutional home for an adult's right to education—with the following key features:

- It is an ethical institution responsible for the collective good of an autonomy-supporting education in service of
- an adequate range of social forms and practices of such importance to citizens' pursuit of the good that it would be unreasonable for those citizens to take individual responsibility for acquiring the knowledge, understanding, and skills key to success in that pursuit and is
- conditioned by liberty-maximizing requirements of justice.

How should these features inform our thinking about the higher education systems that we already have? It is common to critique the fairness of higher education in terms of its impact on the socioeconomic life chances of citizens. But if my account is well-motivated, a more fundamental critique requires that we hold higher education to norms and standards of justice appropriate to any liberal social institution. And these standards refer to ways in which higher education imposes rules and constraints on a citizen's pursuit of the good life. Questions we would want to consider include: do these rules and constraints move society closer to, or further away from, liberty-maximizing requirements of justice? Do they arbitrarily advantage certain conceptions of the good, held by certain kinds of citizens, pursued for certain kinds of reasons, at the expense of other conceptions, held by different citizens, valued for altogether different reasons? Do they prevent citizens from further education for reasons having to do with their unchosen or innate characteristics?

The right to higher education is able to hold the institution of higher education to a more robust standard of justice because it proposes an altogether different relationship between mature citizens and the state provision of education: one where the state has a responsibility for the autonomous well-being of individual citizens and the political authority to ensure that higher education institutions comply in order to meet this responsibility. But there looks to be something contradictory about this relationship on the face of it. How can state responsibility *for* citizens' autonomous well-being and support for personal autonomy—which is very much about self-determination and *independence*—co-exist? Depending on the authority of an institution seems to cut against the idea of independence and self-determination. And what about social forms? Does the state get to tell citizens what kind of education they must undergo in order to access a certain social form? Left unanswered, questions of this nature suggest that the right to higher education looks more about treating mature citizens like children than about supporting their freedom and independence. This is a reasonable worry. In the next chapter, I go into to more detail about what political authority entails for the right to higher education, why its exercise is legitimate, and how it can avoid treating citizens paternalistically.

5
The Right to Higher Education and Political Authority

I have so far argued that institutions of higher education in a free and open society ought to be defined by a foundational moral purpose: a responsibility to support the autonomy of liberal citizens by making available the knowledge, understanding, and skills that enable such citizens to access valuable social forms and practices. And because the provision of these autonomy-supporting educational goods across a complete life is something to which liberal citizens are entitled, we can describe this as a right to higher education.

Conceiving of higher education institutions in this way also makes it subject to what I have called *liberty-maximizing* requirements of justice. This is because the foundational moral purpose of higher education decisively puts it into the pantheon of basic social institutions that together help individual citizens' lives go better, in the spirit of a just liberal society, i.e., the basic structure. Liberty-maximizing justice obligates the state—at least in principle—to ensure that an autonomy-supporting system of higher education is structured in such a way that these requirements are adequately fulfilled.

The question we now have to ask is whether or not the degree and kind of authority required to ensure such compliance is plausibly legitimate. Would such authority hand over too much power to the liberal state, for example?

In this chapter, I make the argument for *liberty-maximizing political authority* over a higher education, a conception of authority that sets out a proactive role for the state in helping adult citizens to autonomously flourish. This argument, if successful, affirms the idea that the liberal state's educational obligations to citizens extend beyond a basic or compulsory education, not only for reasons of political justice, but also because it is politically *legitimate* for the state to do so. I also defend this account against the concern that such authority might be too paternalistic, and I give examples of how this conception of authority would legitimately apply (and not apply) to higher education systems.

The Necessity (and Limits) of Political Authority Over Higher Education

Why does the question of authority matter for the right to higher education? While higher education belongs to the range of social institutions to which principles of political justice should apply (as argued in chapter 4) there are reasons why we might want to restrict the state's authority to demand that higher education institutions fully comply with these principles. We saw in the last chapter, for example, that universities play a politically essential social function. Undermining that function in the interests of justice broadly conceived may do more harm than good. So, the fact that the exercise of some regime of authority can promote justice, in higher education or elsewhere, is not sufficient to justify the authority required to bring about justice. "Can" does not imply "ought." And while in that last chapter I also argued that a viewing higher education as part of the basic structure of a liberal society would not *necessarily* undermine the socially essential values of the university within that same structure, this by itself does not justify the state's authority over higher education in general. There are, in fact, at least two reasons why further arguments are required.

One reason has to do with the general need for an authority that can coordinate institutions to bring about collective goods that they are responsible for providing. In an ideal world, we could imagine that higher education (and other) institutions—were they to be motivated by the idea of autonomy support as an overarching political goal—could voluntarily change how they function in order to realize requirements of liberty-maximizing justice. They would cooperate in order to realize a shared mandate. But in the real world, our institutions are unlikely to have the resources or power do this through their own efforts, even if they wanted to. What university in our current times, for example, has the money to make sure that any student who walks its halls can do so without having to take on a serious financial burden? What board of governors is willing to stand down from the relentless competition for "research excellence" and change their mission statements to target access for all citizens regardless of ability?

Not to mention the fact that while some systems of higher education, the United States most notably, are relatively diverse compared to other nations in terms of what they offer to students, many systems are fairly monolithic and focused on various status-conferring metrics such as research excellence and international recruitment. An autonomy-supporting conception of higher education would therefore likely require new institutions, or at the very least, a willingness among higher education institutions to coordinate in a way the ensures that they collectively offer a curriculum broad enough to support access to an adequate range of valuable social forms and practices. And this would mean curricular offerings that depart (possibly quite widely) from the standard, prestigious academic offerings that we often associate with a modern research institution. My point here is that any principled argument about the values and aims of higher education, and the obligations contained therein, presupposes the political authority to help (or ensure that) institutions of higher education comply with such principles, especially when individual institutions may not have the political, social, or economic power to undertake such reforms on their own.[1]

The second reason has to do with the specific nature of a political authority that acts through institutions in order to maximize the collective liberty of citizens. Higher education is predominantly viewed as an economic decision, and liberalism puts a premium on such decisions being freely made by individuals. We might want higher education systems to do more to promote civic-mindedness and to encourage citizens to value advanced knowledge and understanding for more diverse reasons. We might even think that the state should *force* higher education systems, if necessary, to do more in this respect. However, as systems of higher education internationalize it has become difficult for liberal states to steer higher education policy in directions that serve civic interests.[2] This is because liberalism imposes clear restrictions on what one might call *directive* educational authority: the power to command citizens to acquire specific kinds of knowledge, understanding, and skills in the interests of making their lives better. And with good reason, too. These restrictions follow from the view that the state ought not to ground public policy in the intrinsic merits of, or with the aim of promoting, any one (or several) conceptions(s) of the good. For example, a liberal state that exercises its authority to intervene in its higher education system on the grounds that anyone seeking a higher education will be better off through the study of philosophy would be rightly charged with failing to respect that citizen's own capacity to make judgments about the good, and with illegitimately favoring conceptions that take philosophical reflection to be central to the good life. At most, liberal states today exercise an indirect "spooky authority at distance," manipulating funding models and other incentives in order to nudge the system into bringing about particular economic or social outcomes.[3]

The problem is that this restriction may *also* rule out the very authority we need in order to ensure that higher education systems take the support of personal autonomy to be a core aim.

Here is why: I have described how political philosophers and philosophers of education have appealed to the value and importance of autonomy in order to justify the aims of public schooling in the liberal state and their relationship to political justice. But these arguments also align, or seek to align, with standards of legitimate liberal authority. And here the political value of autonomy also justifies the nature and limits of the authority required to ensure that a system of public education realizes its public and political goals. More specifically, the state has the legitimate *educational* authority to use its power to *direct* children toward an autonomy-facilitating or autonomy-promoting education. Educational authority also obligates the state to exercise its authority in order to ensure that such an education is well funded and that market forces do not impinge on its quality or fairness.

Why, then, can't we just claim that political authority applies to higher education on the same grounds as it does basic education? After all, compulsory and post-compulsory education are both committed to autonomy as a core value. So, we could imagine an argument going something like this: just as public schools are legitimately compelled by the state to foster skills and dispositions conducive to autonomy in young children, so too should higher education systems be compelled to promote knowledge, understanding, and skills that will support the autonomy of mature citizens. Let us say, then, that the right to higher education must be backed by *liberty-maximizing educational authority*.

The problem is that autonomy-grounded arguments for educational authority have a sunset clause built into them. By this I mean that such authority is thought to legitimately apply up until the point at which minimal conditions of personal autonomy are (or are assumed to be) satisfied (usually the age of majority).

This sunset clause arises from familiar liberal concerns about state power and paternalism. Many liberal accounts treat autonomy as an absolute agency right (George, 1995, pp. 129–130). Mature citizens ought to be treated as rational and responsible beings, and this includes a presumption against interfering with their judgments or actions. Childhood is a circumstance where interference is justified. This, because citizens must acquire the competences associated with personal autonomy in order to be recognized as agency-rights-bearing agents. While it's usually not okay to treat adults like children, it's fine to treat children like children (so long as that treatment does not undermine their future ability to function as adults).

We can see how the sunset clause matters for liberty-maximizing authority over higher education. At this stage authority and liberty, which work together at the compulsory level, are ostensibly incompatible. Authority involves being subject to the will or command of another, and such subjection is generally thought to be contrary to autonomous reason. And violating the autonomy rights that I acquire as an adult simply to increase my capacity for autonomy in the long term would seriously weaken those rights.[4]

Therefore, if a state exercised its authority in order to ensure that higher education systems collectively worked to support the autonomy of citizens it would mean *directing* citizens toward a certain limited, or bounded, range of knowledge, understanding, and skill. And while the state would be using its authority to direct citizens toward an education intended to increase their autonomous flourishing, it would involve overruling what those citizens might otherwise have chosen independently if they were in, say, a free-market system where such authority did not exist. And shouldn't autonomous citizens' choices and preferences drive what systems of higher education have to offer? Today, it is more common to see citizens exercise their autonomy as consumer sovereignty,[5] choosing post-compulsory programs that they believe they want, and see the system responding by competing for their dollars and shifting its offerings (or redescribing its offerings in its marketing material!) in order to respond to such wants. The less the state interferes with this arrangement, the better.

The problem, then, seems to be that liberty-maximizing authority involves subjecting institutions of higher education (and the citizens who choose to access them) to the will or command of the state. Even if this interference arises from a good-faith desire to promote autonomy among citizens, it actually *undermines* citizens' autonomy by treating them in a paternalistic-looking manner.

Anti-Perfectionism and Educational Authority

The sunset clause plays an influential role in how we think about the limits of educational authority over systems of higher education. Specifically, it places strong constraints on how far liberal states can go in advancing the educational interests of adult citizens. For example, the state may have educational authority with respect to questions of distributive justice in higher education. Authority in these cases is derived from the state's duty to promote socioeconomic equality of opportunity and does not necessarily involve judgments about the value that education should have in the lives of individual citizens. Further, the state may compel higher education systems to be more conducive to student choice so long as "choice" is neutrally conceived as an economic investment.[6] Unlike a compulsory education, however, it would not be legitimate for the state to structure higher education institutions with the intention to make personal autonomy an explicit educational *aim*. Such a directive would be paternalistic, with the state assuming that it knows better than individual citizens about the kinds of knowledge, understanding, and skills that will lead to valuable social forms and practices.

These constraints are derived from a tension between the nature of authority and personal autonomy. Reassessing this tension requires that we first detail those respects in which it is uncontroversial that the state *can* exercise legitimate authority.

When I talk about autonomy as an agency right, the tradition I have in mind is sometimes called "anti-perfectionist" liberalism. Anti-perfectionist liberals believe that political principles should not be grounded in any notion of the good life, reasonable as such notions may be. Political principles are only legitimate when they respect the (neutrally conceived) autonomy of citizens. They are principles that citizens can observe without such observance threatening their own conceptions of the good.

Debates over the provision of higher education are usually framed in terms of the just and fair distribution of the benefits and burdens of a higher education. We can talk about benefits and burdens in socioeconomic terms without advancing a particular view of the good life—these resources can support many purposes and aims in life. Therefore, directives about how higher education institutions should allocate those benefits and burdens are neutral with respect to the particular reasons that citizens have (or should have) for accessing post-compulsory educational goods in the context of a good life.

Can anti-perfectionists also justify directive educational authority—authority over the kinds of knowledge and understand citizens should experience—and, if so, what would it look like? This question is an important one because I will be arguing that the state should indeed have directive educational authority over post-compulsory education so as to promote the autonomous flourishing of citizens. An account of the merits (and limits) of anti-perfectionist authority can show why a perfectionist account of authority is needed.

In modern societies, the education we acquire as adults is one that should be freely chosen, given that one has a right to make of oneself what one wishes so long as that pursuit does not harm others or oneself. Such freedom goes beyond the choice to attend an institution or program and encompasses decisions about what is worth learning and why. Nonetheless, the fact that citizens require sustained opportunities to acquire knowledge and understanding at various points in their lives is a matter of unavoidable, practical necessity. For example, sometimes it is appropriate to require a person to undertake further training if they wish to keep their job when the demands of the job change. The fact that a person is determined to keep their job also gives them a strong reason to learn. And we already discussed, in chapter 2, why it is legitimate for educational institutions to require that those who choose to enter into professions undertake a curriculum that *is not* of their own choosing.

Citizens depend on knowledge and understanding in order to achieve self-determined goals. Does this fact point the way to directive educational authority? In making choices about the good life, we can and do rely on various educational authorities, especially in complex societies such as ours where one person cannot know everything. A physician needs to learn new procedures in order to stay proficient, and to the extent that he desires to be proficient, he must recognize the authority of what he is learning from the person who is teaching it to him. Insofar as a patient desires to be healthy, he must recognize the authority of that same physician when on the receiving end of advice about an operation. We can call this the *instrumental justification of educational authority*—authority about knowledge and understanding we defer to in order to facilitate the realization of a goal.

Anti-perfectionist liberals can easily justify this kind of educational authority. First, deference to instrumental authority is not contrary to autonomous reason and, as such, fully respects the citizen's autonomy. Such authority does not direct its subjects what to do; it supplies a reason to *believe* that one should do X if they wish to successfully achieve Y. It requires no abdication of a person's right to choose their own ends, nor does it undermine the value of those ends. When successful, instrumental educational authority simply increases the likelihood that the beliefs one has about how best to achieve an end will lead to success. For example, governments often publish vetted health science in the hopes that citizens will use this information to inform their judgments about diet and exercise. No illegitimate paternalism is involved. The state is not acting on the assumption that it is more capable than citizens of making good decisions about their own health; rather, the state has the resources to ensure that this information is accessible.

Second, there is an anti-perfectionist argument for the state to support citizens in this instrumental way. Knowledge is a public good, but public goods can be undersupplied. Therefore, the state has a reason to step in and subsidize the production of knowledge that can facilitate the attainment of aims or goals overlooked or neglected in the market context (Stiglitz, 1999, pp. 311–316). These subsidies do not have to run afoul of liberal neutrality. For example, some might object that the state's efforts to subsidize the research and dissemination of knowledge about a healthy diet—a public value judgment—entails an implicit criticism of those who do not see optimal health as central to their conception of the good and who would like to have their own goals facilitated through educational means. Why shouldn't the state lead an information campaign designed to help interested citizens maximize their fat and alcohol consumption at the lowest cost? The state's choice to advance a healthy over an unhealthy diet, it could be argued, disrespects citizens who wish to live in unhealthy ways.

However, anti-perfectionists generally view it as permissible for liberal democracies to promote social and economic goods on the grounds that all reasonable citizens have an interest in fair access to such goods. If this is the case, the legitimate promotion of knowledge that enables citizens to access goods such as health follows from this view. To be sure, these efforts will have different consequences for different conceptions of the good. Fast-food-loving citizens may see their favorite burger joint getting more expensive as the total number of customers decline, for example. But the state is not making judgments about the intrinsic value of these various conceptions or aiming to advance certain conceptions over others (Arneson, 2003). If the state's support of particular bodies of knowledge and understanding is grounded in the idea that informed decision-making facilitates access to common goods—perhaps by enriching the stock of public knowledge from which citizens make their own decisions about the good life in spheres pertaining to work, health, and education—no illiberal judgment about the value of these various conceptions is involved.

From an anti-perfectionist point of view, then, it would seem that the state has the legitimate authority to promote certain forms of knowledge and understanding. But does such authority warrant *directing* citizens toward particular kinds of knowledge and understanding on the grounds that it would support their autonomy? No, because the instrumental justification of authority we are talking about is essentially limited to *epistemic* authority (Raz, 2010, pp. 299–300). Epistemic authority, unlike practical authority, does not impose obligations or direct others. Epistemic authorities succeed through the giving of expert advice, not by issuing directives on how what someone should do or how they should live their life. When liberal democratic governments publicly disseminate findings in health science, they are acting as epistemic authorities, offering advice in the hopes that citizens will independently recognize the validity of the knowledge grounding that advice and act on it. But they do not direct mature citizens to eat or exercise. Nor do they obligate citizens to go out and learn about diet and exercise—they can at most promote this knowledge and understanding through public channels that citizens are free to ignore. The kind of educational authority that can be justified under anti-perfectionist premises (i.e., instrumental educational authority) is ultimately non-directive. As such, it cannot justify liberty-maximizing authority over the conception of higher education that I have been defending.

Perfectionism and Educational Authority

Anti-perfectionist arguments only allow for non-directive educational authority over adults; that is, the authority to promote knowledge and understanding that will facilitate the attainment of freely chosen ends.[7] But can we justify directive educational authority, that is, authority over the forms of knowledge, understanding, and skills worth making freely available to citizens in order to support their autonomous flourishing? In other words, should the state have the authority to *structure* the range of options citizens may choose from once they opt to take part in a system of higher education?

One might here ask in what respect the exercise of such authority would be in any way directive. After all, it is not as if the state is commanding citizens to pursue a particular program of study, nor is it obligating citizens to undertake an education beyond a basic, compulsory level. However, the exercise of such authority is nonetheless directive. This, because directive educational authority empowers the state to issue commands about the structure of the higher education system, including directives about the forms of knowledge, understanding, and skills to be made freely available to citizens. These directives redound on the range of options that citizens may choose among.

Importantly, these directives can overrule the voluntary choices of individual citizens because they involve replacing some of the options that citizens would normally choose from, in a system free from such authority, with options aimed at ensuring that the total *range* of options is adequate and genuinely autonomy supporting. That is to say, once citizens opt to receive a higher education, their choices are structured by an authority, i.e., they are *directed* to choose among some fixed range required by liberty-maximizing justice. This structure would likely look different from its marketized version.

I believe that what is sometimes called a *liberal perfectionist* account of autonomy is able to justify conditions under which the exercise of directive educational authority is legitimate. This is for two reasons. First, liberal perfectionists see autonomy as an intrinsic good or moral ideal that the state has a duty to protect and promote. Liberal perfectionists should, therefore, be more sympathetic to the idea of a state seeking to promote personal autonomy.

Second, the conception of personal autonomy that I have defended throughout the book is, in essence, a liberal perfectionist one. I have, for example, claimed that the value of personal autonomy lies in the essential role that it plays in enabling people to flourish in specifically liberal societies—what liberal perfectionists often call the socials forms thesis. If liberal perfectionists are sympathetic to the idea of a state that has the legitimate authority to promote autonomy in general we can expect this authority to apply to basic social institutions, such as higher education, that are directly responsible for autonomous flourishing.

While promising, directing a system of higher education to offer a particular range of knowledge, understanding, and skill—even on the perfectionist grounds that such a directive would facilitate citizens' autonomous flourishing—might still be an illegitimate use of government power. This is because using directive authority to promote autonomy seems to defeat the very perfectionist purpose of autonomy promotion, which is to enable adult citizens to flourish *through* self-determined choices (George, 1995, pp. 129–130; Raz, 1986, p. 420).

Why should perfectionist liberals think that such an approach would be self-defeating? Much turns on the nature of autonomous reason and its connection to well-being in the perfectionist conception. We ordinarily think that autonomous reasons are *self-determined* reasons. On this view, submitting to authority—taking the directive or command of another as a reason for acting—is contrary to personal autonomy. When I direct a person to do something, I may aim to increase their well-being in some tangible way, but I cannot increase the kind of well-being that only arises through the realization of self-determined goals. Directing someone to flourish autonomously is, in this sense, a contradiction.

Fortunately, Joseph Raz has developed an influential perfectionist account of authority that aims for greater precision in judging when directives undermine autonomy, and when they do not. In what follows, I provide a brief reconstruction of this account and assess the extent to which, and ways in which, this account can be successfully applied to higher education.

The Pre-Emption Thesis

Raz claims that authoritative directives succeed by excluding some (but not all) of the reasons that a subject herself has for acting, and replaces them with some of the authority's own reasons. Raz uses the example of traffic law (2005, p. 1018). When I drive to work, I have a general reason to drive as safely as I can, and this supplies me with a number of other reasons for acting. Raz calls these other kinds of reasons *first-order* reasons—reasons that directly apply to us when we reason practically about whatever situation we may find ourselves in. In a world before traffic law, an interest in driving safely generated numerous direct/first-order reasons for acting, such as switching between left and right sides of the road as the particular situation required. For example, if another driver, similarly independent and similarly moved to drive safely, was heading straight at us, this would have given us a direct reason to swerve to the other side.

However, if everyone drives in this independent way, our collective ability to conform to reason (i.e., to drive safely) is compromised: drivers will be weaving side to side as circumstance dictates, making overall conformity to reason impossible.[8] Legal authority over traffic, such as the side of the road one must drive on, aims at helping us to better comply with what reason requires of us (to drive safely) by directing us to do what we otherwise would not do (stick to one side of the road at all times). In other words, authoritative directives exclude *some* of our background reasons in order to facilitate our conformity *to* reason. Many of our driving decisions are independent. But in some instances, we have an obligation to obey traffic rules in order to ensure that we can do what reason requires of us in that circumstance.

The directive to drive on the same side of the road pre-empts and replaces some of our first-order reasons—it asks that we follow the authority as opposed to some of those reasons (Raz, 2005, p. 1019)—in order to better conform to the more general reason of driving safely. Raz states this in the more concise terms of a pre-emption thesis:

> [T]he fact that an authority requires performance of an action is a reason for its performance which is not to be added to all other relevant reasons when assessing what to do, but should exclude and take the place of some of them. (1986, p. 46)

The Normal Justification Thesis

Two features are worth emphasizing about pre-emption. First, authority succeeds in what it aims to do—to improve our ability to conform to reasons—by obligating us to follow its directive as opposed to (some of the) background reasons that are already there. Second, because an authority aims to help agents do what they already have reason to do, such directives cannot—nor should they—rely on coercion or manipulation in order to shift the balance of the agent's background reasons in favor of that directive. Put another way, an authority may not compel the agent to act contrary to their own reason. Rather, authority works by pre-empting some of the reasons an agent has and replacing those reasons with directives that help the agent better conform to the reasons that already apply to them, given that agent's end. So, while the pre-emption thesis describes what authorities actually do (pre-emption and replacement), their legitimacy requires an additional feature, which Raz calls the normal justification thesis, or NJT.

> [T]he normal way to establish that a person has authority over another person involves showing that the alleged subject is likely

better to comply with reasons which apply to him (other than the alleged authoritative directives) if he accepts the directives of the alleged authority as authoritatively binding and tries to follow them, rather than by trying to follow the reasons which apply to him directly. (1986, p. 53)

In other words, authority is justified on the merits of submitting to that authority versus the agent relying on their own reason in trying to conform *to* reason (see also Hershovitz, 2011, p. 2).

Before continuing, I'll offer another example for clarity. Anyone familiar with open-water swimming will tell you that many long-distance races require the support of a kayaker as a partner to paddle alongside the swimmer. While some may see this requirement as paternalistic, it is, on a Razian view, an example of legitimate authority. Each swimmer has reason to finish the race in the best time possible and one way to do this is to take the optimal route. But open-water swimming is notoriously difficult to navigate. Fatigue can set in. Swim goggles fog up. Waves make landmarks hard to track. It can be a very disorienting experience. Accordingly, swimmers have reason to defer to the directive authority of their kayaker partner because by following their commands ("correct to the right"; "you're drifting into the current") they are more likely to swim less distance (and finish with a better time) than if they tried to navigate on their own.

Raz's account describes how authority works (the pre-emption thesis) and establishes the normative grounds of its legitimate function (the NJT). Taken together, he calls this the *service conception* of authority. If this conception of legitimate authority is sound, it invites a more nuanced account of the relationship between education, state authority, and personal autonomy. For, while authority might indeed restrict us from acting independently in certain situations, it ought not to require us to act in a manner contrary to reason because the very point and purpose of legitimate authority is to help us conform to such reason.

To be sure, there are many situations where it would be better to rely on the use of our own rational capacities in so conforming. Solving a puzzle is one example. If you direct me where to put all the pieces, the reason for working on the puzzle in the first place has been lost.

But there are many situations where it is rational for me to recognize that it would be best if I allow others to direct my actions. If I am trapped in a room and I do not know how to get out, I will be more than happy for you to direct me to a safe exit. Such examples are not an abdication of reason; rather, we are here *indirectly* satisfying aims and goals that our rational capacities are otherwise designed to serve (Raz, 2005, p. 1003). Further, submitting to legitimate authority is not the sign of a weak or non-autonomous will. Acknowledging that an authority is legitimate entails the rational capacity to judge when it is (and when it is not) better to allow others to direct one's actions as opposed to directly relying on one's own rational capacities. This ability and willingness are themselves markers of autonomy.

When service authority is being exercised legitimately, it is not coercive but in fact *supportive* of reason. Is this by itself enough to justify liberty-maximizing authority over higher education? Recall that we are talking about the authority to structure the range of knowledge, understanding, and skills that citizens may choose from on the grounds that such authority will facilitate or promote their personal autonomy. On a Razian account, such authority is only legitimate when it satisfies the conditions of the NJT in the following way: its directives (such as the laws it passes about the structure and function of a public higher education system) help citizens conform to autonomous practical reason (i.e., the direct and independent use of practical reason) better than they would on their own.

Is it possible for an authority to satisfy such conditions? It's certainly possible in the case of children. Children have reason to develop their rational capacities in general, whether they recognize it or not, including their autonomous or independent use. But they can better conform to this reason when they rely on the direction of good teachers as opposed to doing so independently. In short, children have to be initiated into practical reason, including the independent use of their rational capacities, and this requires guidance from the already initiated.

Adult citizens, however, are in a different circumstance. They have completed a compulsory education and have had sufficient opportunity to develop their rational capacities, including the independent use of reason. They have a reason to choose, on autonomous grounds, the forms of knowledge and understanding that will make their lives better. It would therefore be difficult to show how a mature citizen could be better off in conforming to the *autonomous* use of practical reason by allowing others to direct their educational decisions, that is, unless one assumes that such citizens are like children: plainly bad at conforming to autonomous reason and requiring constant guidance. But if one argues along these lines, one is essentially claiming that adults should not be treated as personally autonomous to begin with. And this would mean that liberty-maximizing educational authority is not "liberty-maximizing" at all.

Liberty-Maximizing Educational Authority

Despite the concerns raised previously, I believe that a Razian argument for liberty-maximizing authority over higher education is one that liberal citizens have reason to embrace. This is because the sunset clause on educational authority rests on a powerful, but nonetheless mistaken, premise about the role of personal autonomy in the good life; namely, that the direct use of one's own capacities for reason is a sufficient explanation of what makes personally autonomous decision-making a distinctively valuable kind of flourishing.[9] By focusing on this premise, I also hope to show why non-interventionist and free market arguments against the role of the state in higher education are misconceived insofar as they appeal to it, either explicitly or implicitly.

Autonomy and Well-Being

Consider that one reason for relying on our own judgment when making decisions about the good life, even when others may be able to make better decisions for us, is because there is something intrinsically worthwhile about making our own decisions. Accordingly, it would be a mistake to think that independent action is merely instrumental to desirable goals—that following directives and acting independently are just different means to the same end.

It is tempting to move from the intrinsic value of independence to the idea that independence fully explains what makes personal autonomy distinct. Independence may be an important or even essential feature of some of our decisions. However, when we make independent judgments about the good life, we do this not only for the intrinsic value of independence; we also do so with the belief that those independent judgments will prove favorable for our well-being or flourishing. That is to say, we think we can get these judgments *right*.

If we really thought that independence was enough for autonomous practical reasoning about the good life, making a judgment independently should always leave us brimming with confidence that the judgment will serve us well. But we don't always approach judgment in this way. We seek advice from others. We hesitate. Sometimes we wait for more favorable conditions to arise. This is because we recognize that part of what it means to be autonomous is to understand the limits *of one's own reason*.

Anyone can be mistaken about the good life for reasons that have nothing to do with our rational capacities. Happenstance, bad luck, missing information, a lack of understanding, and the unpredictable nature of other people are all features of decision-making that can undermine the most judicious among us. I am not arguing that the fallibility of our autonomous judgments detracts from the importance of personal autonomy for living well. Nor am I denying that autonomous judgments are a constitutive feature of a variety of worthwhile goals. And I am not claiming that for any decision we make it would always be better to defer to the judgment of someone who knows better than we do. My point is simply that in order for a personally autonomous action to make a distinctive contribution to our well-being it must satisfy not one but (at least) two conditions: an independence condition and a *value condition* (see Raz, 1986, pp. 378–380).

What is the value condition? If one of the reasons why we have rational capacities is so that we can make decisions about the good but, further, our rational capacities can fall short in making such judgments successfully, it follows that the independent use of reason is not sufficient for autonomous well-being. The value condition explains why this is so: judgments of value are partly agent-independent.

Another way to put this is that we can and should distinguish between one's capacity for personal autonomy and the value of personal autonomy in a good life. While there are situations in which autonomous practical reasons apply to us (i.e., situations in which it is better for our well-being that we decide for ourselves), our successful compliance with such reasons also requires that what we decide on has value. In other words, the social forms and practices that constitute an adequate range of options[10] must be *valuable* options, and this value is independent of one's particular preferences. For example, it is better for my flourishing (in general) that I choose an occupation as opposed to being assigned one. But I may nonetheless choose an occupation that has no recognizable value or may even be harmful for others (e.g., running a violent drug cartel).

Alternatively, if independence were sufficient for personally autonomous decisions to contribute to our well-being, we would have to claim that running a violent drug cartel actually is a worthwhile activity (if only for the person running it), because to choose something independently just is what makes it valuable for one's flourishing. But this also seems wrong. We have reason to lead a good life (the value condition) defined by self-determined choices (the independence condition). But we can satisfy the independence condition while missing the value condition entirely. When we do, we have failed to conform to the autonomy-based reasons that apply to us. Autonomous lives, one might say, can be misdirected.

Finally, it is of course true that the independent exercise of reason can be its own reward. The puzzle-solving example I offered is one such example. The exercise of reason in that example is linked to an activity (puzzle-solving) that, when well-designed, allows for the exercise of our rational capacities as an end in itself. Puzzle-solving and other games belong to a broader class of activity: activities that are worthwhile because they allow for the direct and intrinsic enjoyment of our capacities. But not all activities are like this.

Liberty-Maximizing Authority Over Value, not Independence

If my interpretation of Razian authority and the conditions of personal autonomy is correct, it opens up a slightly different way of framing the problem of educational authority. It does so in three steps.

First, political authority may be legitimately applied in order to help citizens lead better lives when doing so helps them conform to the autonomy-based reasons that apply to them. Successfully conforming to such reasons is important because it contributes to their autonomous flourishing.

Second, by distinguishing between a *capacity* for personal autonomy and the *value* of personal autonomy, we can see how political authority can help adult citizens conform to autonomy-based reasons without undermining autonomy. This is because political authorities may in principle issue directives that target the second condition (value) without illegitimately interfering with the first condition (independence).

Is it possible to do this, in practice? Can some authority direct citizens in ways that leave them better able to satisfy the value condition than if those citizens tried to do so on their own *without* those directives compromising the independence condition (and so undermining the agent's personal autonomy)? I believe that in at least some circumstances the answer to this question is "yes," and the design of educational institutions is one such circumstance.

As I have already argued across several chapters, liberal citizens have reason to make self-determined choices about the acquisition of knowledge, understanding, and skills that will contribute to their well-being. These goods enable citizens to access a variety of valuable social forms and activities, that is to say, knowledge renders such social forms and activities "choosable" for the agent. Self-determination matters crucially in this picture. It may be the case that a citizen has a specific social practice in view and that it requires knowledge, understanding, or skill. The cases of the aspiring athlete and the political activist that I discussed in the previous chapters come to mind here.

But the decisions we make about knowledge makes some social forms more accessible than others even when our self-determined goals are only beginning to form or are imprecise and broad. Studying urban planning might enable one to become an urban planner. Studying philosophy might enable one to become a philosopher. Urban planning and professional philosophy are both worthwhile activities. But many who choose such programs end up becoming neither. Each path nonetheless enables the graduate to access a variety of other social forms and activities that were largely unavailable beforehand, and the activities opened up to our student philosopher does not always overlap with the social forms opened up to our student urban planner. Further, it is likely that the social forms and activities opened up through the study of urban planning share important intellectual, affective, and aesthetic features different from some of those opened up by philosophy. Therefore, students who flourish *in* their chosen pursuit of knowledge, understanding, and skill are likely to derive value from the social forms that are opened up by virtue of that pursuit and, further, they are more likely to flourish through their participation in those forms.[11]

My point is that autonomous choices about education make a distinctive contribution to the good life—it really does matter that such decisions be arrived at independently—because they enable the graduate to choose among and access *other* social forms and activities that are likely to help them flourish. And this holds both for the citizen who has a clear and distinct idea about the social forms and practices that they want to partake in, as well as the citizen who is in a formative process of self-discovery about what they want from life.

Third, and finally, note that we are justifying the right of the state to shape the context of choice for citizens who opt for a higher education as opposed to allowing that context to be defined by the voluntary choices of citizens. To put this in technical terms, when a citizen chooses to receive a higher education, they accept the state's directive—the commands that structure the higher education in such a way that contingent choices are repealed and replaced with choices that matter—because they are more likely to succeed in complying with the autonomy-based reasons which apply to them if they accept that directive and abide by it rather than trying to follow the reasons which apply to them directly.

This account of the value of knowledge and understanding in the lives of mature citizens has implications for why, and under what conditions, independence matters in the post-compulsory context. In a system of higher education defined by competition for students and the proliferation of degree options and other credentials, it is all too easy to overstate in what respect independence matters when citizens make autonomous choices about their education.

For example, if each and every educational program on offer opened distinctly valuable social forms and activities that cannot be accessed through other educational programs—if one could link every program of study to some uniquely comprehensive goal, for example—the level of independence needed for personally autonomous choices to contribute to well-being would be very high. And I suspect that many students really do think of their choices in this way. They think that the specific sub-specialization in undergraduate psychology, hosted at a specific institution, is a straight path to those things they want out of life. But such cases are rare. It is a choice among broad categories of programming that dovetail with meaningfully different forms of knowledge, understanding, and skill that matter for the agent, and so it is the provision of an *adequate range of meaningful options* among these categories where the independence condition really matters.

Accordingly, an argument for liberty-maximizing authority over higher education doesn't have to deny independence. It is possible to distinguish between those features of an educational decision that ultimately matter for an agent's autonomously pursued well-being and those features that are merely contingent. When I drive a car, for example, I have many reasons that apply to me directly, but not all of those reasons play a constitutive role in the value I derive from driving a car. It is no threat to my autonomy to direct me to stay on one side of the road, for these direct reasons are merely contingent on my background reason, which is to drive safely. And I think that we can say something similar about students navigating complex, and highly marketized, systems of post-compulsory education. Some choices really are "options" in the sense that choosing between them will make a real difference for flourishing because they have consequences for the kinds of social forms and activities one will be able to take part of. But many choices are like the direct reasons we have for switching between left and right sides of the road in a world before traffic law: they are merely derivative of the background reasons we have for making choices to begin with and, as such, can be pre-empted and replaced without compromising our independence. Liberty-maximizing educational authority, we might say, should help citizens navigate between educational signals (meaningful choices) and educational noise (like marketing).

Applying Liberty-Maximizing Authority to Higher Education

Recall that a legitimate conception of liberty-maximizing educational authority must help adult citizens to make autonomy-based decisions in a way that leaves them better off than if they were to make such decisions on their own. The question was whether an authority could ever do this without compromising the independence condition. The answer is "yes." Practical authorities such as the state may direct higher education systems to structure themselves in a way that ensures citizens are more likely to succeed in making self-determined choices about the knowledge, understanding, and skill that will contribute to their autonomous well-being than if they were to do so on their own. One key way to do so is to ensure that, at a system level, higher education provides access to an adequate range of meaningful educational options, where "meaningful" refers to the role that such options play in enabling access to various social forms and practices that can define a good life.

It is worth pointing out how this conception of authority shifts the relationship between citizens, their educational entitlements, and the state. Normally we think that higher education should serve a collective or public good, or that it should serve the private economic interests some citizens may have in a higher education. These purposes are otherwise thought to justify a fairly limited role for the state in higher education. But the argument we have been pursing stakes out a public and political role for higher education in serving an individual interest that every liberal citizen has in flourishing through a personally autonomous life. In the last chapter,

I argued that this role can be justified on grounds of political justice (and, more specifically, liberty-maximizing requirements of justice). The problem is that realizing this role in practice looked to require an illegitimate exercise of political power that state. However, the service conception is able to justify terms (and limits) under which it is legitimate for the state to exercise its authority in order to see this role fulfilled.

For example, imagine a post-compulsory system that finds it increasingly difficult to attract students to arts programs. Many such programs are offered but because students are acting on the reasons that apply to them directly, choosing between these many different programs spreads them too thin, making each arts program unsustainable. (It becomes too expensive for institutions to fund them and too expensive to have students cover the cost.) One consequence is that a valuable educational option (or class of options) may be lost to many citizens, making it more difficult for them to access related social forms and activities that matter for their well-being in the long run. Some citizens who want to pursue art as part of their conception of the good will be frozen out, not to mention citizens who are not entirely sure what their self-directed goals should like. These citizens may be intuitively drawn to social forms and practices that put a high premium on aesthetics.

According to liberty-maximizing authority, in such a case the state has the authority to direct the system to adopt reforms that make arts programming a viable option for citizens. The specific policies may be something best left to be negotiated between specific higher education institutions. For example, we could imagine a proposal to merge some of the existing arts programming in order to ensure a critical mass of students. The aim of such a policy is to ensure that all citizens have access to an adequate range of educationally valuable options.

However, imagine that this approach was undesirable. Perhaps a good case is made that merging such programs elides important educational differences. The state could take a different approach.

For example, it could use its authority to pay students to enroll in arts programs, making them more attractive.

There is a troubling objection to this policy. Note that in this example the state is using its authority to change the balance of reasons for or against humanities programming by introducing an incentive. Does the state have the authority to change the balance of reasons in this way? It looks as if this is simply a case of pre-emption and replacement: the payment replaces some of the existing reasons for acting and replaces them with the authority's own reasons. But one could object that the state has crossed a line by interfering with the independence condition—some students who would have chosen sciences will choose otherwise.

However, this claim is only cause for concern if we assume that there is some intrinsic or "natural" balance of reasons and that changing the balance is an instance of illegitimate or paternalistic interference.[12] Personally autonomous agents decide on the merits of the various available options, including the costs and benefits of that choice, which may change depending on the circumstances or the actions of others. There is no natural balance. So long as the state is changing the balance of reasons in order to help citizens lead good lives and, in the case of post-compulsory education, ensuring that an important educational good remains an option for all those making self-determined education choices, the interference is justified.

Of course, as with any form of authority, liberty-maximizing authority must be marshaled in a responsible way, with a keen awareness of the conditions and limitations of its application to institutions of higher education. It is especially important that the state not undermine the independence condition through coercion and manipulation. Liberty-maximizing educational authority may not achieve its service goals by directing citizens to *particular* forms of knowledge, understanding, and skill. For example, they may not structure systems aimed at ensuring all citizens were enrolled in STEM programs. Pushing citizens to a particular option would detract from the role of independence in making choices about the role of knowledge in a good life.

What then, would this look like for actual post-compulsory institutions? To the extent that the state is able to satisfy the conditions of the service conception it may issue authoritative directives in the form of educational policies that change the structure of higher education institutions for (autonomy-based) perfectionist reasons, including the authority to intervene in the higher education system for reasons other than distributive justice or economic efficiency. For example, under the right circumstances the state may have the authority to establish educational institutions, or direct existing institutions to offer educational opportunities, that enable access for all citizens to valued social forms and practices currently underserved in the market context. This authority permits the liberal state to ensure that its system of higher education is compliant with liberty-maximizing requirements of justice.

Conclusion

I have argued that the liberal state has legitimate authority over post-compulsory educational institutions for perfectionist reasons in general and for the support of personal autonomy in particular. Liberal political authority is therefore compatible with the right to higher education.

Specifically, the state has the authority to promote conditions that help citizens pursue valuable conceptions of the good through the use of directives that put citizens in a better position to independently choose among valued forms of knowledge, understanding, and skill. Such authority goes beyond anti-perfectionist reasons of egalitarian justice or liberal neutrality (Chan, 2012), and in this respect establishes a broader role for that state in promoting worthwhile civic goals through post-compulsory education than politically liberal conceptions of educational justice permit.

The right to higher education puts the autonomy of individual citizens at the forefront. It is motivated by a social vision in which all such citizens, regardless of their age, background, or ability, are able to freely pursue a good life. I have contrasted this conception of higher education with conceptions that have focused on the distribution of socioeconomic benefits and burdens. On my account, institutions of higher education have a political responsibility to enable citizens to access social forms and practices that will contribute to their autonomous flourishing, and the state has the legitimate authority to ensure that they are fully compliant with this responsibility. Claims about fair distribution in higher education must be informed by this more fundamental responsibility. But how exactly does the right to higher education inform difficult questions about how to allocate higher education and who should pay for it? In a perfect world, liberal states would have more than enough revenue to fully fund this conception of higher education. But the fact is that resources can be scarce, and any public funding that the state puts into the system is likely to come from individual taxpayers, many of whom may not (at present) choose to access the system. Therefore, in the next chapter I will show how the right to higher education can inform decision-making about distributive justice when resources are scarce and concerns about the fair distribution of benefits and burdens are at the forefront. I will do this by addressing the ongoing controversy over educational debt and the public funding of higher education institutions.

6
The Right to Higher Education and the Problem of Unequal Benefits

Over several chapters I have defended a conception of higher education understood as a right. Along the way, I have identified the central educational values and aims of this conception and its relationship to political justice and political authority. In particular, I have argued that we should think of higher education as a basic social institution responsible for helping citizens in their pursuit of a good life regardless of race, class, gender, or ability. All citizens are entitled to such assistance (what I have called an "autonomy-supporting" education) by virtue of the fundamental interest that all citizens have in liberty. Access to higher education is, on this view, a basic right of all liberal citizens.

In this chapter, I turn to the question of who should pay for a system of higher education founded on such a right. First, I explain how moral intuitions about fair funding can challenge the claim that an autonomy-supporting education should be allocated as an entitlement or primary good. Second, I show how these intuitions are conventionally justified in terms of a distribution's effects on socioeconomic equality. Third, I argue that there are also liberty-based reasons for the public to fund higher education. Finally, I argue that these liberty-based reasons take on a special significance in the context of a right to higher education, warranting full public funding so long as two other distributive conditions (non-exclusivity and support for diverse conceptions of the good) are satisfied.

Why the Distribution of Benefits and Burdens (Still) Matters

How systems of higher education should be funded—how much of this burden should be shouldered by society in general, and how much should be paid for by those receiving a higher education—is no easy question in a world of imperfect, unequal institutions. Consider the situation for many students today: a higher education has become synonymous with rising tuition and educational debt. Social scientists and economists have contributed to a growing literature on the impact of fees and debt on important life decisions regarding access to further education, choice of occupation, and household planning.[1] While this state of affairs may seem unfair to students, there are good reasons for thinking that having them shoulder some of the costs of higher education is reasonable.

To be sure, higher education is an important pathway to upward social mobility for many citizens. It would be plainly unjust if the upfront costs of higher education prevented them from setting out on this path. This might look to be a *prima facie* reason in favor of making higher education free for all and fully funded by the public. However, as the costs of higher education rise it becomes increasingly unfair to require the public to match those rising costs. For example, public funding would require citizens who never opted for a higher education—or more importantly, never qualified to be admitted into one—to shoulder a greater tax burden so that others can go for free. It may even involve shifting tax funding away from valuable goods, such as health care, that clearly benefit all citizens. On top of this, those who attend for free will also experience a college premium—an increase in average earning power after graduation—while those who helped to pay for it will not. The belief that a free higher education under such conditions is unfair follows from a moral intuition about fair distribution: that it is unfair to obligate some people to contribute to a system or scheme that will bring most of the benefit to others.

But should this intuition matter for an autonomy-supporting conception of higher education? It might be tempting to think that it does not matter at all because such a conception justifies access to higher education as a right, not a privilege. Requiring all citizens to pitch in for a higher education might be unfair in a world where many students pursue a higher education for the income boost, where a growing demand for labor market credentials and social status empowers institutions to increase private fees to astronomical levels, and where many potential students are turned away or would never qualify for admission to begin with. But according to the autonomy-supporting conception, citizens throughout adult life ought to have access to the system. This includes citizens whose working lives are largely over and done with, as well as citizens who aim to participate in social forms and practices that are not linked to the labor market. In this picture, the distribution of benefits and burdens arising from full public funding is far less troubling.

But this is too hasty a move. While the *particulars* of a system founded on an autonomy-supporting conception will differ in many important respects from the system we currently have, intuitions about fair distribution persist. For example, we can expect many citizens to exercise their right to an autonomy-supporting education. But there will be many others who see no reason to do so at all. Those who opt in will benefit from an increased capacity for autonomous flourishing (whether that flourishing comes in the form of success on the job market or access to some other desired social practice) while these non-opting citizens are required to contribute.

Is it fair to require these other citizens to take on the burden of funding? If the answer to this question is "no"—if it is more just to require users to pay—it could be argued that framing autonomy-supporting higher education as a right is cogent in principle but unjust in practice. The benefits and burdens of society should be distributed fairly across its members, and the sheer unfairness of a policy of free, autonomy-supporting higher education makes any case for the right to higher education implausible at best.

Therefore, the question of how higher education ought to be funded presents a challenge to the claim that higher education should be a basic entitlement. We need to show that intuitions about the fair distribution of benefits and burdens, which ordinarily rule against full public funding for higher education, do not apply in quite the same way under its autonomy-supporting, rights-based version.

The Socioeconomic Argument for Higher Education Funding

Before determining whether or not moral concerns about the fair distribution of benefits and burdens rule against full public funding as part of the right to higher education, we need a more precise understanding of how these intuitions inform egalitarian reasoning about the distributive fairness of higher education under actual, non-ideal conditions. Two philosophical contributions to the funding debate are especially instructive.

First, Harry Brighouse (2004) has argued for means-tested public provision. "Means-tested" refers to the idea that a person is eligible to have their access to a good funded by the public if they do not have the economic means to access that good through their own efforts. His argument runs like this. First, we have to realize that students should be responsible for their choices, and because the economic benefits of higher education mainly go to the student, it is reasonable to require them to pay. Second, we also have to consider the fact that there are many students who will be discouraged from attending if they have to pay upfront, either because they do not have the money in the first place, or because taking on student debt is too risky an investment. Therefore, fairness requires that relatively well-off students pay, while those less well-off should receive public support. In this context, debt financing looks to be a good solution. Students who are so poorly off that any financial costs are a barrier to accessing the system should qualify for public funding. These students are clearly worse off than many citizens, and receiving higher education as a benefit will help to level the socioeconomic playing field. But there are some students who are not especially wealthy and cannot afford to pay the upfront costs of higher education, yet are well-off *enough* that if the public paid for their attendance it would go beyond what is "fair."

Why would it go beyond fairness? Because these students are already better off than many of the citizens who would be asked to help fund their access. Educational loans enable access for students of a certain socioeconomic background, that is, the middle class. This is why debt financing can be understood as a just policy. It enables people of average income (or family backgrounds with average income) to access the system without placing an unfair burden on the public. The relatively wealthy pay for access, while the least well-off receive public funding.

Second, Paul Bou-Habib (2010) has argued that a fair scheme of cost sharing is that which most improves the lifetime income of the worst off (p. 493). He emphasizes that his argument will leave the actual scheme dependent on empirics about the distribution of income in any given society. Therefore, he does not in principle rule out full public funding or full private funding. Nonetheless, it is reasonable to assume that some students would qualify for public funding because funding these likely lower-income students will improve the socioeconomic prospects for the worst off. Meanwhile, requiring the remaining students to pay or borrow improves the worst off because these likely middle- or high-income students contribute resources that can fund students closer to the bottom.

Both Brighouse and Bou-Habib converge on something important about the fairness of higher education funding. While they each establish principled grounds on which the public should financially support citizens' access to higher education, they also recognize that the burdens of such support should be distributed fairly. For example, when resources are scarce and the costs of higher education are rising, a concern for socioeconomic equality should place a redistributive "check" against policies that shift too much of the cost to students. Higher education has become a gateway to improved socioeconomic fortunes, and so it is unjust to ask low-income students to pay or borrow in order to pass through that gateway.

However, this does not entail full public funding for all. Why? A concern for socioeconomic equality also places a redistributive check against policies that shift too much of the burden on the public. A regime of full funding, for example, would involve paying for students who are already quite well-off in socioeconomic terms. Citizens should not be obligated to contribute more than equality demands because it places an unjustified burden on the public, compelling them take on an additional burden simply in order to help those who are already privileged to access even more privilege.

It looks, then, as if socioeconomic equality is able to explain the extent (and limits) of public funding for higher education. But are reasons of socioeconomic equality the *only* kind of reasons why the public should pay? Perhaps there are non-economic reasons why citizens should contribute to the funding of higher education. Could these reasons justify public funding above and beyond what socioeconomic equality alone requires?

There are many candidate reasons why funding access to higher education has value. Examples abound in the debate on higher education funding: that knowledge and understanding is intrinsically worthwhile, that higher education is emancipatory, or that a liberal arts education makes for more competent citizens (see Barnett, 1990; Collini, 2012; Nussbaum, 2010). Perhaps one could bundle all of these goods together and argue that citizens should support higher education, not only in the interests of socioeconomic equality, but because all citizens of a democracy benefit from the production of able thinkers (where "able" is construed widely). To the extent that a higher education does produce such thinkers, the public should contribute more public funding than what socioeconomic equality alone calls for.

Making good on such a claim would require a public that prefers to boost the number of able thinkers in a democracy beyond what a funding regime based on socioeconomic equality would generate incidentally. But even if the idea of producing more able thinkers were uncontroversial in and of itself, obligating the public to pay for the production of such thinkers surely is.

One might ask why citizens' actual preferences about supporting higher education should bear on the public funding of higher education in the first place. People often complain about being taxed for public health care and basic schooling, for example, and yet these complaints are not usually seen as strong enough to call the public funding of these goods into question. Nonetheless, the public funding of institutions involves compulsory taxation, and such compulsion must be justifiable to citizens. Rutger Claassen (2013) has described this as the problem of unequal benefits: "Which goods should be provided, given that for almost any good some citizens will not see an interest in its provision (but must contribute through taxation?)" (p. 272).

Initially, unequal benefits may not seem like much of a problem at all. There are some goods that are beneficial to everyone but are undersupplied by the market. And some of these undersupplied public goods serve an interest shared by all, sometimes referred to as presumptive public goods (Klosko, 1987). Health care, mentioned previously, is a paradigmatic case. Each citizen has an individual interest in health care, and supplying health care to others benefits the individual supplying it (by reducing communicable diseases, for example). We could make a similar argument about funding for basic education.

However, some goods that depend on large-scale cooperation clearly are not of interest to every individual. These are goods such as the arts, libraries, and sport facilities, which clearly have value but are discretionary in terms of the interest they hold for individual citizens (Klosko, 1990). Individual citizens are free not to observe an interest in such discretionary public goods even when they are widely recognized as having value.

The difference between discretionary and presumptive public goods highlights the relevance of citizens' preferences to the justification of public funding for higher education. A case needs to be made for why a particular public good ought to be supported by the state and, given the role that taxation plays in such support, this case must include reasons why it is fair to place an additional financial burden on individual citizens in exchange for that good. For goods that are presumptively beneficial, these reasons will be easy to come by. You have a hard-to-deny interest in such a good. If you want to satisfy that interest, you must pay. However, in cases where many citizens have little to no interest, a stronger argument for why those citizens should pay for the good in question is needed.

Many of our claims about the goods of higher education are claims about its discretionary value. They reflect goods that some citizens will find to be worthwhile, but certainly not all.[2] As such, they do not serve as a convincing basis for public funding. In fact, the presumptive/discretionary distinction helps to explain the power and appeal of arguments for public funding from socioeconomic equality. Brighouse's and Bou-Habib's arguments, for example, do not rest on the discretionary value of higher education. Rather, they focus on higher education's role in supporting the *presumptive* public good of justice. If someone asks why citizens should support higher education at all, given that people choose it at their own discretion, they can point to the fact that it is nonetheless an essential means to a good that all can benefit from: socioeconomic equality. That is to say, they would be better off if the society that they found themselves to be in were one where socioeconomic equality was one of its characteristic features.

Klosko has cited this approach as a plausible justification for the public funding of discretionary public goods. As he puts it, the justification of discretionary goods rests on "the *practical indispensability* of certain goods . . . presumptive goods are necessary for an acceptable life for all members of society . . . though discretionary public goods are not directly required for individual wellbeing, [some] are required indirectly" (Klosko, 1990, pp. 205-206). Discretionary public goods are justly funded if it can be showed that they are necessary for propping up presumptively public goods.

This approach offers an additional advantage. One might be tempted to think that the argument from socioeconomic equality works in the following way: because justice is a presumptive good and a higher education is instrumental to justice (due to its role in indirectly allocating socioeconomic opportunities), citizens should *prefer* to contribute. However, even if every citizen preferred to contribute it would not mean that they *must* contribute. If justice were like this—simply one preference among many—a citizen could contribute on a voluntary basis. They could claim, for example, that while they prefer a socioeconomically just society over an unjust one, they also have an overriding preference on this particular tax year—a preference for greater disposable income, perhaps—that overrules contributing. Yet, the term "presumptive good" should not be understood as a preference but as something closer to what Rawls would call a primary good, or, as Klosko defines it, a good where the importance of the benefits derived from cooperating in the supply of that good trumps a person's ordinary right to opt out of the scheme (Klosko, 1990, p. 198). By establishing that higher education is instrumental to justice understood as a presumptive good, the argument from socioeconomic equality is able to explain why citizens do not merely have a preference to pitch in, but are legitimately obligated to do so.

The Liberty-Maximizing Argument for Higher Education Funding

The socioeconomic argument for public funding can tell us some helpful things about the justification of public funding for higher education in general. First, the kinds of reasons that are sufficiently weighty to motivate public funding are those that point to the instrumental role of higher education in contributing to presumptive public goods—goods that all citizens will benefit from and have an obligation to contribute toward. Second, *justice* is the presumptive public good that is best able to motivate these obligating reasons.

Can we adopt this approach in order to justify funding higher education as a universal benefit? Again, one might here argue that if higher education is indeed an individual right, the state simply has an obligation to ensure that it is provided at no cost to all. Fulfillment of this obligation is itself a matter of justice. One does not need to claim that higher education is instrumental to some presumptive public good such as socioeconomic justice.

The problem, however, is that, unlike a right to health care or compulsory education, a right to higher education that entailed full public funding could nonetheless lead to a distribution of benefits and burdens that is intolerably unfair. That is, the right to higher education may not necessarily justify funding higher education like a universal benefit. Here is why:

> Let us grant that citizens have a right to educational goods that will support their autonomous flourishing. And a higher education system founded on such a right should ensure that no adult citizen is prevented from accessing educational pathways that support that flourishing. But there is an important distinction between a right qua right and the conditions necessary and sufficient in order for a citizen to make good on that right. The right to higher education is no different.
>
> First, citizens should be admitted simply on the basis of their declared interest in receiving a higher education. Failure to realize this condition would violate the right on the face of it.
>
> Second, such a system should host a range of institutions sufficiently diverse enough to ensure that access to an adequate range of valuable social forms and practices are being supported. Failure to realize this condition excludes citizens whose self-directed

goals require educational support but are not represented in the system.

These two conditions (non-exclusion and diverse offerings) are necessary to make good on a person's moral claim to a higher education on autonomy-supporting grounds. Without them, many citizens would be unable to access a higher education system for reasons that are, on the account I am offering, arbitrary.

But full funding by the public is not necessary in order to make good on such a claim. There are many young citizens who come from families that can afford to pay. In many cases, older students will have already acquired a great deal of wealth over the course of their working years. Private costs would be unlikely to prevent these citizens from accessing the system. And we could implement means-tested loans similar to what we already have in many liberal states, such as the United States and Canada, that ensure a person's financial background will never get in the way of their right to a higher education. One serious advantage of this approach is that the benefits and burdens of that system will be distributed more equally than if it were fully funded by the public. Wealthy citizens would be required to pay their fair share. And citizens who prefer not to opt in, or whose self-directed goals are not of the kind that would necessitate an autonomy-supporting higher education, would not be expected to shoulder this additional funding burden. In short, the right to higher education requires non-exclusion and diversity. But it does not require full public funding.

Is this an insurmountable problem? The right to higher education is founded on the idea that personal autonomy is essential to liberal citizenship. Therefore, reasons in favor of public funding must be grounded in liberty-maximizing justice, that is, claims about how that funding will advance the personal autonomy of citizens. What specific liberty-based reasons justify public funding, and can these reasons justify *full* funding without being guilty of an unfair distribution of benefits and burdens? In other words, does the argument for a right to higher education necessitate full public funding as a condition for making good on that right? Let's take up this challenge by first setting out how exactly it is that liberty-based reasons could motivate public funding at all. Then we can see how *far* these kinds of reasons can take us before they run into the problem of unequal benefits.

First, recall that on my account higher education goods must support citizens in the realization of self-directed goals. It does this by providing them with knowledge, understanding, and skills that make those self-directed goals more achievable. This account is grounded in the idea that access to higher education is instrumental to citizens' free pursuit of the good life. Such freedom is a matter of basic justice, and basic justice is valuable to all citizens. Individual citizens' freedom to pursue the good should not be constrained for arbitrary or morally irrelevant reasons. Such constraints are unjust.

Now, picture a scenario where those who choose a higher education are deemed fully responsible for the upfront costs of such support. We can quickly see why some public funding would be warranted. Many citizens would be unable to realize their self-determined goals for the morally arbitrary reason that they do not have the resources to pay for these up-front costs. Therefore, liberty-based reasons justify at least *some* public funding.

What about students from middle-class families? These families are fairly well-off, but do not have enough resources to cover the up-front costs of attending. One could argue that these students are in no better a position than students from families that have no resources at all. Therefore, society has an obligation to fully fund these students, as well.

The problem is that this courts the same unequal benefits problem as the funding argument from socioeconomic equality. Middle class students have relatively more resources than other citizens in society, so this argument goes, and as such they are already in a better position to exercise their basic liberties in the pursuit of the good life. They have the money, the cultural capital, and the leisure time to exercise personal autonomy in directions that many other citizens do not. Therefore, while poor students should get full funding, this support should be gradually lessened as we move closer to the middle class. But this still leaves us with the problem of an unjust constraint on freedom. There are certain options in life that may only be accessible through some form of post-compulsory education, and the fact that a person is not rich *enough* should not get in the way of the pursuit of such options. One might conclude, then, that individuals in such a position should be permitted to borrow, and pay back after graduation. The wealthy, meanwhile, can pay the up-front costs.

This line of reasoning puts liberty-based arguments for public funding in roughly the same place as arguments grounded in socioeconomic equality. But must we stop here? No. One important way in which higher education is supposed to support the autonomy of citizens is to widen the range of valuable options from which a citizen is empowered to choose. Now compare the range of options for the student who borrows with the range of options for a student who does not. First, consider the consequences of debt financing for autonomy support. Suppose higher education is free at the point of use, and I choose to study creative writing. Becoming a novelist is my self-directed goal. I have no realistic expectation of making very much money from my novels, but I don't mind that because a high income and other trappings of upward social mobility are not part of my conception of the good. If it were, it is likely that my interest in earning a high income would override my desire to write novels. Of course, some minimal degree of financial security is necessary, and so I'll need to plan accordingly. I'll probably have to pick up casual employment after graduation as a means of supporting my self-determined goal—publishing creative works. It will be up to me to decide how much casual work I need to take on to maintain an acceptable level of material comfort. While it is unfortunate that my personal goals are not likely to be financially rewarding, it is not unjust: after all, I'm doing what I want with my life. And in this scenario, I am able to acquire the knowledge and understanding I need for the kind of life I have chosen. I am also able to do so without taking on burdens beyond those I am willing to accept as part of that life.

But now suppose that higher education is debt-financed and I must decide whether a creative writing degree is a good investment—something that will enable me to pay off the debt. The prospect of this debt, of which I may never be free if I follow my preferred career path, acts as a significant constraint on my freedom of choice. As a borrower, I must always be mindful of my debt obligation, which drastically alters my appraisal of the options open to me. If I try to pursue my conception of the good, I may fail to meet my debt obligation, and the consequences of this failure (accumulating interest, higher loan repayments, a lower credit rating, etc.) will further undermine my ability to pursue that conception. The life of a novelist is no longer a serious option for me: it is a luxury I cannot afford.

The hardship imposed by student loans is of a different character from those imposed by our freely undertaken, widely reflective choices about what kind of life to live. Autonomous choosers have a degree of control over the latter hardships: they recognize that different choices bring different mixes of costs and benefits, and they accept responsibility for the mix they choose. But borrowing students incur a hardship that stretches across all of their choices and has severe consequences for their autonomous flourishing. Debt profoundly changes the context of choice, reducing students' educational options by forcing them to weigh all their options on the basis of economic considerations.

Under this funding regime, of course, not *all* students' choices are constrained in this way. Higher education remains autonomy-supporting for those wealthy enough to avoid having to borrow. And we can probably include citizens who are in pursuit of high-paying jobs and expect to pay off their loan once they are successfully employed. The rich can still choose to be novelists because the choice doesn't involve taking on a debt they cannot repay. Debt financing makes freedom of educational choice a luxury for those who can afford it and a risky proposition for those who can't. Alex Gourevitch describes the different situations of the indebted and the debt-free student as follows:

> ... the indebted student knows he will face a unique constraint [on his freedom]. He will have to pay back his loans. Knowing that, even if he is no more risk-averse than his fellow student, he is much more likely to make a conservative choice about his educational and subsequent professional choices. He will be guided toward choosing degrees and career paths that promise better earning potential. To pursue his education with the same intellectual freedom and experimental attitude as the other student would require the indebted student to be much less risk-averse than his colleagues. (Gourevitch, 2012, p. 144)

Student loans thus amplify existing inequalities in terms of citizens' ability to set and successfully pursue self-determined goals by requiring already less well-off students to give much greater weight to prospective income than their well-off counterparts.

When upward social mobility is the fundamental aim, then, debt-financing makes sense because those who succeed in their efforts at upward social mobility should be able to pay off that debt.[3] But when personal autonomy is the fundamental aim (of which upward social mobility is but *one* kind of self-directed goal that a person seeking a higher education might have) debt-financing can frustrate a citizen's efforts at charting a self-directed life from the outset. Consequently, liberty-based arguments for public funding can rule against debt-financing and in favor of greater public funding.

For example, a student who will not qualify for student loans on socioeconomic grounds might qualify for funding on autonomy grounds for the reason that the sheer amount of borrowing they have to do in order to access the system would unjustly constrain his or her choices. Furthermore, the fact that such reasons can be linked to the presumptive good of liberty-maximizing justice militates against the complaint of unfair benefits. Recall that upfront costs frustrate higher education's efforts at socioeconomic equality by closing off valuable opportunities to those with little or no resources. This is unjust, and so it is reasonable to obligate the public to fund some students and permit loans for others. But loans frustrate higher education's efforts at equality of liberty by subverting the autonomy-supporting value of such an education for those with not *enough* resources. Loans do not solve this particular access problem. It is therefore reasonable to obligate the public to fund access for both lower- *and* middle-class students.

One final consideration: this argument has yet to take into consideration the fact that an autonomy-supporting conception of higher education should help citizens access social forms and practices that have no direct relationship to the labor market. In such instances, loan repayments are sure to be an arbitrary restriction on freedom. Nor does it consider that such an education ought to support adult citizens at various stages of life achieve their goals, including senior citizens (some of whom may have little remaining income). For example, imagine that I want a higher education simply to broaden my understanding of the world. Perhaps I've long held certain religious commitments, but I want to delve into the theological underpinnings of various religious points of view. I don't want a change of career; in fact, I've only ever made a modest living. The educational goods that I'm interested in will add little to my credentials. However, I need a loan to cover the upfront costs. The possibility of having to pay back such a loan would almost certainly place an unreasonable constraint on my choices. I would quickly find myself wondering if I should switch to a program that will open up work opportunities that will enable me to pay off that loan. My original reason for seeking out an education would be all but lost.

In this section, I have showed how liberty-based reasons can plausibly motivate public funding for higher education. I also showed how these reasons can justify, all things being equal, a stronger role for public funding than arguments from socioeconomic equality can do on their own. But we have yet to show that liberty-based reasons can justify *full* public funding. There are at least three important objections we have yet to consider.

First, one might argue that liberty-based arguments for funding overstate who will benefit and understate who will be burdened from that funding. The fact is that there are many citizens who will never qualify for, let alone desire, a higher education. For these citizens the fact that a system supports "autonomy" as opposed to "social mobility" makes no practical difference. And yet we are asking these citizens to support the liberty of other citizens. Therefore, we need an argument from liberty to show why such a funding regime would not be unfair to citizens excluded from receiving a higher education. Let us call this the *unequal liberty objection*.

Second, liberty-based arguments have yet to show why we have to go all the way to full public funding when there are plausible alternatives to student loans. The most promising among these alternatives are income-contingent loans. These loans take financial pressure off of graduates by linking their repayment rate and amount to their income. Call this the *alternative repayment scheme objection*.

Finally, liberty-based arguments have yet to show why the public should pay for citizens who can fully afford the upfront costs of accessing the system. Why is it important that we be able to cover such citizens? Let us call this the *overshooting objection*. Next I will deal with all three of these objections.

The Right to Higher Education and Unequal Benefits

In the last section, I showed how liberty-based arguments for the value of higher education can justify public funding beyond what might be warranted by the view that higher education is merely instrumental to socioeconomic equality. But this line of argument has yet to carry us across the crucial threshold: can these arguments justify full public funding for higher education without being subject to the charge of unequal benefits? I believe that the answer is "yes." In making the case I address three objections that stand in the way of full funding.

The Unequal Liberty Objection

In order to answer this objection, we need to first find out what *distributive conditions* would have to be satisfied in order to avoid the charge of unequal benefits. Then we can determine if an autonomy-supporting system of higher education can satisfy those conditions. What distributive conditions are we talking about? The obvious, but frankly unhelpful, answer is that such a system would have to distribute its benefits more or less equally. But we can build on this (initially) unhelpful answer by distinguishing between two versions of these distributive conditions. One version says that the distribution must benefit me by putting resources and welfare-promoting goods directly into my pocket (a child tax benefit, for example). It's fairly obvious to see that, for the case of higher education at least, we can never satisfy such conditions unless we *forced* everyone to receive a higher education.

But we can also say that a distribution can benefit citizens by ensuring that there is a pool of resources available for them *should the need for those goods ever come*. In fact, knowing that such a pool of resources is there is itself a kind of civic benefit or welfare-promoting good even if one is not actually availing of those resources at a given point in time.[4] We might say that such goods a have a diachronic value, in the sense that one can foresee circumstances where those goods may be of direct benefit at some point in the future, either for myself or those that I care about. For example, it can benefit me by promoting my sense of security or peace of mind. Or it can empower me to act in ways that I would not otherwise were I responsible for covering the cost of those benefits on my own. A social insurance scheme is an archetypical example. I pay into an employment insurance scheme even when I may never come to require the benefits that the scheme makes available. But the fact that the benefit is there to claim, should I need it, militates against the claim that those who draw employment insurance are benefitting unfairly.[5] We could think of public funding for an autonomy-supporting system of higher education in similar terms.

In order to understand how, consider by contrast a conception of higher education focused on fair access to valuable opportunities. As we have already seen, full public funding of such a system is very much open to the charge of unequal benefits. And for good reason, too. Even when the availability of such opportunities satisfies commonly recognized requirements of fair equality of opportunity, many citizens obligated to contribute to the funding of such opportunities are nonetheless excluded from those benefits. First, these citizens may be deemed not to merit the receipt of those benefits because they lack the requisite talent or qualifications. The second form of exclusion is subtler. Citizens may not opt to access a higher education because they do not desire a higher education. Now, one way to account for this lack of desire is that such citizens have no love or appreciation for knowledge, or do not value the hard work necessary to succeed in that system. While such explanations may have the occasional grain of truth to them, they are superficial at best. At least part of the reason that some citizens do not desire a higher education is because the opportunities (including the predominant forms of knowledge and understanding on offer, as well as the way that that knowledge is shared and learning assessed) do not fit with those citizens' conceptions of the good or their self-directed goals. They are excluded, one might say, because the point and purpose of the system is designed in such a way that these citizens will *not* desire a higher education, not because they do not desire educational goods in general.

Imagine a health insurance scheme where you must pay in, but you can only make an insurance claim if you were hurt in the course of participating in professional sports. We can anticipate some citizens would not be able to claim such benefits because they do not have the talent to become a professional athlete, not to mention the fact that many citizens might benefit from free health care but have no desire to be professional athletes. It is plainly obvious that an insurance scheme of this kind would be unfair from a benefits point of view. A system of free higher education that excluded citizens who pay into that system on the grounds that they do not merit access, or because the nature of the benefit only applies to those who value further education for a fairly narrow set of possible goals, looks to be no different. It is unfair.

However, a fully funded system of higher education that takes autonomy-support as its fundamental aim is different. It entails distributive conditions that go some way to meeting the charge of unequal benefits that accompany a regime of full public funding.

First, it should be non-exclusive. An autonomy-supporting conception of higher education may not exclude citizens from accessing that system on the grounds that the citizen in question is insufficiently talented or lacks merit. To do so would contradict the fundamental educational aim of the system, which is to support— through educational means—citizens' shared interest in the free pursuit of a good life. For example, universities are free to admit (or not to admit) students based on a judgment about whether or not the applicant is able to benefit from the forms of knowledge, understanding, and skill that the university has to offer. This is quite different than selecting "the most talented" and is an entirety reasonable educational judgment that does not violate requirements of liberty-maximizing justice.[6] However, the judgment that a citizen is not ready to benefit from a particular educational pathway does not justify their exclusion from an autonomy-supporting higher education across the board. Liberty-maximizing requirements obligate higher education systems to provide educational pathways and opportunities for citizens of varying degrees of talent and preparedness.

Second, it should support an adequate range of self-directed goals suitable for citizens in a plural liberal society with diverse talents and interests. Liberty-maximizing justice requires institutions (or programs within existing institutions) that can organize the transmission of knowledge, understanding, and skill in a manner that facilitates access to valuable social forms and practices. The upshot is that such a system, ideally, should be less likely to exclude citizens on the grounds that what it offers does not connect with what those citizens want from life.

These two distributive conditions (non-exclusivity and support for diverse conceptions of the good), are the *same* conditions that we claimed were necessary in order for individual citizens to make good on their claim to a right to higher education. And it should work out this way. The conditions necessary for citizens to make good on a claim to higher education must be in place for all citizens in order to neutralize the problem of unequal benefits. In other words, the benefits and burdens of a rights-based system of higher education is unfairly distributed when that system, from the perspective of liberty-maximizing justice, arbitrarily restricts some citizens from accessing the system but requires all citizens to help pay for it.

Therefore, we can speak of three jointly necessary and sufficient distributive conditions that must be fulfilled in order for a liberal society to make good on a citizen's right to higher education:

(i) Non-exclusion
(ii) Adequate options

And the fulfillment of these two conditions, in order to avoid the charge of unequal benefits, motivates the necessity of a third distributive condition:

(iii) Full public funding

These three distributive norms are justified on the grounds that their fulfillment ensures that any citizen can in principle derive benefits from the system. Therefore, they are robust enough to defeat the charge that fully funding such a system would involve an unfair distribution of benefits and burdens. Put differently, they show how a publicly funded, rights-based system of higher education is not inherently distributivity unfair. With this more general objection taken care of we can now turn to two specific variations on the problem of unequal benefits.

The Alternative Repayment Scheme Objection

Recall that a key feature of the liberty-maximizing argument for public funding is that the debt financing of higher education *changes* the value of educational goods for those required to take on such debt. Put simply, making future debt repayment part of a citizen's judgment about the educational pathway that best facilitates their self-directed goals undermines the very autonomy-supporting point and purpose of higher education provision. However, one could argue that a debt repayment scheme sensitive to such a problem can avoid self-defeat.

Income-contingent loans are a good candidate. These loans allow the students to avoid the upfront costs of attending while also removing the financial stress of loan repayment. This is because borrowers are not required to repay their loan if their income does not rise above some established repayment threshold. For example, in the United Kingdom this repayment threshold is £26,575 a year, £2,214 a month, or £511 a week.[7] This means that higher education is essentially free for graduates who do not fare well in terms of post-graduate income. Income-contingent loans target graduates with jobs that pay well but who, as students, could not afford to pay upfront.

Can these loans thread the needle of upfront costs while minimizing or removing altogether constraints on choice that would otherwise be motivated by the specter of debt repayment? If the educational pathway I desire is unlikely to lead to an income premium on graduation, the income-contingent repayment threshold of the loan (if high enough) ought not to prevent me from choosing that pathway that best fits with my self-determined goals.

I concede that if educational loan policies can avoid distorting constraints on student choice, we have little reason to reject them on purely liberty-maximizing grounds. But this concession is also the key to why alternative repayment schemes are not sufficient grounds for objecting to full public funding. This is because in order for income-contingent (and similar alternative) loans to avoid placing an unjust constraint on student choice they must be loans *in name only*. Here is why:

Income-contingent loans strive to achieve two goals. The first is to prevent educational debt from undermining the autonomy of citizens (the goal of non-distorting debt). The second is to ensure that the public does not pay for the higher education of citizens who can repay, after graduation (the goal of repayment to the public). The loan scheme succeeds when students pay for their higher education but in such a way that these repayments do not impose an unfair restriction on their autonomy relative to students who do not have to borrow. But the policy faces a dilemma at the level of principle.

In order to understand this dilemma, consider the background conditions that would be necessary in order for such a policy to succeed in both its aims. If the private costs of higher education were sufficiently low it would surely succeed. Borrowers would owe very little on graduation in any case, and one could get away with a very low repayment threshold so that the public can gets back almost all of what they lend out. Of course, under these background conditions there is not much of a distributive justice issue to begin with. There is little to no scarcity of resources getting in the way of citizen's accessing the system. The amount that the public would need to lend out for the few citizens who cannot access the system through their own money would be negligible and unlikely to burden the public. In short, the income-contingent policy works beautifully in a situation where there is little or no need for educational debt financing to begin with.

The real test of the policy comes under conditions of scarcity. In this scenario, the private costs of higher education are out of reach for a substantial number of citizens. Under such conditions these two goals (repayment to the public and non-distorting debt) cannot be simultaneously pursued. This is because in order to achieve the goal of non-distorting debt the repayment threshold and repayment rates will need to be so low that the public is unlikely to receive much back relative to what they lend out. And in order to achieve the goal of repayment the threshold and rate will have to be so substantial that it would be implausible to claim that borrowers would not experience a distortion of their educational choices relative to those who do not have to borrow.

My point is that income-contingent loans and similar policies must ultimately choose between one of two policy goals. If income-contingent loans value debt repayment over non-distortion they will inevitably be unjust on liberty-maximizing grounds. This, because such policies must insist that the borrower repay *even if* the threshold/repayment rate of payment required to fulfill the debt obligation unjustly constrains the borrower relative to the non-borrower. If income-contingent loan policies value non-distortion over debt collection, they cannot really be loans in practice. This, because such policies must refrain from demanding substantial repayment or, depending on the graduate's employment situation, any repayment.

The real appeal of income-contingent loans and similar finance strategies comes down to optics. They message that the state is reticent about having the public pay into a robust scheme of higher education public funding (even if it actually does this, in practice). And they signal to higher education students that there is an expectation that they pay their fair share (even if they don't really have to, in practice). But the merits of these loans, either from the point of view of political justice or financial efficiency, are not so obvious.

One final, and quite important, consideration is that under a rights-based conception it isn't obvious that institutions of higher education should be free to charge whatever they want. And rising tuition fees appear to be a substantial part of the funding problem in higher education, not absolute resource scarcity per se. For example, we can anticipate that it would be unfair to fund student X orders of magnitude more than student Y for the same educational pathway simply because the latter chooses an institution that charges much more.[8] The discussion of fees, under a rights-based conception, should be directed at the question of how much higher education institutions may reasonably bill the state for different programs, not how much students should pay.

Why Should the Public Pay for the Wealthy? The Overshooting Objection

Finally, one might object that a system of higher education fully funded by the public overshoots by allocating resources to wealthy citizens who do not need them. Citizens who can afford to pay for the upfront costs of a higher education should be expected to pay. Such a requirement will certainly not be a barrier to accessing the system, nor will it be likely to place constraints on the self-directed goals they hope to realize through that access. We cannot, therefore, say that liberty-based reasons apply to them.

This objection fails because it is mistaken about the potential harms of making higher education free for everyone but for the wealthy. In order to understand why, we need to look to the role of fair play in the argument for public funding.

Recall that a successful argument in favor of public funding must show that this funding is instrumental to a presumptive public good. The fact that citizens will benefit from such a good generates an obligation for them to contribute. But why? The moral intuition often appealed to in explaining obligations that arise through social cooperation (such as the provision of public goods) is the norm of fair play (or the principle of fairness). Fair play has already come up in chapter 2, but a more detailed discussion is warranted, here.

The norm of fair play states that the acceptance of benefits within a cooperative scheme is sufficient to generate a cooperative obligation to contribute to that scheme. H. L. A. Hart's (1955) original formulation is as follows:

> When a number of persons conduct any joint enterprise according to rules and thus restrict their liberty, those who have submitted to these restrictions when required have a right to a similar submission from those who have benefited by their submission. (p. 185)

In its most basic form, the norm of fair play asks that we not act as free riders—if we benefit from a cooperative effort, we have a duty to pitch in. In political philosophy, this norm has been used to justify political obligations, where the cooperative scheme in question is a stable state and where the obligation is to obey the law. However, the norm of fair play demonstrates considerable range both with respect to the kinds of cooperative schemes it may be applied to and the scope of the obligation generated by those schemes. For example, fair play varies depending on whether the cooperation is aimed at perfect public goods (Klosko, 1987), discretionary goods (Claassen, 2013; Klosko, 1990), neighborhood cooperatives (Nozick, 1974; Simmons, 1979), and everyday financial transactions (Arneson, 1982). In fact, the moral expectation that we "play fair"—that we do not ride free when we benefit from the cooperative efforts of others—can range from interactions between neighbors to political legitimacy.

How does the argument from fair play apply to the right to higher education? When an individual citizen receives a costless higher education, it is ultimately society that supports their autonomous flourishing. However, it is also true that that individual's obligations to a free and open society now runs deeper. When the community acknowledges my claim and provides me with an opportunity to support my self-directed goals, I am both recognized and respected as a full member of society. When I understand myself *as* a respected member of society, I am more likely to be moved by the idea that, having received such support, I have an obligation to use this support in a way that contributes.

Therefore, from the point of view of fair play we might say that the right to higher education entails a corresponding moral duty to use one's developed talents for the betterment of a liberal democratic society. Those who enjoy the benefits of a higher education, and enjoy those benefits through the cooperative efforts of others, incur a moral debt to the society that has contributed. Why? When students receive benefits that allow them to make the most of what a free and democratic society has to offer, they incur an obligation to use the talents and skills that a higher education helped make possible in ways that give back to that larger democratic society. That is to say, they ought to contribute to the collective liberty of society. These contributions can take many forms. It could involve using one's developed talents to address injustices in democratic society as they understand them, or to challenge conventional assumptions about how society ought to be, in ways big and small. The possibilities can range from getting involved in the political process to cultural contributions that disrupt unjust social norms to pro bono work related to their occupation. In sum, such contributions should be aimed at promoting the social conditions that enable citizens to live freely.

This might seem like a contradiction of my earlier claim, in chapter 2, that we ought not see higher education as preparation for citizenship as a kind of special vocation. But note several important differences between the two claims. First, the obligation to contribute to society is a voluntary moral duty. I again stress that this is not a political obligation, rather, it is a moral one. The state may not compel citizens to contribute. Second, the obligation to contribute does not justify the imposition of particular educational aims on adults. Graduates are free to give back in the ways that best fit, in accordance with their liberty. Finally, the obligation to contribute is derived from the benefit of a higher education, not by virtue of their entering into a valuable job or office. Any graduate, *regardless of their economic or social position*, therefore incurs a moral obligation to contribute.

Understood in this light, upfront payments and debt financing dramatically change both the scope of this obligation and the relationship between one's self-development and the larger society. The personal financing of social goods is both de-socializing and de-democratizing. It transforms a political arrangement that is supposed to support the social vision of a free and open society into a transactional and highly individualistic one. By requiring the individual to supply a basic good as opposed to making a claim on society (Gourevitch, 210, p. 135), that individual sees his obligation as extending no further than what he can pay back monetarily, either by paying up front or by using a private lender. In turn, the community has no morally legitimate claim on citizens to share their developed talents in the spirit of a larger social vision of society.

If we required the rich to pay, we would essentially be exempting such citizens from the cooperative obligation to contribute to a free and open society. And yet many of these students come from backgrounds defined by the wealthy and elite—the very kinds of people that a society would seriously benefit from if they were to make a strong personal commitment to public service and the promotion of democratic ends. My point is that a system of higher education that aims to contribute to personal autonomy as a collective good is one that must include all citizens. But a system that requires the rich to pay essentially excludes them (or lets them off the hook, depending on your point of view) from being a full party to that liberal social vision.

The idea that we can at best hold the wealthy to a voluntary, moral obligation to contribute in return for a publicly funded higher education may seem unsatisfying. However, there is one sense in which these citizens are constrained in a manner that might tame our egalitarian sensibilities. Note that the receipt of a free, autonomy-supporting public higher education means attending a publicly funded higher educational *institution*. By this I mean that a system of higher education founded on the right to education, one that fully complies with distributive norms of non-exclusion and diversity, will be one that is open to citizens of different talents, stages of life, working backgrounds, and so on. Wealthy citizens who receive a publicly funded education will be attending institutions that are much different than the elite institutions that the wealthy cluster around and that today contribute greatly to social stratification.

In a free and open higher education system of the kind I am defending, we can expect that fully funded students from wealthy backgrounds will therefore be mixed in with a more diverse population of citizens than anything that they might otherwise experience.

There is an important public good arising from such a constraint on the wealthy. Many political philosophers have argued that higher education systems should be more diverse because such diversity can help to ensure that new generations of elites know and understand the experiences and challenges faced by less-advantaged citizens and marginalized communities, as well as ensuring that higher education is well-represented by traditionally non-elite populations who themselves can take on influential roles in society and work for change (Anderson, 2007; Morton, 2019).[9] My claim is that a higher education system that is non-exclusive and supportive of diverse conceptions of the good will be much more effective at realizing these epistemic benefits than, say, trying to make the elite institutions that we currently have more "progressive" or "conscientious." In a rights-based system we can expect that wealthy citizens will have a much harder time concentrating themselves around institutions that insulate them from the preoccupations, worries, and civic interests of the rest of society. And we can expect that the peer effects arising from the right to higher education to do far more to produce a civically minded elite than the systems that we rely on today.

There is still one final reply to the overshooting objection that we have not yet considered. The claim that it would be permissible to require wealthy families to pay for access to higher education assumes that students coming from these families will be just as free to choose whatever educational pathway they desire as their publicly funded counterparts. But this fails to consider that fact that it is the parent, not the student, who is wealthy and who pays. Students from wealthy families will, at least in some cases, experience pressure to choose educational pathways that have been vetted by their parental benefactors.[10] Consider, for example, students who wish to pursue civic-minded, or perhaps even downright bohemian, goals that could lead to downward intergenerational income mobility and are dissuaded from that goal with the threat of non-payment. This arrangement may be tolerable in the systems of higher education we have today. But it is unacceptable from a liberty-maximizing point of view. Students from wealthy families (like any citizen in this framework) should be free to pursue worthwhile self-directed goals that may nonetheless be undesirable from the family's point of view. That fact that these students are born into wealth is not a reason to deny them access to resources and opportunities that will enable them to stake out in a direction that would not meet with the approval of their family. We often think of the lesser-off as the group whose educational choices can be constrained by the economics of higher education. But students from wealthy families, to the extent that they rely on their parents to pay the bills, may experience constraints on choice from a different direction.

Conclusion

In this chapter, I addressed the worry that full public funding will unavoidably lead to an unfair distribution of benefits and burdens and that this unfair distribution would undermine the case for a right to higher education. First, I argued that linking higher education access to private funding or loans undermines the autonomy-supporting aims of the system. Second, the distributive conditions entailed by a right to higher education require that the benefits of the system be open to all regardless of talent and ability, and must aim to support as many conceptions of the good as is reasonably possible. These conditions can only be sufficiently satisfied through a regime of full public funding. Finally, funding should support access for all citizens, even the wealthy. Otherwise, that system risks exempting some citizens from the liberal social vision that such a conception of higher education aims to bring about simply by virtue of the fact that these citizens happen to have more resources than others. I also pointed to some civic benefits arising from a system that requires the wealthy to pursue their education and training alongside citizens from all walks of life, as well as the potential autonomy-undermining constraints facing students from well-off families when they are required to pay.

Higher education is a right. The ability and opportunity to freely pursue the good is essential to liberal citizenship, and higher education plays an instrumental role in ensuring that citizens can freely pursue that good. The justification of this right does not depend on higher education's usefulness in bringing about any other kinds of goods, nor does a citizen's claim on this right depend on how much (or how little) they have in terms of other goods such as income. As such, full public funding should be a characteristic feature of a system of higher education founded on such a right.

7
What Should the Right to Higher Education Look Like?

Across six chapters I have argued that liberal democratic citizens have a right to higher education. My defense of this right has required an analysis of several key elements including its basic educational aims (chapters 2 and 3), the institutional framework justified by such aims (chapter 4), the legitimate authority of the liberal state to ensure that this framework is oriented toward these aims (chapter 5), and the distributive norms necessary and sufficient for the benefits and burdens of a rights-based system of higher education to be justly and fairly apportioned across a liberal citizenry (chapter 6).

In this chapter, I address some key objections to my argument in order to provide a fuller picture of what the right to higher education can look like at the level of public policy and institutional practice. First, I revisit the rationale for the argument. My aim here is to show how a rights-based conception can better inform public debate over the justice, fairness, and purposes of higher education. Second, I apply this account to Martin Trow's famous conceptualization of higher education systems into "elite," "mass," and "universal" stages of growth and development in order to demonstrate how the right to higher education can inform higher education policy. Finally, I address the worry that the right to higher education overstates the importance of post-compulsory education for a liberal society. Here I engage with issues about the role of higher education in the promotion of human welfare and the level of "idealization" built into my argument.

The Argument Revisited

In chapter 1 I claimed that there is an imbalance, or asymmetry, in liberal political reasoning about the justice and fairness of higher education. By "asymmetry" I mean that the analysis is trained on the distributive *consequences* of higher education. My point has been that, in order to fully understand these consequences, we require an equally robust consideration of the freestanding *individual* value of education for adult liberal citizens. By "freestanding" I mean educational values and aims understood independently from premises about institutional frameworks or distributive norms. These premises matter, of course, but their relevance only becomes clear once we understand this freestanding value.

Let there be no mistake: the fact that the individual returns of a higher education are hierarchically stratified (especially the U.S. higher education system with its emphasis on elite Ivy League admissions) makes the scholarly and public policy emphasis on distributive consequences understandable and entirely appropriate. Interestingly, however, there are also good *conceptual* reasons why one might be reluctant to focus on the individual value of post-compulsory education independent of (or logically prior to) these distributive norms. These reasons derive from an aim often held up as fundamental to the compulsory education of liberal citizens: personal autonomy. Here is how: if the common aim of compulsory education in a liberal society is to prepare future citizens to lead autonomous lives, it appears to follow that the stipulation of common values and aims for higher education disrespects the autonomy of such citizens. It tells them what they should desire from a higher education regardless of their autonomously determined chosen goals or interests.

Does this conceptual problem mean that debates about higher education provision must proceed on the assumption that such provision serves no common value or purpose? If so, it would be an unfortunate conclusion to have to draw. A rational consensus on the distribution of a good whose value is fundamentally subjective or contestable is a consensus forever out of view.

However, there is a clear alternative: one can frame the values and aims of higher education as *social* returns that arise when sufficiently large numbers of citizens consume higher education goods. This approach is attractive for two reasons. First, social returns can be objectively measured using economic methods. But more significantly, these returns are desirable *irrespective* of each individual citizen's own autonomous reasons for seeking them out. We are here talking about positive externalities or "public goods" such as citizenship, culture, economic growth, socioeconomic equality, public knowledge, and so on.

So long as these social returns are undersupplied by the market, we have a solid rationale for state intervention in higher education in the form of, for example, tuition subsidies and other widening participation efforts. But how reliable is this rationale? A public goods argument for a better funded, more diverse, and more accessible higher education system is precarious, I think. Its convincing force depends on social and economic contingencies. If such goods were no longer undersupplied, or they were no longer seen as important for society, or if other public goods became more pressing, states would be justified is withdrawing their support. We would also lose the desirable spillover effects of a more accessible higher education system for individual citizens such as improved affordability and access. Social returns have served to prop up a policy regime that looks something like a right to higher education. But public goods do not touch on the question that we are interested in, here: whether or not liberal citizens have a right to higher education, social returns or no.

Getting at this question means taking the conceptual problem of autonomy and individual returns head on. I do this by showing how the reasons any given citizen might have for receiving a higher education are logically connected to the demands of personal autonomy and autonomous flourishing. The promise of such a connection is that it can explain why just and fair access to higher education is not just a social, but an *individual*, imperative. Accordingly, much of my argument for the right to higher education is founded on a philosophical reassessment of personal autonomy and its relationship to educational goods. More specifically, I argue that while an individual's desire for further knowledge, understanding, and skills may be conditioned by the cultural and economic realities in which they find themselves, the impetus (and legitimacy) of this desire can be traced back to the widespread and largely unavoidable demands that a complex, open, and pluralist liberal society makes on adult citizens in the lifelong pursuit of a good and happy life. In short, educational goods are not merely an essential foundation for personal autonomy, rather, they also support adult citizens' capacity for autonomous flourishing by helping them to realize self-determined goals that would otherwise be out of reach. They contribute to the broader infrastructure of opportunity that enables liberal citizens to carry out their life plan(s).

This account introduces a potentially profound shift in the terms of reference through which liberal publics reason about the value of higher education. To use a rough example, some critics bemoan the fact that most young citizens see higher education mainly as a pathway into the labor market. They complain that a higher education should open students to new and better ways of understanding the world, raise their conscience about important social issues and so on, not just lead them to a higher income. Surely higher education, being education, should have *something* to do with these other goals! But these criticisms can sometimes come across as too detached from the social and economic realities that young citizens face. In recent decades, higher education has become the dominant path to decent, meaningful work. These critics, one might argue, are lost in the memory of a traditional university education whose time has long passed.

But now we have a conceptual basis for recognizing this false dichotomy for what it is. On the one hand, it seems entirely reasonable for citizens to pursue the knowledge (and credentials) they require for full participation in the labor market. This is especially the case for citizens in desperate need of upward mobility. The freedom to pursue, and succeed in pursuing, self-determined goals requires adequate economic conditions. Not to mention the fact that meaningful work can itself be a source of autonomous flourishing. On the other hand, a system that sees access to the labor market as *one and the same* as the pursuit of the good life will distort the value of educational goods. Such a system will emphasize the availability and accessibility of vocational training as opposed to forms of understanding characteristic of the liberal arts, for example. It will emphasize the availability and accessibility of higher education for young and other underemployed citizens, and it will say that the underemployed must make future/improved employment a priority as a condition for any higher education goods that they might wish to receive. It will also neglect the value of such an education for its more senior members, who have self-determined goals that may have nothing directly to do with the labor market.

The intuition that higher education is too focused on human capital does not have to lead us to the conclusion that it is founded on the wrong educational aims; rather, it can motivate us to resist a narrow view of the contribution of higher education to the autonomous flourishing of liberal citizens. The push for justice in higher education, then, should not be about rediscovering its "true" aims nor a more effective socioeconomic levelling so much as improving opportunities for citizens from many walks of life to lead better (autonomous) lives.

An analysis of higher education provision that takes the pre-institutional, individual value of educational goods for liberal citizens as its starting point changes the normative trajectory of how one reasons through the problem of justice and fairness in higher education. This trajectory intersects with a number of key political philosophical questions, such as the place of higher education within a larger (liberal) system of social cooperation, its relationship to legitimate political authority, and the requirements of distributive fairness, and it does so at different points than does the conventional approach. Finally, this trajectory lands at a much different place: higher education founded on a right of liberal citizenship and firmly established as an institution essential for any liberal society.

Toward a Normative Stage Theory of Higher Education

It is one thing to identify conditions necessary in order for higher education systems to, in principle, support diverse citizen's autonomous flourishing.[1] It is quite another to claim that we ought to embrace reforms that move existing higher education systems closer to these conditions. For example, one might claim that even if such an account is justifiable in basic liberal political terms it cannot be appropriately applied to the higher education systems that we actually *have*. Such an application might even be harmful to the present interests of citizens. The most that we can take from such a conception, such a critic might argue, is that it is merely a description of the foundations of a higher education that might have been.

For example, one might argue that the development of basic institutions is a path dependent phenomenon, and in the case of higher education the ship has already sailed. For example, if early liberal governments had the wisdom to recognize post-compulsory education as an opportunity to promote human freedom among all citizens regardless of talent, income, and so on we could imagine having eventually arrived at a rights-based conception, or something like it. But the fact is that these societies chose otherwise. They opted to see higher education as key to the formation of elites, or as a means to specific public policy goals such as Research and Development (during World War II) or, in the United States especially, civic public service (spurred by the Morrill Act and land-grant education). Therefore, as a basis for reform and social criticism this conception is far too ahistorical. We should pursue reform that aims to improve the purposes that we have already inherited, not what might have been.

This charge, if sound, applies not only to the conception of higher education defended in this book but to almost any such philosophical conception. And yet, ahistorical vices can be philosophical virtues.[2] The growth and expansion of higher education is not an end in itself. Everything depends on the direction that this growth and expansion takes. We need a standard (or standards) by which liberal citizens can judge what directions of growth and forms of expansion are desirable and undesirable, adequate and inadequate, fully realized and incomplete, just and unjust. A rights-based conception does this by offering a normative perspective on the long-term growth and development of higher education systems in free and open societies. Far from setting out a vision of what could have been, it can help us to understand those respects in which the higher education systems we have inherited are a merely partial fulfillment of more widespread contribution to the good lives of citizens.

In order to get a more grounded sense of what such a perspective offers, I apply the right to higher education to Martin Trow's famous classification of higher education into three stages of development: elite, mass, and universal (1976, 2000, 2006). His conceptual scheme aimed to describe (in Weberian "ideal-typical" terms) the massive transformation of higher education occurring throughout the 20th and early 21st centuries. A key aim of his analysis was to anticipate how the expansion of higher education by governments around the would have serious implications for student selection, university management, and public attitudes about its value.

Trow defined an elite higher education as a highly selective and academically rigorous form of provision aimed at preparing citizens for leadership in society. Mass higher education is characterized by an expansion of the system aiming to select for and maximize the talents of the population in order to contribute to the industrial and technological demands of the economy. But most significant for our purposes was his prediction of, and characterization of, the last stage of higher education development: *universal* higher education. Universal higher education is supposed to mark a more or less complete transition from education as elite formation to education as egalitarian entitlement (Scott, 2019, p. 502). But it is also the least developed of Trow's stages.

In order to get a more precise picture of this final stage I have extracted some characteristic, though by no means exhaustive, features as described his landmark paper, *Problems in the Transition from Elite to Mass Higher Education* (1973).

On the aims of a universal higher education:

> In institutions marked by universal access there is concern for the first time with the preparation of large numbers for life in an advanced industrial society; they are training not primarily elites, either broad or narrow, but the whole population, and their chief concern is to maximize the adaptability of that population to a society whose chief characteristic is rapid social and technological change. (p. 8)

On its mutigenerational clientele:

> In institutions of universal access there is much postponement of entry, "stopping out" (i.e., periods when the student is not in attendance), and large numbers of students with experience in adult occupations. The emphasis on "lifelong learning" is compatible with the softening of the boundaries between formal education and other forms of life experience. (p. 11)

On the non-exclusionary nature of its institutions:

> In the institutions of universal higher education, which by definition are wholly "open" either to anyone who wishes to join or to those who have certain minimal educational qualifications, the

criterion is whether an individual has *chosen* to associate himself with the institution voluntarily. (p. 14)

Imagine that Trow's description is on the mark and that a universal conception is the direction in which systems of higher education are trending. Is this the direction in which they ought to go? Is Trow offering various descriptions of a desirable outcome, or is a universal higher education something that liberal societies are better off doing without?

Trowian Aims of Universal Higher Education

The adoption of an autonomy-supporting conception of higher education as a normative standard for the growth and development of higher education systems can help to answer these questions. First, we can note a broad similarity between the aims of a Trowian universal system of higher education and the aims of a higher education system founded on liberal rights. Both are concerned with a citizen's successful engagement with the demands of a complex society. Recall, for example, that the ideal of personal autonomy is derived from the Razian claim that autonomy is necessary for flourishing in a modern society. As Raz puts it:

> [autonomy] is an ideal particularly suited to the conditions of the industrial age and its aftermath with their fast changing technologies and free movement of labour. They call for an ability to cope with changing technological, economic and social conditions, for an ability to adjust, to acquire new skills, to move from one sub-culture to another, to come to terms with new scientific and moral views. (Raz, 1986, p. 369)

Where the Trowian account merely describes such an aim, an autonomy-supporting conception justifies it. But it can also identify, by virtue of that same justification, those respects in which the aims of Trowian universal system may fall short. For example, Trow claims that the "chief concern" of such a system is to "maximize the adaptability" of citizens to social and technological change. But what does this mean? One could imagine two interpretations, each with divergent policy implications.

One could take adaptability to refer to a citizen's ability to participate in a fast-changing labor market, linking personal autonomy to vocational self-directed goals. Such a system could, in principle, be quite diverse given continual changes in the kind of knowledge, understanding, and skill required in response to technological change. However, a system founded on the relationship between autonomy and vocational self-directed goals would diverge from a rights-based approach in two major respects. First, universal higher education would only be obligated to structure the availability of educational options in response to the changing demands of the labor market as opposed to the interests of a diverse citizenry. It would not be obligated to support educational pathways that have no direct bearing on those technological changes. Second, educational options would be structured on the assumption that a citizen's reasons for accessing the system are (or ought to be) *vocational* participation in valuable social forms and practices. This will have implications for teaching and learning within such a system. It would not, for example, need to account for the significance that the individual assigns to successful participation in a given social form. Labor market (re)entry just is the significance that any rational individual should assign to such participation.

In contrast, one could take "maximizing adaptability" to refer to any citizen's ability to participate in a changing *society*, linking personal autonomy to self-directed goals, broadly conceived. A system founded on the relationship between personal autonomy and self-directed goals writ large is more in line with a conception of higher education in the autonomy-supporting sense. This conception also supplies now-familiar reasons why this latter interpretation is more desirable and better attuned to a liberal social vision, reasons relating to the non-arbitrariness of institutional constraints and freedom to pursue the good.[3]

Trowian Elite Higher Education

Second, Trow claims that institutions of universal higher education should be open to all regardless of any prior qualifications. But here we run into the question of how "universal" universal institutions of higher education really are in his conceptual scheme. As Scott (2019) rightly points out, Trow thought that "mass" and "universal" systems are not successors to, or replacements of, elite institutions so much as co-existing layers of a larger system. Therefore, the distributive conditions that hold for "universal" institutions within this larger system (openness, diversity, free for the individual) need not apply to either its elite or mass counterparts. In fact, this picture appears to be a formalized version of the kind of institutional stratification we already see in many higher education systems with elite, expensive, highly selective institutions at the top (Harvard, Oxford), followed by more open, less expensive but also less status-conferring institutions in the middle (state universities in the United States, "red-bricks" in the United Kingdom), and largely open institutions at the bottom (trade schools, community colleges, adult and continuing education).

What does an autonomy-supporting conception have to say about this arrangement? We can see some superficial alignment. Recall, for example, the argument from chapter 4 which saw traditional universities as a distinctive social form in its own right. This distinctiveness justifies (rough) protections on how far the liberal state can go in requiring these universities to conform to liberty-maximizing requirements of justice. It means, for example, that it is not *prima facie* arbitrary from a liberty-maximizing point of view to require citizens to demonstrate minimum levels of academic preparedness as a condition of admission into traditional universities.

However, this does not entail nearly the same degree of hierarchical organization that a Trowian conception might permit. First, the distributive conditions that make it possible for citizens to claim higher education as a right must be *universally applied*. They apply differently depending on the particular institution and its purposes. But they apply, nonetheless. For example, the requirement that such a system ought to support access to an adequate range of options (the diversity condition) fits with a picture in which elite, mass, and universal institutions support access to different self-directed goals at a collective level because it allows for specialism and differentiation within that system. We do not want to force adult citizens who have little desire to pursue disciplinary forms of knowledge and understanding to attend institutions that take such pursuits as its main focus; but nor is it obviously desirable to require such institutions to accommodate the interests of such citizens, either.[4]

But the other two conditions (openness and full public funding) must also apply to the system as a whole. What does this mean? It means, for example, that elite institutions can no longer define themselves by either their exclusivity or their costliness. Consider the openness condition. Should elite institutions be required to accept every citizen who makes a claim to them? One might say that an educational institution that cannot be selective is one that cannot carry out its mission. This is almost certainly true. But we can distinguish between the idea that all citizens (regardless of talent) should have a right to a higher education, on the one hand, and the idea that all citizens (regardless of talent) have a right to access every institution at every level of programming, on the other. The latter surely takes us out of educational reality: people's progression through different educational pathways should be built on prior educational achievement. It makes no sense for someone without any such prior learning to arrive at a course on the principles of aesthetics, or on advanced automotive design, without a sufficient degree of preparation.

How then, does the openness condition apply to elite and other institutions that are normally highly selective? The rationale for educational selection should be, as Ben Kotzee and I have argued, logically connected to an institution's legitimate purposes (Kotzee and Martin, 2013). More specifically, we argued that incoming students must be "ready" for the learning opportunities available at any given institution (p. 637). By this we mean that they have experienced enough prior learning in order to derive benefits from admission into a specific educational pathway.

However, what counts as readiness for a learning opportunity will depend on the *specific* benefits that this opportunity is supposed to promote.[5] The overarching purpose of higher education is, on my rights-based account, autonomy support. This purpose applies to elite institutions as it would to mass and universal. We must therefore ask: how does this bear on readiness for elite admissions?

In a rights-based Trowian framework, highly selective educational institutions should drop what we might call positional selectivity. Positional selectivity refers to the idea that we set the bar for qualification higher and higher so as to make that institution harder to get into and, therefore, more desirable in terms of social esteem or status. We should reject positional selectivity because it has no logical connection to the minimal level of preparation that a student would require in order derive autonomy-supporting benefits from their educational experience. It is inconsistent with openness.

Positional selectivity should be replaced with what I call *sufficientarian selectivity*. Sufficientarian selectivity is derived from the idea that we may permissibly set the bar for admission to an educational institution at a fixed level reflecting the minimum preparedness that a student would require in order to derive the relevant benefits. More specifically, openness extends only to those students who would experience *autonomy-supporting benefits* from their admission into a particular educational pathway. Admitting students who would be unable to derive such benefits—students who are not ready—would be more likely to have the achievement of their personally autonomous goals frustrated.

But what about selection for the most talented? This approach involves setting the bar higher and higher in order to ensure that only the "brightest and best" students enter the institution. In practice we could imagine that such selection will end up looking a lot like positional selection. As more citizens apply, more will be turned away. But this superficial resemblance is not a reason for rejecting selection for the most talented. This is because both "most talented" and "sufficiency" select for reasons that are logically connected to student learning. One selects for the best learners while the other selects for those who *can* learn. The defender of highly elite selection can therefore claim that (i) selection for the most talented is not intentionally exclusive and that (ii) such selection is logically connected to student leaning and in full compliance with a higher education system defined by openness.

However, this defense of elite selection does not take into full consideration the educational purposes that justify selection in a rights-based system in the first place. Recall once again the collective good that ought to be served by the right to higher education: support for citizen's access to valuable social forms and practices. Sufficientarian selection is justified because there will be cases in which a citizen is unable to derive autonomy-supporting benefits from the forms of knowledge, understanding, and skill offered by different institutions. This does not mean that they will never be able to so benefit. And it does not mean that they cannot access different educational pathways within the system for which they are prepared.

Can this broader purpose also accommodate selection for the brightest and best? One strategy could be to show that elite selection is consistent with this broader purpose: the aim of highly selective, elite institutions is to ensure that certain social forms and practices should be reserved only for, or should be more likely to be populated by, the most talented in a society. A fuller defense of this aim might go something like this: many social forms and practices should be open to all. But we do not want citizens of merely average intellectual and moral character moving into, say, key positions in society. We want the best among of us taking up these roles. And we all benefit when these key positions are held by highly competent people. Therefore, we all have an interest in elite selectivity. While Trowian universal and mass institutions of higher education should abide by a more open, sufficientarian approach, we are justified in making elite intuitions an exception to this more general rule.

The problem with this strategy, once again, comes down to purposes. It is plausible to think that an elite institution could select on a brightest and best basis if its only legitimate purpose was to help citizens compete for the rare few jobs in, say, professional political philosophy. Elite selection is simply one leg of the competition. But note that it could not select on a brightest and best basis if its only legitimate purpose was to initiate citizens into an understanding of, and intrinsic care for, values and principles of political philosophical inquiry. This is because lots of able but relatively less talented citizens may have a curiosity and passion for such inquiry. There is no reason to exclude them.[6]

The problem is that elite *autonomy-supporting* institutions ought to support citizens in their pursuit of *either* goal. Imagine, for example, a system in which elite institutions happen to be the only ones offering full degree programs in political philosophy.[7] In such a system, some few citizens will want to become professional philosophers. But a good number of citizens will see the study of political philosophy as an important means of realizing self-determined goals that lie beyond the institution. Brightest and best selection would crowd out these other purposes.

The defender of brightest and best selection might still press: this does not address the concern that there will be some positions in society—key leadership roles such as in politics and industry—where we all have an interest in the best citizens occupying such positions. The rigor that an elite system would require in order to achieve this purpose would suffer under sufficientarian requirements. Let there be political philosophy programs, populated by the best teachers and writers in the field, in elite institutions for those who are the most talented, and similar programming and less rigorous selection in the mass system for those who are less promising but interested in the topic, nonetheless.

There may be good reasons for separating out educational programs in terms of citizens' reasons for accessing them—one system for the would-be professionals and one for the would-be amateurs. But a loss of rigor does not look to be one of them. First, it is not obvious that high selectivity entails a higher quality education. Take again the example of a political philosophy program that only selected among the brightest and best. Such a program may well be intellectually impoverished relative to their more open counterparts. Seminars in which students from very different walks of life, different lived experiences, and different self-directed goals would be far livelier and more educative than one where almost everyone aspires for an academic job. We can imagine the same concern applying to other elite programs.

Second, elite selection assumes that the talents, abilities, and inclinations of students are fixed in advance of such selection. However, personally autonomous citizens have the ability to revise their self-determined goals. For example, we can all think of intellectual "late bloomers" who did not discover an interest or aptitude for such pursuits until well into an educational journey. John White offers a version of this argument (2016). He suggests that one of the functions of educational institutions is to *develop* ability, not merely to select for it. Elite selection will exclude citizens who have the potential to make important contributions by occupying key positions in society.

Interestingly, White also suggests that the "readiness to learn" selection criterion that Kotzee and I advanced, and which I use here in order to justify a sufficientarian conception of selection for a rights-based system, does not go far enough in acknowledging this developmental role. Asking if higher education institutions should see the development of ability as its function, or take ability as given, he answers:

> Kotzee and Martin appear to hold the latter position. They advocate, for instance, the incoming student's being "ready (based on previous learning) for the learning opportunities available at the university" (p. 637). But why rule out the development alternative? (p. 508)

On this view, elite selection should not only be sufficientarian but developmental as well. This means admitting not only those who are ready to derive benefits, but also students who are not yet ready but can be helped into a position where they are.

White's critique trades on what is admittedly a certain vagueness of mine and Kotzee's account of what it actually means to be ready for a learning opportunity. How much developmental effort and support should an educator to be tasked with undertaking in order for a student to derive benefits from a given learning opportunity before it is reasonable to say that the student in question is just not ready (yet)? I do not take the view that *any* such developmental efforts are sufficient to deem a student unqualified for admission into a particular educational pathway, elite or no. But nor do I have a particularly strong view on where that line ought to be drawn. Much will depend on empirical judgments about learning. And the larger institutional context would surely also matter. For example, one important consideration is whether or not there are suitable alternative pathways for a student who is not selected.

However, sufficientarian selection should mark a rough distinction between persons who, with some additional support, can participate with others in learning a certain forms of knowledge, understanding, and skill and those who would require support that has few, if any, connections to that form. To use a very basic example, the student who seeks admission into a drafting program but has poor geometrical knowledge would require a drafting instructor to teach them something—geometry—entirely different from what the instructor is qualified to teach in order to bring that student into the fold. In such cases it is reasonable to think that such an effort, even on a developmentally sensitive conception of sufficiency, puts us beyond educational reality. But the larger point stands—judgments about readiness to learn should not be too rigid and should take into account a student's developmental potential.

This leads to a third reason why we should not assume that more open approaches to elite selection will reduce the overall quality of who gets into elite positions in society. Sufficientarian selection, even in its developmentalist version, is not "anything goes." As citizens work their way up through educational pathways into more specialized programming, we can expect the requirements of sufficiency to become more specific and demanding. This fact is of no disservice to citizens whose reasons for being in the system are nonvocational. Their educational interests are likely to be satisfied long before arriving at a potentially exclusionary level of sufficientarian selection. The citizen interested in political philosophy does not need to petition for admission into a PhD program in political philosophy. The citizen interested in medicine does not need to apply to medical school. And the citizen interested in law does not have to go to law school. My point here is that elite institutions could continue to select in ways that would have the *consequence* of absorbing the most talented and supporting access to leading positions in society *without* having to intentionally exclude citizens for morally arbitrary reasons. In fact, it will likely catch a larger number of students with diverse backgrounds and experiences who might otherwise never have moved into such positions, along the way.

From a liberty-maximizing point of view, selection must be sufficientarian and logically connected to the minimum standard required in order to participate in learning a form of knowledge, understanding, or skill. But the minimum standard can be quite high depending on the particular program, the level of specialization, and how closely it is connected to social roles where there is a public interest in ensuring that those who occupy those roles are competent (the professions, for example).

Social Forms, Expensive Tastes, and Ideal Institutions

The last section applied the rights-based conception of higher education in the form of a normative standard by which different features of a Trowian system could be justified or revised. But this was an admittedly brief treatment, and we can debate precisely how this conception best applies to existing higher education systems without overturning the conception itself.

There is, however, a more fundamental objection to the application of this conception to existing higher education systems. This objection says that the right to higher education overstates the importance of post-compulsory education for a liberal society already under the strain of scarce resources. Adding another entitlement— another social guarantee—even if philosophically cogent, will be politically unfeasible or perhaps even undesirable. This objection can take two major forms.

The Right to Higher Education and Expensive Tastes

The first version states that the fact some citizens have self-directed goals that require educational goods in order to support their achievement, while other citizens have self-directed goals that will not require such goods, makes higher education an *expensive taste*. Individuals should be responsible for their expensive tastes, and it is unfair to require some citizens to pay for the expensive tastes of others. This makes the right to higher education fundamentally unfair.

This objection is somewhat different from the problem of unequal benefits that was the focus of chapter 6, and addressing it requires that we say more about the relationship between autonomous flourishing and social forms and practices.

Before taking this objection head on, we should first understand the general terms under which the expensive tastes problem is thought to apply. Simon Keller illustrates the objection through the following helpful example:

> Suppose that resources have been successfully distributed in our community in such a way as to leave us all with equal levels of welfare. Then, imagine that one person, Alan, cultivates expensive tastes; he takes a wine-appreciation course, pays close attention to the latest developments in personal computing technology, and so on. Once Alan has developed his expensive tastes, it will take more of the community's resources to keep him at the level of welfare enjoyed by the rest of us; he will no longer be happy with everyday wines and everyday computers. If equality of welfare is to be restored, then we will all have to put up with a smaller allocation of resources so that Alan can be given the things that he needs in order to bring himself up to our (now slightly reduced) level of welfare. But this is surely not what justice requires. Welfare egalitarianism, the objection concludes, is false. (Keller, 2002, p. 529)

In what respects could the expensive tastes objection apply to the right to higher education? It applies because this right takes a certain unit of welfare—autonomous flourishing—as a central moral concern. For example, I have the self-directed goal of becoming skilled in carpentry. I have no intention of pursuing carpentry as a trade. There will be no social return (in the form of taxation) for the carpentry work that I do. But this self-directed goal is considered a valuable social practice in its own right, and so I am entitled to receive the educational goods required to support my access to that practice. You, on the other hand, have self-directed goals that require no claim to educational goods. Consequently, in order to ensure that everyone experiences the same degree of autonomous flourishing I should receive a greater share of resources than you and others like you. In fact, my need for greater resources leaves the rest of you will a little less. This seems unfair: why should I have the right to satisfy a preference that leaves everyone else a little worse off?

The first line of defense against this objection is to point out that a right to autonomy-supporting education goods is not same as a right to autonomous flourishing. Consider again my pursuit of carpentry as a social practice: if autonomous flourishing were a right, it would follow that society would have to allocate to me the resources (educational and otherwise) necessary in order to experience success in the pursuit of that goal. If carpentry were not a practice in my community, it might require the establishment and subsidization of something like a carpentry society in order to ensure that the practice was there for me to flourish through. But the right to higher education only states that I have *a right to the opportunity* to experience autonomous flourishing in existing social forms and that this opportunity may not be constrained for morally irrelevant reasons.[8] The expensive tastes objection does not apply to the right to higher education because the right to higher education is not founded on the idea that all citizens ought to experience equality of welfare.

One might still insist that the fact that the resource costs involved in creating opportunities for my autonomous flourishing are much higher than the resource costs for other citizens makes my goal an expensive taste. My freely chosen preference to learn carpentry is therefore one that I should be responsible for. There are a number of points we can raise against this objection.

First, it is simply not accurate to claim that educational resources are being allocated to me in order to satisfy a mere preference. If opportunities for autonomy-support were one and the same as opportunities for preference satisfaction the objection would be warranted. But as Arneson puts it, "satisfaction of these expensive and trivial preferences does little to advance the person's genuine well-being. Social resources devoted to satisfaction of preferences the individual mistakenly deems important are rightly viewed with a jaundiced eye as money down the drain" (2000; p. 513). The desire to become a carpenter may seem trivial to some. However, as I have argued (most especially in chapter 4) the allocation of educational resources is warranted *in virtue of the significance that the individual assigns to successful participation in that social form in the context of a self-determined life*. That is to say, we are talking about opportunities that will contribute, in a meaningful way, to the autonomous flourishing of citizens. These are not the same as an opportunity to satisfy preferences.

What if I were to pursue a self-directed goal that was significant for me but was in reality trivial in just the sense that Arneson speaks? Recall, once again, that the right to higher education obligates the state to provide a range of educational pathways sufficiently diverse in order to ensure that citizens can access an adequate range of valuable social forms and practices. But the fact that an individual believes that a self-directed goal counts as a valuable social practice does not make it so. Social forms and practices depend on recognition by, and participation of, other citizens.[9] They must have some welfare-conferring properties that make engagement in that practice worthwhile for a critical number of citizens. In fact, investment in valuable social practices (unlike the mere satisfaction of preferences) entails an obvious social return logically connected to personal autonomy: citizens who are interested in a particular social practice are better off—more likely to flourish—when there are more citizens engaged in that same practice. The tri-athlete who has nobody to race with—even though they may spend many months training entirely on their own—cannot flourish through their practice.[10]

The characterization of higher education provision as an individual, subjective taste is inaccurate. Nothing in a rights-based account requires that the state ensure that higher education institutions provide opportunities for citizens to realize goals that are obviously frivolous and make no serious contribution to a person's (or the larger community's) well-being. As Arneson also puts it, whims and mistaken obsessions are expensive tastes. But it is not unfair to allocate resources so that citizens can obtain objectively worthy goods (such as autonomous flourishing) (p. 514).

Second, the charge of expensive tastes is arbitrarily "backwards" looking, given the role of educational goods in the support of citizen's autonomous flourishing. My self-directed goal is to become a professional carpenter. I am allocated some amount of educational goods in support of the pursuit of that goal. Let us also say that carpentry is a valuable social practice and that my successful participation in that practice will contribute to my autonomous flourishing. Now imagine three different scenarios. In the first scenario I graduate and realize my self-directed goal: I am a professional carpenter. In the second scenario I graduate and end up doing something valuable but altogether different from carpentry. Educational goods still supported my access to that other activity. In the third scenario I graduate but cannot find any work, and I end up doing something frivolous with my time instead. According to the expensive tastes objection, the allocation of goods was just in the first and second scenarios, but unfair in the third. But this makes little sense: the justness of an allocation would here depend on unpredictable outcomes that arise after the fact. What makes the allocation of educational goods (as opposed to an expensive taste) just should turn on the extent to which such allocations furnish *opportunities* for autonomous flourishing, not on an individual's success or failure in capitalizing on those opportunities after graduation.[11]

Third, the expensive taste objection loses even more of its force when we recognize that the right to higher education functions to support autonomous flourishing alongside other liberty-maximizing institutions within the basic structure. To be sure, some citizens will have self-directed goals that will not require as much an allocation of higher education goods as other citizens. But these citizens may require support from other basic social institutions. Health care is an obvious example. And some citizens pursue goals that require a greater use of the legal system (for non-nefarious reasons) than others. Citizens with children consume more educational resources than those without.

If the fact that citizen A's self-directed goals require a mix of supporting goods different from citizen B were a sufficient reason to judge that the self-directed goals of citizen A are an expensive taste, it would follow that *any* citizen who requires a mix of autonomy-supporting goods different from some other group of citizens has an expensive taste. And if this were true, it would mean that in order to avoid resource allocations that do not run afoul of the expensive tastes objection, the basic structure would have to ensure that each citizen receives exactly the same package of educational, health, and other related goods. This would be a disastrous constraint on a liberty-maximizing conception of justice whose point and purpose is to ensure that citizens can freely pursue self-directed goals and in which the allocation goods, in order to succeed in this purpose, must be responsive to those choices.

Finally, the role of choice in the allocation of goods leads to one final version of the expensive tastes objection. This objection states that citizens should take some responsibility for their freely chosen goals. For young citizens this threshold of responsibility is perhaps higher than that of children, but not by much. But there are citizens who are further along in life and may have failed in their pursuit of such goals. Or they may have failed to set any goals at all. Consequently, they find themselves in need of educational goods. For example, there are adult citizens who forgo attending a university in their younger years and come to see that this choice was a mistake. Or they went to a university and should have pursued a trade. Some citizens choose social forms and practices that die out, either in the labor market or in community life more generally. Such citizens, not the state and the public purse, should take responsibility for their choices. Educational goods become an expensive taste when they are allocated to citizens who make imprudent choices. Why should the prudent citizen experience a decrease in resources in order to provide additional chances for these citizens?

Here we need to take great care in terms of what it means to be responsible for the costs of failure. When a person fails to realize a self-directed goal—or to set goals at all—they experience costs to their autonomous flourishing and their self-worth, opportunity costs in term of the time and effort they could have allocated to other pursuits (or worthwhile pursuits, in the case of the non-goal setter), and so on. It is appropriate to require citizens to take responsibility for these costs. But it is not clear why taking moral responsibility for one's failure requires that one be disqualified from receiving public support in the pursuit of further opportunities. For those who experience success without adversity, self-directed success might seem like a matter of pure agency. Take talent, stir in some effort, and the magic of human flourishing will be sure to follow. But it almost never plays out that way, in reality. Failure is not an expensive taste. It is part of the human condition. If failure were an expensive taste, it would mean a society where good luck reigns morally supreme.[12]

The Right to Higher Education and Ideal Theory

The second version of the "unfeasibility" objection says that the ideal grounds on which the right to higher education is justified will, once we take into consideration the non-ideal realities of our world, *fail* to justify allocating resources to a system of higher education founded on that right. Where the expensive tastes objection proceeds from the fact that some citizens choose self-directed goals that require higher education goods and others do not, this objection proceeds from the fact that some citizens cannot choose higher education goods through no fault of their own, and this makes the allocation of educational resources to higher education unfair. Here is how this objection might go:

The argument for the right to higher education is grounded in the claim that educational goods have a key role play in supporting the autonomous flourishing of citizens—a key metric of welfare in a liberal society. The argument also claims that this role has political and public relevance over a complete life, for young citizens developing basic capacities for autonomous reflection and judgment as well as older citizens living out a good life *in media res*. In this picture, compulsory education sets the foundation for autonomous flourishing. Post-compulsory education helps to ensure that all citizens have opportunities to realize such flourishing throughout life. Taken together, these two institutions help to realize liberty-maximizing requirements of justice in which citizens must be free to pursue the good without arbitrary or unjust constraints. However, in order for these requirements to be satisfied in practice, we must assume that the compulsory education system functions under "ideal conditions." By ideal conditions we mean this system is in full compliance with liberty-maximizing requirement of justice: it is fairly funded and ensures that all citizens sufficiently develop their capacity for personal autonomy.[13] This, because otherwise they will not be in a good position to take advantage of the autonomy-supporting resources that a right to higher education would have to offer.

In order for this objection to work we have to assume that the prevailing inequalities in compulsory schooling come down to a lack of resources. But systemic inequalities in education can arise for a host of reasons that have nothing to do with the absolute level of resources: the structure of the system, the way that current resources are allocated, efficiency issues, class and racial discrimination, and so on. But it's certainly possible that more resources could reduce inequality, and addressing this objection head-on allows us to emphasize other aspects of the argument. Therefore, I will accept this assumption and carry on.

There are many ways in which the compulsory educations systems that we currently have are unequal and a long way off from full compliance. This has two implications. First, it means that shifting resources into a rights-based higher education system is going to do more to benefit those who are lucky enough to have experienced a decent compulsory education. And it would empower these people, but not others, to lead flourishing lives simply because of the unequal circumstances many children find themselves in. This would go against liberty-maximizing requirements of justice. Second, the way to mitigate this problem is to make investment in the compulsory education system a priority until that system gets close to something like full compliance, or the ideal, and only then should we focus on allocating resources to higher education. And because we are unlikely to ever achieve full compliance in the compulsory system, the right to higher education must always remain an *unrealizable* ideal.

The objection supposes that the successful justification of the right to higher education depends on ideal conditions, i.e., what higher education should look like in a society where resources are allocated fairly and everyone is in full compliance with norms of justice and fairness. But this is not how the argument works. To be sure, *if* we had an ideal society a rights-based system of higher education would have to be a part of it. Yet, this is not because such an institution would be required in order for society to realize some kind of distributive ideal. My justification is grounded in what is necessary (but not sufficient) in order for a society to be a fully liberal one. The claim is that *the practice* of higher education as a right-based institution is a constitutive feature of any politically liberal framework, and that our current institutional practice should strive for better alignment with the rules and constraints stipulated by this right. In this respect, my approach is closer to what James Gledhill (2014) calls "transcendental institutionalism" in order to distinguish it from theories that aspire to "perfect justice." The right to higher education is, on a transcendental view, a fuller realization of what education must mean for *our* social world and not (only) for a perfect world of ideal theory (see Gledhill, 2014, p. 675).

Should the fact that an institution necessary for such a society might incidentally generate a certain amount of inequality be a sufficient reason to abolish that institution? The answer is clearly, "no." It would be like saying that the legal system should be abolished because, in our non-ideal world, some citizens have more access to justice than others. Of course, we can argue for distributive norms that regulate the allocation of resources *between* different institutions of the basic structure once the right to higher education (and its endogenous distributive norms of openness, diversity, and public provision) has been established at an institutional level. Defending the right to higher education does not require that we bury our head in the sand about difficult trade-offs, efficiency considerations, and the like.

What if one were to insist that the practice of allocating public resources to colleges, universities, and trade schools instead of K-12 schools is unjust, regardless? That is to say, the correct inter-institutional distributive norm for the allocation of limited resources between compulsory and post-compulsory schools is one that makes compulsory schooling a priority.

The force of this objection derives, in part, from the egalitarian intuition that we should make sure that everyone has a decent capacity *for* autonomous flourishing before we allocate resources to boost the attainment of autonomous flourishing among those who have already acquired such a capacity. An allocation of educational goods to a personally autonomous adult (who was lucky to have received a good basic education) could have gone to improve the foundational educational experiences of a less well-off child in our "non-ideal" school system. The allocation to educational resources to adults with a decent basic education therefore increases the inequality between those who were lucky to get that decent basic education and those who were not.

Such an intuition, insofar as it fails to consider other moral goods, is too demanding. Consider the principle that this intuition calls for: scarce resources that promote the well-being of citizens over a complete life should always be allocated on a priority basis to more "foundational" stages of that life. But consider what this prioritarian principle would warrant in practice. For example, massive investments in pediatric care could arguably do a great deal to mitigate the unjust health outcomes that many children experience through no fault of their own. But health care resources are scarce. The principle therefore recommends that we should hold off making significant public investment in adolescent, adult, or senior health care provision until we have perfected the pediatric system. There are three reasons for thinking that this arrangement is undesirable.

First, it would commit us to denying health care to citizens who need it simply because they happen to be older. But if the rationale for allocating resources to health care in the first place is because such care plays an important role in one's capacity to lead a good life, we need an argument for why the good life of very young citizens has more value than that of older citizens.

Perhaps a utilitarian argument could suffice. We could say that younger children have more flourishing ahead of them, and we want more flourishing in the world. So, let's make them a priority. But this leads to a second objection: citizens would not get very much value from the excellent foundational health care that they received as children if there were little to no allocation of resources for them later on in life where accidents and illness are common. In fact, the absence of public health care provision for adults would place less well-off citizens at a disadvantage relative to other citizens in terms of the value that they can derive a quality childhood healthcare experience. The latter can afford to pay for such care, privately, for example, while less well-off citizens would not have access to that infrastructure.

Second, the principle leads to something of a slippery slope. Perhaps we can reallocate health care resources away from seniors to more foundational stages of life. But then, why not reallocate away from middle-aged adults for the same reason? And we can get even better, more just pediatric health care if we cut public provision to young adults, and even more if we cut provision for adolescents, and then older children. The principle gives us no reason to stop. The same considerations apply to education: by cutting funding for grade 12 we can make grades 1–11 that much more funded, that much more just. And so on.

The natural solution to this slippery slope is to incorporate a stopping point: priority investment in health care (and education) should extend right up until that point at which citizens reach the age of majority and can take moral responsibility for any future decisions they make in either sphere. But note how the incorporation of such a "responsibility-sensitive" criterion transforms the principle. It would no longer be justified on the grounds that there is greater utility in allocating resources to more foundational stages of life, with the fact that there are fewer resources left over for later stages being an unfortunate consequence. It would mean there *is* no right to such resources *in principle* beyond the age of majority because citizens at this stage and after should take full responsibility for any distributive differences that may arise between them in terms of their autonomous flourishing.

How, then, could the principle be altered in order to stave off all these morally counterintuitive outcomes? The answer just is that the right to education (across all stages of life) places moral constraints on how far an egalitarian regime may permissibly go in seeking to mitigate non-ideal circumstances in more foundational stages (in the provision of, say, early childhood education). Once we recognize these moral constraints, we can make further arguments about the relative priority and utility of certain approaches to educational resource allocation between different stages of life. But we cannot justify an allocation that leaves the higher education system a merely "formal" right. In other words, the unfeasibility objection does not defeat the right to higher education; rather, the right to higher education explains why one cannot appeal to "unfeasibility" in order to justify the refusal to allocate resources to the post-compulsory level in favor of a more "ideal" compulsory education. Distributive perfection can be the enemy of the good.

Third, there is an important sense in which the argument for the right to higher education is more attuned to "non-ideal realties" than the objection itself. It would be a good thing if a system of compulsory schooling perfectly funded and fully compliant with norms of justice meant equal prospects for autonomous flourishing later in life, socioeconomically as well as in other domains, with any differences coming down to talent and effort. But is this feasible? Autonomous flourishing depends on the realization of self-determined goals. But as I have argued, the fair allocation of resources is no guarantee of success. In our non-ideal world people can fail to take advantage of educational opportunities and resources, or take advantage of those resources but fail to succeed nonetheless. Sometimes this is due to plain bad luck.

Good people can make bad decisions. And if we want citizens to set goals and strive to achieve them, we should be willing to provide further opportunities in the event of failure. Part of the value of the right to higher education is that it provides opportunities for people who want to try again. And these opportunities will be especially important for citizens who may not have gotten a fair deal in their compulsory school experience in the first place and, as adults, are willing to invest time and effort in order to compensate for that earlier, unfair treatment.[14] When it comes to the pursuit of self-determined goals, our intuitions about luck and fairness should run in a humanistic direction.

Conclusion

In this concluding chapter I have addressed a number of potential objections to the right to higher education. My aim in addressing these objections is, in part, to provide a more detailed picture of what this conception could mean for higher education policy, governance, and practice. First, I showed how this conception can be treated as an end state by which current and future developments in the growth and expansion of higher education can be judged as desirable or undesirable, just or unjust. Second, I addressed two variations of the charge that the right to higher education places too much value on the importance of higher education goods, leading to allocations of liberal state resources that leave citizens worse off and less equal. The upshot of my reply to these objections is that the liberal democratic right to higher education is a distributive priority. This, because it is necessary for any open society that takes citizens' free and equal pursuit of the good life seriously.

Notes

Chapter 1

1. This does not mean that the provision of higher education proceeds without any concern for public and political interests. For example, the Universal Declaration of Human Rights stipulates that a "higher education should be *equally accessible* to all on the basis of *merit*" (UNDHR Article 26, emphasis mine).
2. Once having chosen a higher education, a number of student rights and guarantees may apply. The evolving U.S. tradition of *in loco parentis* is a good example (see Szablewicz and Gibbs, 1987).
3. Higher education is out of reach for many, even though the returns from higher education remain high, in large part because its costs continue to rise. But why do they rise? One explanation is that higher education is delivered as a service and not a product. Therefore, the cost of a higher education can remain fixed unlike, say, a television, which gets cheaper as the technology used to produce it becomes more efficient. For a detailed discussion of this and other causes see Archibald and Feldman (2014). For an economic analysis of the role of market competition and income inequality in contributing to the social stratification of the American higher education system see Clotfelter (2017).
4. When that cosmetic need interrupts our normal range of function, as in the case of severe disfigurement, cosmetic surgery is seen to be necessary on medical grounds and is therefore free. Citizens can, of course, debate what counts as necessary and this can/will change over time.
5. For an excellent example of such a policy, see the U.K. government's Department for Business, Innovation and Skills (BIS) Economics Paper No. 14 (2011b).
6. For a contemporary policy example, see *Higher Education: Students at the Heart of the System* (BIS, 2011a).
7. There is an important debate in the literature about the extent to which higher education institutions, especially elite ones, should train their students to be citizens who work to mitigate the injustices of our imperfect societies. I engage with this debate in chapter 2.

8. McCowan (2012a) offers one of the few attempts to justify higher education as an individual right. His account is highly recommended for anyone interested in the question of educational rights and higher education. While my approach shares some broad similarities (the relevance of access across various stages of life, for example) his account is justified in reference to international law and conceives of the right as opening access to *universities* as traditionally understood.
9. These educational interests—though they may be *implemented* differently across different national systems—define what higher education systems look like in liberal states. Student and professors may not explicitly have these interests in mind. The history professor who is fascinated by Rome's fall and is trying to show her students why they should also find it fascinating is not (usually) thinking of their students as "sovereign" consumers (until course evaluations are due, perhaps). Nor is she necessarily seeing herself as part of a larger system that allocates valuable socioeconomic opportunities in accordance with some ideal of distributive fairness and fairness. But these are interests define the way that system functions, all the same.
10. This approach to the justification of basic rights, and its relevance for higher education, is described in greater detail in chapter 3.
11. The justification of an education for autonomy and the legitimate authority of the liberal state to promote such an aim is a contested one. I address this debate in chapter 2, and again in chapter 5.
12. I further discuss the relationship of the right to higher education to the basic structure in chapter 4.
13. For a Dworkinian analysis of higher education funding, see Colbun and Lazenby (2016).
14. There is a debate over which of these two conditions of distributive justice should take priority. In the Rawslian tradition these conditions are given lexical priority, with individual equality of opportunity taking priority over the difference principle, which states that inequalities should benefit the least well of in society (Rawls, 1971/1999). Brighouse (2014) and Brighouse and Swift (2006) have argued that there are grounds for thinking that the difference principle should take priority in the educational domain. Bou-Habib (2010) has defended the lexical priority of the difference principle in higher education. I discuss distributive implications of a right to higher education in chapter 6.
15. Note that I do not claim that scholars and policy makers have never argued for what a higher education should look like in terms of aims and goals.

Much has been written on this topic (see, for example, Gibbs, 2017). My point is that arguments for the justice and fairness of higher education are not usually informed by strong claims about what individual adult citizens are owed in terms of an education. I discuss this shortcoming in more detail in chapter 3.

16. Recent data suggests that in the United States a strong economy has led to higher education applicants placing less emphasis on economic interests and a greater focus on personal and intellectual development in contrast to the years following the Great Recession (Eagan et al., 2016).

17. "The desires and aspirations that individuals happen to have at any given moment enjoy no default moral authority. Antecedently, there is no more reason to endorse the status quo with respect to the distribution of desires and interests than there is to endorse the existing distribution of property" (Scheffler, 2006, p. 104). See also Rawls: "Combined with an index of primary goods the principles of justice detach reasons of justice not only from the ebb and flow of fluctuating wants and desires but even from sentiments and commitments" (1999, p. 190).

18. This can include the ways in which different institutions within a system of higher education behave. For example, the contemporary higher education context has seen a dramatic rise in status competition between institutions, which arguably both wastes resources and generates inequalities between individuals who are best able to access the most "status-conferring" elite institutions, and those who cannot. See Brown (2018).

19. For a philosophical analysis of the ethical costs many citizens from less well-off backgrounds may incur through their pursuit of upward social mobility through higher education, see Morton (2019).

Chapter 2

1. McCowan (2012b) highlights an important distinction between the contributions that higher education makes to civic or public culture incidentally through disciplines such as philosophy and the creative arts, on the one hand, and the effects of a higher education curriculum that aims to directly increase the civic capacities of citizens, on the other.

2. For an excellent overview of the terms of the debate, see Schouten (2018). For a civic educational defense of autonomy education, see Callan (1997) and Gutmann (1995).

3. There are some notable exceptions to this formulation. Ben Colburn (2010) has argued that a commitment to liberal neutrality actually entails a commitment to autonomy. I share Colburn's view that the state should be concerned with equality of autonomy between citizens, and that this means a state that protects equal access to those conditions that support autonomy (pp. 84–85). I do not think that this position requires a commitment to liberal neutrality, however, for reasons I detail in chapter 5.
4. For a helpful discussion of the liberal-communitarian debate in education, see Feinberg (1995).
5. I challenge the applicability of the neutrality restriction on liberal political authority to higher education in chapter 5.
6. As Davis and Neufeld point out, there are actually (at least) two versions of the convergence thesis (p. 48–49). The first version states that both autonomy and civic education draw from the concept of equal moral respect for persons, and so they do not really differ in terms of their practical educational commitments. The second version, which they attribute to Eamonn Callan (1996;1997), is the version I deal with here. This is because I agree, along with Davis and Neufeld, that the first version underplays the difference between politically liberal and comprehensively liberal conceptions of respect.
7. This is based on a well-known distinction between neutrality of aim, neutrality of justification, and neutrality of effect. Neutrality of effect is generally understood to be an unreasonable restriction on liberal political authority. See Arneson (2003).
8. As McDonough (2016) also puts it, "The long-term survival and flourishing of liberal democratic political values and institutions *depends to some extent on a critical mass of individual citizens* having certain dispositions, attitudes and qualities of character rather than others" (p. 229, emphasis mine).
9. Not everyone needs to bear the costs of civic engagement in all spheres of civic life. See, for example, a rule-utilitarian explanation for voter turnout (Coate and Conlin, 2004).
10. This amounts to the idea that a compulsory civic education in higher education is justified if it were successful in the creation of a civic elite. In addition to the downsides of such an approach for personal autonomy, which I address later, we can also add some empirical doubts. Jennifer Morton (2021) has advanced an argument showing that the very citizens who we might wish to enter into such a civic elite (such as marginalized citizens) are so transformed by their educational experience that it undermines their ability to advance the interests of the marginalized groups from

whence they came. In short, an elite civic education seems to create a new interest group: civic elites.

11. As Galston (1991) puts it, "If citizenship means anything, it means a package of benefits and burdens shared, and accepted, by all. To be a citizen of a liberal polity is to be required to surrender so much of your own private conscience as is necessary for the secure enjoyment of what remains. To refuse this surrender is in effect to breach the agreement under which you are entitled to full membership in your community." (p. 51).

12. For a variation on this claim see Brighouse and McAvoy (2009). They argue that higher education allows citizens to access unearned advantages and, for this reason, these institutions should shape such students so they that they are motivated to work for the benefit of the less advantaged. Note that this, and arguments like it (Anderson, 2007, p. 621) apply to a non-ideal higher education system that works to distribute advantages to the few through elite and highly selective institutions, especially in the United States (Brighouse and McAvoy, 2009, p. 168). They are not intended, as far as I can tell, to serve as a justification for the basic aims of higher education in a liberal society, ideally conceived.

13. This is a debatable empirical claim, however, with some arguing that absolute income level is what matters for political stability (see Posner, 1997).

14. One could object that many post-compulsory students are not "adults." For example, one could claim that young people high school graduates are not fully mature and should be treated in a paternalistic fashion. If this were true, the objection looks to be more in favor of the idea that we should raise the age of a compulsory, paternalistic education, not extend paternalistic norms into the post-compulsory context.

15. This touches on the larger debate in political philosophy about the role of "ideal" and "non-ideal" theorizing in general and the philosophy of education in particular. Readers interested in this distinction should at work by Valentini (2009; 2012) and the symposium issue of the journal, *Educational Theory* (2015) which features a number of articles on the contribution of ideal and non-ideal theorizing to questions of educational justice. I address the ideal/non-ideal distinction in more detail in Chapter 7.

16. There is some empirical data the supports the view that more education actually serves to *increase* political polarization. See for example Drummond and Fischhoff (2017).

17. For a recent example see the introduction of compulsory Indigenous course requirements (ICRs) in some Canadian universities. Tanchuk et al (2018), mirroring the political stability argument outlined in this chapter,

have claimed that such requirements are justified, in part, on the grounds that graduates are likely to become members of a civic elite and therefore must have a robust understanding of the nation-to-nation relationship for a successful post Truth and Reconciliation Era. Does a commitment to autonomy mean that ICRs and similar initiatives would be impermissible in higher education on the face of it? Not necessarily. The value of autonomy is just that—a value. This value has to be balanced against other values that define a liberal society. It may mean, for example, that the aims of transitional justice are warranted given the exceptionally nonideal circumstances of states with a colonial history, such as Canada. But it is important that we explicitly understand such policies as being exceptional, warranted by the intolerable non-ideal conditions, and that such policies put a strain on the core values and aims of higher education in a liberal society.

18. There is one final way to rescue practical convergence worth noting. One could argue that citizens who see higher education as a way to advance their own aims and goals are simply mistaken. They should understand that the aim of higher education is just to prepare citizens for service to society and that an interest in being qualified for this role should be their main reason for voluntarily choosing it. That is to say, any student who really understands what a higher education is about should see civic education as being logically connected to their self-determined goals. The consequence of this move, however, would be that the argument from civic education has nothing to do with the value of autonomy at all. Under this conception, a higher education restricts the range of meaningful educational options for citizens to a single path: a civic education focused on public service. To be sure, a small number of citizens might see an alignment between their own educational goals and this aim, but such alignment is a matter of luck, not purpose. The public and political role of higher education outlined here may cut closer to what one might call a "civic republican" conception of higher education, one defined by the cultivation of civic virtues and a sense of public purpose. The idea of this role has a long tradition in the American higher education context (Boyte and Kari, 2000) and has growing influence in the United Kingdom, likely as a reaction to the marketization of U.K. universities (Annette, 2005). Perhaps an argument could be made that a civic republican conception can be justified as basic to a civic republican political framework. I leave that argument to others. But my wager is that it would be a difficult argument to pull off. It is not clear to me how the civic virtues and public purposes ascribed

to a civic republican system of higher education would not be more appropriately sought out through compulsory basic education for all. This is especially so given the neo-republican emphasis on the value of *equal* citizenship (Pettit, 1989). The idea that you would have one class of citizens who are "excellent" citizens, and another class who are even more "excellent," seems to run decidedly counter to the republican ideal of equal citizenship.

19. I set aside a possible variation on Huemer's argument that I believe the defender of compulsory civic higher education would need to address: that just as citizens in general may reasonably differ on matters of justice, students may reasonably differ both in terms of the extent to which their access to higher education unfairly advantages them in some way, the extent to which that unfair advantage warrants extra civic effort on graduation, as well as the *form* that this extra effort should take. For example, is the political libertarian who, on graduation, dedicates his or her best years to advancing libertarian public policy—in a civic and well-reasoned manner—making up for the advantages that they received by virtue of their higher education? The defender of civic education who would say "no" has the burden of showing that their beliefs about injustice and unfair advantage are not an illiberal imposition of their (reasonable) conception of justice on the student's (reasonable) conception. My point is that there appears to be an assumption that the way graduates will compensate for their advantages (or recognize them as advantages that require redress in the first place) will align with the theorist's own views about justice and fairness. But insofar as a graduate's views are reasonable we have no reason to expect, or require, them to address their advantage in precisely the same way that the theorist expects.

Chapter 3

1. I go into greater detail about the implications of my account for the public funding of higher education in chapter 6.
2. This is sometimes referred to in the Rawlsian literature as "the original position" but sometimes more broadly in the liberal tradition as "the moral point of view" (Habermas, 1990), the Categorical Imperative (Kant, 1964/1785) or the "judicious spectator" (Hume, 1978/1888). The aim here is to identify *generalizable* interests—interest that apply equally to each and every individual.

3. The political conception of the person as a method for reasoning about justice falls within the broader tradition of transcendental theories of justice. For a discussion of this tradition and its distinctiveness from "transcendent" theories of the more Platonic variety, see Gledhill (2014).
4. An account of primary goods, or needs, "must be combined with a political conception of citizens as free and equal. With this done, we then work out what citizens need and require when they are regarded as such persons and as normal and fully cooperating members of society over a complete life" (Rawls, 1999, p. 178).
5. Though this is disputed on grounds of liberal neutrality. See chapter 2 and chapter 5.
6. The distributive political ideal underlying this claim is termed "luck egalitarianism." For an overview see Knight (2013).
7. Segall (2007) has argued that this broadened interpretation of equality of opportunity is not open to Daniels. He counters that, for Rawls, opportunity is linked to competition. Yet, those aspects of a life plan that citizens later focus on (by Daniel's lights) are not by nature competitive (pp. 351–352). Note that this does not mean that Daniels could not broaden the idea of a life plan and, on this basis, argue that a principle of justice other than equality of opportunity can explain health care as a primary good. That is to say, Segall's objection is focused on equality of opportunity as the principle that best explains health care as a primary good, not on health care *as* a primary good.
8. For a helpful account of the implications of the Razian account for basic education see the many works of John White, including his *Education and the Good Life* (1990).
9. While an individual may not have the capacity to live autonomously in the achievement sense of the term, they nonetheless retain the status of a being with intrinsic moral value and deserving of basic moral respect. Such citizens are entitled to the basic goods or resources necessary for a decent life owed to any person, which may include access to a certain kind of education. The implications of these entitlements for arguments about distributive justice fall outside the scope of the argument developed here, but see Nussbaum (2009) and Kittay (2013).
10. "The mistake . . . is the hidden assumption that while an environment supports autonomy through providing adequate opportunities to individuals, this fact does not affect the nature of the opportunities it provides" (Raz, 1986, p. 392).

11. Rutger Claassen, building from capability theories of justice, has cached out this distinction in terms of a conception of agency (autonomy and freedom) divided between internal and external capabilities (2017). Claassen offers a complex theory that aligns with many of the features that I take to be informative of the value of education in adulthood, such as entry into and exit from social practices and effective freedom. However, while his account rightly stresses the relationship between agency and *access* to real options in life (as opposed to, say, mere rational deliberation about such options) he endorses an exclusively instilling conception of education, where education is essential for cultivating the internal mental and physical capabilities needed for setting and pursuing ends *in general* (p. 1293). Access to options is here mainly a problem of negative freedom (non-interference) which downplays what I wish to stress: the role of education in enabling individuals to enter into *particular* social practices successfully and flourish within them.

Chapter 4

1. Similarly, Simmons (2001) has defended what he calls the *external justification* view of institutional obligations: "Institutions, in short, are not normatively independent, and the existence of an institutional 'obligation' is, considered by itself, a morally neutral fact. Institutional obligations acquire moral force only by being required by external moral rules" (p. 96). In our case, the relevant external moral rule is the provision of needed goods to liberal citizens. There are also "internally" justified role obligations: obligations that arise by virtue of a person's role within the institution itself. For example, the fact that many hospitals are centrally located may justify an obligation on the part of hospitals to provide swift transportation to outlying citizens in the event of a medical emergency. But such obligations come after the external justification, not before. If there were no moral obligation to provide health care, the internal obligation to provide an ambulance service would be a much weaker one, normatively speaking.
2. One could argue that we have grounds for denying free shelter to those who can afford to pay for it. True enough. However, there are instances in which paying for a good undermines the value of that good, even for those who can afford to pay. See chapter 6, in which I argue that students who can afford to pay or borrow for a higher education nonetheless can

experience unreasonable constraints on the autonomy-supporting value of that education.
3. O'Brien does not describe them as policies that universities and colleges could be *compelled* to undertake subject to the political authority of the liberal state. But if higher education is part of the basic structure, and political principles apply to the institutions of the basic structure, this seems to be the right way to describe them. (Harvard, for example, is unlikely to abolish legacy admissions through their own initiative.)
4. For more on the implications of parental partiality for political justice and equality, see Swift and Brighouse (2009) and Kolodny (2010).
5. For a similar conclusion, but from an epistemic justice perspective, see Kotzee (2018).
6. For an example of such an analysis applied to the parental choice of school see Swift (2003; 2004) and Brighouse and Swift (2009).
7. A similar account is offered by Neufeld and Van Schoelandt (2014). See also Steven Wall's critique of John Rawls' account of the special value of political liberty over non-political basic liberties. As Wall puts it, political liberties are "rightly subordinate to liberties that make it possible for people to pursue a wide range of different, but valuable, conceptions of the good" (2006, p. 265).
8. Hodgson is well aware that Rawls sees citizens as having a capacity for justice alongside a capacity for a conception of the good, but his account of the basic structure rests on a "person's *interest in developing and exercising* her capacity for a conception of the good" (2012, pp. 312–313, fn 24, emphasis mine).
9. For a detailed theoretical and empirical analysis of the role of existing social services in supporting autonomy, see Ben-Ishai (2012).
10. In the literature on distributive justice this is sometimes called "levelling down." See Temkin (2002).
11. Readers familiar with the philosophical literature will recognize that I am employing a concept/conception distinction in the manner most famously used by John Rawls in his *Theory of Justice* (2009).
12. Note that O'Brien comes close to something similar (footnote 56, p. 35): "[O]n some versions of political liberalism, a privileged subset of basic liberties, the political liberties, are to have their fair value for each citizen, i.e., are to have the *same* value for each person who wishes to exercise them. (Normally, basic liberties will enable different people to get different amounts of what they want, given their different situations and endowments of natural and social primary goods.) And it might be

thought that, in a modern liberal democracy, only if the higher-education sector is reformed in the ways suggested in the representative proposals could this condition be met."

13. In fact, one serious challenge faced by the modern university is the demand that it supports scholarly life as a valuable social form while at the same time functioning as a nearly exclusive gateway to many other external social forms and practices (gainful employment being most prominent among them). For a thoughtful discussion of such pressures, see Collini (2012).

14. See chapter 5, for example, where I argue that the state may exercise political authority to protect forms of knowledge and understanding that are plausibly linked to valuable social forms, but are underfunded or undersupplied.

15. The precise threshold at which liberty-maximizing justice puts too much pressure on the fixed values of the university would require a more detailed account of what is sufficient for a university to function. This account lies beyond those scope of the present argument. But see chapter 7, where I discuss admissions standards under a rights-based conception.

16. For a detailed account of a basic education for autonomous flourishing and why participation in the labor market is insufficient for such flourishing see White (1990).

17. I have argued that the right to higher education is not justified in terms of social returns or public goods. So, is this not a contradiction? No, because the social returns arising from this right are one and the same as the individual benefit that the right is meant to protect. Support for individual autonomy redounds on the environment through which individuals flourish by enabling other citizens to *join us* in our engagement with valuable social forms and practices. This is quite different from the claim that we should support higher education by virtue of contingent outcomes that have no direct relationship with the *telos* of the institution.

Chapter 5

1. This problem is not specific to the conception of higher education that I'm defending. The question of political authority and higher education is something that anyone who wishes to make strong claims about the values and aims (and consequent reforms to) higher education must contend with. For example, educational theorists have made a variety of arguments

about the goods that higher education should be aiming for, such as emancipation, social justice, and civic virtue (Barnett, 1990; Furlong, Furlong, and Cartmel, 2009; Newman, 1996; Nussbaum, 1997). But it is implausible to think that institutions of higher education have the ability and motivation to pursue such goods through their own efforts, especially when doing so may be a threat to their ability to persist under free market conditions. Accordingly, one way to assess an argument for the public and political values and aims of higher education is to look carefully at the justifiability of the kind and degree of political authority that would be necessary in order to make those values and aims possible in real terms.

2. See, for example, the policy future envisioned by Ernst and Young (2012).
3. See, for example, a proposal by Canada's Conservative Party to cut federal funding to Canadian universities that do not adequately protect freedom of expression (Levitz, 2017). In the United Kingdom, the right to raise tuition fees is being linked to student satisfaction and well-being (Hall, 2017).
4. Gerald Dworkin has defended a freedom-maximizing argument for paternalism based on Mill's claim that it is legitimate to prevent someone from selling themselves into slavery (1972, pp. 75–76). Arneson counters that this argument undervalues the right of persons to freely choose conceptions of the good that deviate from often idealized, but no less particular, freedom-loving conceptions of the good (1980, p. 474).
5. See chapter 1.
6. A good example would be the U.K. White Paper *Students at the Heart of the System* (Department for Business, Innovation, and Skills, 2011a), which argues that student choice should be in the "driving seat" of the higher education system.
7. A liberal state philosophically committed to anti-perfectionism could nonetheless endorse educational policies aimed at promoting the good life. For a discussion on the distinction between philosophical and political perfectionism, see Chan (2000, pp. 34–38). Chan claims that perfectionist policies can be defended on the basis of arguments that are essentially neutral with respect to questions of the good life. For example, a democratic majority of citizens might vote in favor of a sugar tax on soda. The policies arising from such a vote are perfectionist in character because they involve the state playing an active role in promoting good lives, but the legitimacy of the policy rests on a neutral, anti-perfectionist, decision-making procedure. My argument is aimed at the idea that higher education systems should be philosophically committed to liberal perfectionist ideals.

NOTES 231

8. Raz argues that there are certain common situations in which directives are helpful. This example highlights situations where there is a need to co-ordinate the behavior of individuals. For a list of these common situations, see Raz (1986, p. 75) and Hershovitz (2011).
9. This is sometimes called the procedural independence, or internalist, conception of autonomy. Procedural independence conceptions see successful autonomous decision-making as the outcome of an internal, reflective process.
10. I discuss "range of options" as a necessary condition of autonomous flourishing in chapters 3 and 4. I also discuss the relationship between this condition and political authority, shortly.
11. One prominent example would be what Denise Réaume calls *participatory goods*, goods in which each individual requires the participation of other individuals in order to enjoy that good (1988, p. 9). Examples include different cultural activities and athletic pursuits.
12. See Raz (1988, pp. 1234–1235). See also *The Morality of Freedom* (Raz, 1986, pp. 49–53).

Chapter 6

1. See Elliott and Lewis (2015), Cooke et al. (2004), Haultain et al. (2010), and Rothstein and Rouse (2011).
2. One might object that personal autonomy is just as discretionary as other goods that are generated through a higher education. Therefore, one cannot justify full public funding higher education as a right on autonomy-supporting grounds. However, recall that I have argued (in chapter 3) that personal autonomy is a basic interest, primary good, or presumptive public good. It is essential to liberal citizenship irrespective of the actual preferences of citizens. Following from this claim, I argue that higher education is one critical way in which the liberal state can realize this presumptive public good.
3. Note that this argument does not take into full account the risks for students who take on student loans but do not graduate. These students are left with loan repayments while experiencing little to no college premiums to help support such repayments. See Bowen and McPherson (2017). Some critics counter that debt and payment—having skin in the game—plays an important role in motivating students to work hard and succeed. This looks to be a psychologically plausible claim. But should we see this kind of motivation as being *right* or *necessary*? An autonomy-supporting

account does not take the view that economic motives ought not play a motivational role. But it sees legitimate economic motives as but one type of a broader spectrum of motives, i.e., motives linked to a person's self-determined goals. I say "legitimate" because there is a difference between a person who freely acts out of economic self-interest and someone who must act out of economic self-interest in spite of what they actually take to be their self-determined aim or goal. Put differently: an autonomy-supporting conception of higher education argues that citizens should be motivated by their interest in autonomous flourishing and the realization of their self-determined goals. Economic success is but one of a number of goals that a person can have. But students should not be *compelled* to receive a higher education for economic reasons.

4. The right to higher education is premised on the free pursuit of a good life as an essential feature of liberal citizenship (chapter 3). Autonomy-supporting goods are facilitative of that pursuit. But we can also understand such goods as a way of mitigating the risks endogenous to that pursuit. People's life plans can go awry for reasons of Sowellinan cosmic injustice. They can fail to achieve their self-determined goals. The value of the goals that they put their faith in may curdle through no fault of their own. Life is full of precarity, and in a free and open society whose social forms and practices presume a certain degree of knowledge, understanding, and skill, education becomes essential to the mitigation of (and perception of) these risks. From this perspective, educational goods address what, in the old welfare state language of the Beveridge and Marshal Reports, are Universal Risks (as opposed to mere Employment Risks). For an overview of these foundational reports and the distinction between Universal and Employment Risk see Jaffary (1943). I address this relationship between risk and autonomy in chapter 7, as well.

5. Colburn and Lazenby (2016) apply Dworkin's hypothetical insurance argument to justify public funding for higher education. But because they see higher education access as (partly) dependent on desire and talent they do not conclude that an argument would justify full public funding. In reviewing the insurance argument for full public funding, for example, they say that "[there are reasons that] speak in favour of taking out some kind of insurance to ensure that you have the option to attend university if you have the desire and talent. However, it is also important to remember that when the time comes you may not have the desire or the talent to attend university. You will therefore want the option of not attending university to remain a good option" (p. 594). See my comments that follow

about desire and talent as criteria that undermine the equal benefits of public funding.
6. I discuss the implications of the right to higher education for the ethics of admissions in chapter 7.
7. "Repaying Your Student Loan." 2018. UCAS. January 11, 2018. https://www.ucas.com/student-finance-england/repaying-your-student-loan.
8. One could perhaps claim that "status" is a self-determined goal for some, and that status-conferring institutions by their very nature require students to pay more. The exclusivity is the point. I don't see any good argument for recognizing "status" as a social practice, and so it does not make sense as a self-determined goal, conceptually speaking. But even if it were, "status" is incidental to the value of education on an autonomy-supporting conception. By this I mean that educational goods advance self-determined goals by virtue of the knowledge, understanding, and skill they confer. "Status" has no obvious relationship to these goods. It is simply a carry-over effect of exclusivity.
9. Interestingly, recent empirical data (Brint et al., 2020) suggest that contemporary U.S. elite higher education does not produce political and economic leaders so much as *cultural* elites (writers, artists, journalists). If true this may have implications for the non-ideal analysis of elite higher education. It raises questions about how effective, for example, diversifying such a system of elite formation would really be in creating better informed political and economic leadership.
10. For an empirical study of parental anxiety about upward social mobility and educational competition for college places among the wealthy see Ramey and Ramey (2010).

Chapter 7

1. I not only argue that higher education *can* serve this function, but also that it *ought* to do so. See especially chapter 4. However, in this section I am addressing a line of criticism likely to arise among those with an historicist mindset. Such critics might agree that a rights-based conception of higher education is the best among all possible alternatives but, even so, maintain that the historical "critical period" in which such an institutional framework could have come about has long passed. And rather than indulge in a desirable "what if," or counterfactual, it is better to hold a higher education system accountable to the normative presuppositions of its own era.

2. As Strauss said of political philosophy and history,

> Without the experience of the variety of political institutions and convictions in different countries and at different times, the questions of the nature of political things and of the best, or the just, political order could never have been raised. And after they have been raised, only historical knowledge can prevent one from mistaking the specific features of the political life of one's time and one's country for the nature of political things. Similar considerations apply to the history of political thought and the history of political philosophy. But however important historical knowledge may be for political philosophy, it is only preliminary and auxiliary to political philosophy; it does not form an integral part of it. (1949, p. 30)

3. Scott (2019) claims that Trow came to embrace technologically driven aims of a universal system: "In the 1970s Trow, like many of his contemporaries, focused on Higher Education's responsibility to educate all citizens, which was no longer adequately discharged by their universal participation in secondary education. Later, again like many others, his gaze shifted to Higher Education's responsibility for producing the more highly skilled workforce demanded by advanced economies" (p. 502). On my account we should see Trow's thinking as moving in the normatively wrong (or more accurately, narrow) direction.

4. This does not mean that, say, students pursuing a trade should never be required to engage with the humanities or basic sciences as part of their training. But the place of such teaching—its justification and consequent pedagogical approach—will differ. For example, there is a relevant difference between teaching philosophy as a research discipline, on the one hand, and as a cognitive perspective that can transform how one can understand oneself and the world around them, on the other.

5. In Kotzee and Martin (2013) we link these benefits to scholarly success and achievement. This assumes that the singular goal of the university, as distinct from higher education more generally, was the production of certain epistemic goods.

6. It would be more accurate to say that the conception of talent following from brightest and best selection is too narrow given the broader aims and purposes of the institution. The virtues required for success in political philosophy as a profession are not likely to fully overlap with the excellences necessary for enjoying the discipline for its own sake.

7. Nothing about my account is meant to suggest that political philosophy should only be found in elite institutions. I use this example because I want

to highlight how the openness condition applies in a way that is consistent with the right to higher education but can also recognize good-faith arguments in favor of a high bar for selection.
8. See Arneson (2000) for an extended discussion of the distinction between welfare and opportunity for welfare. Here Arneson claims that opportunity for welfare defeats the expensive tastes objection on a number of counts. Note that Arneson's account is an early example of "luck egalitarianism," and I deal with luck egalitarian features of my account in section three of this chapter.
9. For a detailed discussion of Razian social forms and their source of value see Crisp (1997).
10. During the Covid-19 lockdowns of 2020, many endurance athletes flocked to virtual racing, which was then heralded by some as the future of endurance sport. Since then, enthusiasm has greatly waned and athletes have become impatient for a return to racing. There are many features of the practice of racing—camaraderie, encouragement, anticipation at the start line, the hugs and celebrations at the finish line, the shared sense that everyone has endured and persevered—that the virtual events do not at all capture.
11. For any system of social cooperation there will be free riders who take advantage. We could imagine some citizens choosing higher education goods and failing to do much with those goods. But rejecting a rights-based system (or any system that involves public allocation) in order to abolish free riders is a scorched earth approach to distributive fairness that does not do much good for anyone.
12. The reader well-versed in the distributive justice literature will note the luck egalitarian sympathies in this part of my argument. See Knight (2013).
13. Laura Valentini (2012) draws a distinction between three different meanings that one can ascribe to the ideal/non-ideal distinction. One of them is "full compliance" versus "partial compliance." The objection I am engaged with in this section is based on this distinction. But another distinction is between "end-state" versus "transitional" theory. End-state ideal theory uses a conception of justice in order to determine goals, or the broader direction, in which our reforms should move society in order to make it more just. My application of the right to higher education to Trow's stage theory of higher education would be one example of an "end-state" approach. Note that Sen (2006) has offered an influential critique of end-state theory. I agree with Simmon's (2010) rejoinder to that critique: we

need end-state accounts in order to know both the moral permissibility of, and progress of, our transitional efforts.
14. There is one further counterargument one can make against the unfeasibility objection. It is worth factoring in the returns of a right to higher education for the family. We have reason to think that the benefits of educational goods and opportunities allocated to adults, especially adults from less well-off circumstances, will redound on their families and their children in a positive way.

Works Cited

Anderson, E. (2007). Fair opportunity in education: A democratic equality perspective. *Ethics, 117*(4), 595–622.
Annette, J. (2005). Character, civic renewal and service learning for democratic citizenship in higher education. *British Journal of Educational Studies, 53*(3), 326–340.
Archibald, R. B., & Feldman, D. H. (2014). *Why does college cost so much?* Oxford University Press.
Arneson, R. J. (1980). Mill versus paternalism. *Ethics, 90*(4), 470–489.
Arneson, R. J. (1982). The principle of fairness and free-rider problems. *Ethics, 92*(4), 616–633.
Ameson, R. J. (1990). Liberalism, distributive subjectivism, and equal opportunity for welfare. *Philosophy and Public Affairs, 19*(2), 158–194.
Arneson, R. J. (2000). Welfare should be the currency of justice. *Canadian Journal of Philosophy, 30*(4), 497–524.
Arneson, R. (2003). Liberal neutrality on the good: An autopsy. In S. Wall (Ed.) *Perfectionism and neutrality: Essays in liberal theory*, 191–218. Rowman and Littlefield.
Assembly, U. G. (1948). Universal declaration of human rights. *UN General Assembly, 302*(2), 14–25.
Austin, D. A. (2013). The indentured generation: Bankruptcy and student loan debt. *Santa Clara Law Review, 53*(2), 329–420.
Barnett, R. (1990). *The idea of higher education.* Society for Research into Higher Education and Open University Press.
Ben-Ishai, E. (2012). *Fostering autonomy: A theory of citizenship, the state, and social service delivery.* Penn State Press.
Bishop, B. (2009). *The big sort: Why the clustering of like-minded America is tearing us apart.* Houghton Mifflin Harcourt.
Blake, M. (2001). Distributive justice, state coercion, and autonomy. *Philosophy & Public Affairs, 30*(3), 257–296.
Bou-Habib, P. (2010). Who should pay for higher education? *Journal of Philosophy of Education, 44*(4), 479–495.
Bowen, W. G., & McPherson, M. S. (2017). *Lesson plan: An agenda for change in American higher education.* Princeton University Press.
Boyte, H. C., & Kari, N. N. (2000). Renewing the democratic spirit in American colleges and universities: higher education as public work. In

T. Erhlich (Ed.) *Civic Responsibility and Higher education*, 37–59. Rowman & Littlefield.

Brand, J. E. (2010). Civic returns to higher education: A note on heterogeneous effects. *Social Forces, 89*(2), 417–433.

Brighouse, H. (1998). Civic education and liberal legitimacy. *Ethics, 108*(4), 719–745.

Brighouse, H. (2004). Paying for higher education: Are top-up fees fair? *Éthique et Économique, 2*(1), 1–11.

Brighouse, H. (2009). Moral and political aims of education. In H. Siegel (Ed.) *The Oxford handbook of philosophy of education*, pp. 35–52. Oxford University Press.

Brighouse, H. (2014). Equality, prioritising the disadvantaged, and the new educational landscape. *Oxford Review of Education, 40*(6), 782–798.

Brighouse, H., & McAvoy, P. (2009). Privilege, wellbeing, and participation in higher education. In Y. Raley and G. Preyer (Eds.) *Philosophy of Education in the Era of Globalization*, 165–180. Routledge.

Brighouse, H., & Swift, A. (2006). Equality, priority, and positional goods. *Ethics, 116*(3), 471–497.

Brighouse, H., & Swift, A. (2009). Legitimate parental partiality. *Philosophy & Public Affairs, 37*(1), 43–80.

Brint, S., German, K. T., Anderson-Natale, K., Shuker, Z. F., & Wang, S. (2020). Where ivy matters: The educational backgrounds of US cultural elites. *Sociology of Education, 93*(2), 153–172.

Brown, R. (2018). Higher education and inequality. *Perspectives: Policy and Practice in Higher Education, 22*(2), 37–43.

Callan, E. (1996). Political liberalism and political education. *Review of Politics, 58*, 5–33

Callan, E. (1997). *Creating citizens: Political education and liberal democracy.* Clarendon Press.

Chan, J. (2000). Legitimacy, unanimity, and perfectionism. *Philosophy & Public Affairs, 29*(1), 5–42.

Chan, J. (2012). Political authority and perfectionism: A response to Quong. *Philosophy and Public Issues, 2*(1), 31–41.

Claassen, R. (2013). Public goods, mutual benefits, and majority rule. *Journal of Social Philosophy, 44*(3), 270–290.

Claassen, R. (2017). An agency-based capability theory of justice. *European Journal of Philosophy, 25*(4), 1279–1304.

Clotfelter, C. T. (2017). *Unequal colleges in the age of disparity.* Harvard University Press.

Coate, S., & Conlin, M. (2004). A group rule-utilitarian approach to voter turnout: Theory and evidence. *American Economic Review, 94*(5), 1476–1504.

Cohen, G. A. (1997). Where the action is: On the site of distributive justice. *Philosophy & Public Affairs*, 26(1), 3–30.
Colburn, B. (2010). *Autonomy and liberalism*. Routledge.
Colburn, B., & Lazenby, H. (2016). Hypothetical insurance and higher education. *Journal of Philosophy of Education*, 50(4), 587–604.
Collini, S. (2012). *What are universities for?* Penguin.
Cooke, R., Barkham, M., Audin, K., Bradley, M., & Davy, J. (2004). Student debt and its relation to student mental health. *Journal of Further and Higher Education*, 28(1), 53–66.
Costa, Victoria M. (2004). Rawlsian civic education: Political not minimal. *Journal of Applied Philosophy*, 21(1), 1–14.
Crisp, R. (1997). Raz on well-being. *Oxford Journal of Legal Studies*, 17(3), 499.
Cullity, G. (1995). Moral free riding. *Philosophy & Public Affairs*, 24(1), 3–34.
Daniels, N. (1985). *Just health care*. Cambridge University Press.
Daniels, N. (2001). Justice, health, and healthcare. *American Journal of Bioethics*, 1(2), 2–16.
Davis, G., & Neufeld, B. (2007). Political liberalism, civic education, and educational choice. *Social Theory and Practice*, 33(1), 47–74.
Dee, T. S. (2004). Are there civic returns to education? *Journal of Public Economics*, 88(9–10), 1697–1720.
Department for Business, Innovation, and Skills. (2011a). *Higher education: Students at the heart of the system*. Department for Business, Innovation and Skills, UK.
Department for Business, Innovation, and Skills. (2011b). BIS economics paper no. 14: Supporting analysis for the Higher Education White Paper. Department for Business, Innovation and Skills, UK.
Department for Business, Innovation, and Skills. (2013). BIS research paper no. 133: Things we know and don't know about the Wider Benefits of Higher Education: A review of the recent literature. Department for Business, Innovation and Skills, UK.
De Wijze, S. (1999). Rawls and civic education. *Cogito*, 13(2), 87–93.
Drummond, C., & Fischhoff, B. (2017). Individuals with greater science literacy and education have more polarized beliefs on controversial science topics. *Proceedings of the National Academy of Sciences*, 114(36), 9587–9592.
Dworkin, G. (1972). Paternalism. *Monist*, 56(1), 64–84.
Eagan, K., Stolzenberg, E. B., Ramirez, J. J., Aragon, M. C., Suchard, M. R., & Hurtado, S. (2016). *The American freshman: National norms fall 2016*. Higher Education Research Institute, UCLA.
Eaton, C. *The ivory tower tax haven: The state, financialization, and the growth of wealthy college endowments* [Research brief]. Hass Institute for a Fair and Inclusive Society, UC Berkeley.

Elliott, W., & Lewis, M. (2015). Student debt effects on financial well-being: Research and policy implications. *Journal of Economic Surveys, 29*(4), 614–636.

Englund, T. (2002). Higher education, democracy and citizenship—the democratic potential of the university? *Studies in Philosophy and education, 21*(4-5), 281–287.

Ernst & Young. (2012). *University of the future: A thousand year old industry on the cusp of profound change.* https://www.bu.edu/edtechcouncil/files/2012/10/Ernst-Young-Higher-University-of-the-Future-2012.pdf

Feinberg, W. (1995). The communitarian challenge to liberal social and educational theory. *Peabody Journal of Education, 70*(4), 34–55.

Ferdman, A. (2019). A perfectionist basic structure. *Philosophy & Social Criticism, 47*(7), 862–882.

Fowler, T. (2011). The limits of civic education: The divergent implications of political and comprehensive liberalism. *Theory and Research in Education, 9*(1), 87–100.

Fullinwider, R. K., & Lichtenberg, J. (2004). *Leveling the playing field: Justice, politics, and college admissions.* Rowman & Littlefield Publishers.

Furlong, A., Furlong, P. A., & Cartmel, F. (2009). *Higher education and social justice.* McGraw-Hill Education (UK).

Galston, W. (1989). Civic education in the liberal state. In N. L. Rosenblum (Ed.), *Liberalism and the moral life* (pp. 89–101). Harvard University Press.

George, R. P. (1995). *Making men moral: Civil liberties and public morality.* Clarendon Press.

Gibbs, P. (2017). *Why universities should seek happiness and contentment.* Bloomsbury Publishing.

Gledhill, J. (2014). In defense of transcendental institutionalism. *Philosophy & Social Criticism, 40*(7), 665–682.

Gourevitch, A. (2012). Debt, freedom, and inequality. *Philosophical Topics, 40*(1), 135–151.

Gutmann, A. (1995). Civic education and social diversity. *Ethics, 105*(3), 557–579.

Habermas, J. (1990). *Moral consciousness and communicative action.* MIT press.

Hall, R. (2017, June 19). Why should I care about the teaching excellence framework? – explainer. *The Guardian.* https://www.theguardian.com/higher-education-network/2017/jun/19/why-should-i-care-about-the-teaching-excellence-framework-explainer

Hart, H. L. A. (1955). Are there any natural rights? *The Philosophical Review, 64*(2), 175–191.

Haultain, S., Kemp, S., & Chernyshenko, O. S. (2010). The structure of attitudes to student debt. *Journal of Economic Psychology, 31*(3), 322–330.

Heath, J. (2005). Liberal autonomy and consumer sovereignty. In J. Christman and J. Anderson (Eds.) *Autonomy and the challenges to liberalism: New essays*, 204–25. Cambridge University Press.
Hershovitz, S. (2011). The role of authority. *Philosopher's Imprint, 11*(7), 1–19.
Hodgson, L. P. (2012). Why the basic structure? *Canadian Journal of Philosophy, 42*(3–4), 303–334.
Huemer, M. (2013). *The Problem of Political Authority*. Palgrave MacMillan.
Hume, D. 1978 (1888). *A treatise of human nature* (L. A. Selby-Bigge, & P. H. Nidditch, Eds.; 2nd ed.) Oxford University Press.
Jaffary, S. K. (1943). Social security: The Beveridge and Marsh Reports. *Canadian Journal of Economics and Political Science/Revue canadienne de economiques et science politique, 9*(4), 571–592.
Julius, A. J. (2003). Basic structure and the value of equality. *Philosophy & Public Affairs, 31*(4), 321–355.
Kant, I. (1964/1785). *Groundwork of the metaphysic of morals* (H. J. Paton, Trans.). Harper Torchbooks.
Keller, S. (2002). Expensive tastes and distributive justice. *Social Theory and Practice, 28*(4), 529–552.
Kittay, E. F. (2013). *Love's labor: Essays on women, equality and dependency*. Routledge.
Klosko, G. (1987). Presumptive benefit, fairness, and political obligation. *Philosophy & Public Affairs, 16*(3), 241–259.
Klosko, G. (1990). The obligation to contribute to discretionary public goods. *Political Studies, 38*(2), 196–214.
Knight, C. (2013). Luck egalitarianism. *Philosophy Compass, 8*(10), 924–934.
Kotzee, B. (2018). The epistemic goods of higher education. *Philosophical Inquiry in Education, 25*(2), 116–133.
Kotzee, B., & Martin, C. (2013). Who should go to university? Justice in university admissions. *Journal of Philosophy of Education, 47*(4), 623–641.
Labaree, D. F. (2016). An affair to remember: America's brief fling with the university as a public good. *Journal of Philosophy of Education, 50*(1), 20–36.
Lang, D. W. (2005). Financing higher education in Canada. In M. Kretovics and S. O. Michael (Eds.) *Financing higher education in a global market*, 71–120. Algora Publishing.
Levitz, S. (2017, August 16). Andrew Scheer's free speech pledge wouldn't apply in Toronto case: Spokesman. *CTV News*. https://www.ctvnews.ca/politics/andrew-scheer-s-free-speech-pledge-wouldn-t-apply-in-toronto-case-spokesman-1.3548920
Martin, C. (2019). The case against (actually existing) higher education: Human capital, educational signaling, and justice. *On Education. Journal for Research and Debate. 2*(6), 1–5.
McCabe, D. (2001). Joseph Raz and the contextual argument for liberal perfectionism. *Ethics, 111*(3), 493–522.

McCowan, T. (2012). Opening spaces for citizenship in higher education: Three initiatives in English universities. *Studies in Higher Education*, 37(1), 51-67.

McCowan, T. (2019). *Higher education for and beyond the sustainable development goals*. Palgrave-MacMillan.

McKay-Panos, L. (2016). Universities and freedom of expression: When should the Charter apply? *Canadian Journal of Human Rights*, 5, 59.

Miller, S. (2010). *The moral foundations of social institutions: A philosophical study*. Cambridge University Press.

Morton, J. M. (2021). The miseducation of the elite. *Journal of Political Philosophy*, 29(1), 3-24.

Morton, J. M. (2019). The miseducation of the elite. *Journal of Political Philosophy*.

Morton, J. M. (2019). *Moving up without losing your way: The ethical costs of upward mobility*. Princeton University Press.

Murphy, L. B. (2017). Institutions and the demands of justice. In D. Reidy, (Ed.) *John Rawls* (pp. 3-44). Routledge.

Neufeld, B., & Van Schoelandt, C. (2014). Political liberalism, ethos justice, and gender equality. *Law and Philosophy*, 33(1), 75-104.

Newman, J. H., & Turner, F. M. (1996). *The idea of a university*. Yale University Press.

Nozick, R. (1974) *Anarchy, State, and Utopia*. New York: Basic Books.

Nussbaum, M. C. (1997). *Cultivating humanity: A classical defense of reform in liberal education*. Harvard University Press.

Nussbaum, M. (2002). Education for citizenship in an era of global connection. *Studies in Philosophy and Education*, 21(4-5), 289-303.

Nussbaum, M. C. (2009). *Frontiers of justice: Disability, nationality, species membership*. Harvard University Press.

Nussbaum, M. C. (2010). *Not for profit: Why democracy needs the humanities*. Princeton University Press.

Pettit, P. (1989). The freedom of the city: A republican ideal. In A. Hamlin & P. Pettit (Eds.), *The good polity*. Blackwell Publishers. 141-68.

Posner, R. A. (1997). Equality, wealth, and political stability. *The Journal of Law, Economics, and Organization*, 13(2), 344-365.

Ramey, G., & Ramey, V. A. (2010). The rug rat race. *Brookings Papers on Economic Activity*, 41(1), 129-200.

Rasmusen, E. (2004). An economic approach to gratitude, with implications for political obligation [Unpublished Manuscript]. http://rasmusen.org/papers/backburner/elves.pdf

Rawls, J. (2001). *Justice as fairness: A restatement*. Harvard University Press.

Rawls, J. (2005). *Political liberalism*. Columbia University Press.

Rawls, J. (2009). *A theory of justice*. Harvard University Press.

Raz, J. (1986). *The morality of freedom*. Clarendon Press.

Raz, J. (1988). Facing up: A reply. *Southern California Law Review, 62,* 1153–1235.
Raz, J. (2005). The problem of authority: Revisiting the service conception. *Minnesota Law Review, 90,* 1003–1044.
Raz, J. (2010). On respect, authority, and neutrality: A response. *Ethics, 120*(2), 279–301.
Réaume, D. (1988). Individuals, groups, and rights to public goods. *The University of Toronto Law Journal, 38*(1), 1–27.
Ronzoni, M. (2008). What makes a basic structure just? *Res Publica, 14*(3), 203–218.
Rothstein, J., & Rouse, C. E. (2011). Constrained after college: Student loans and early-career occupational choices. *Journal of Public Economics, 95*(1–2), 149–163.
Scheffler, S. (2006). Is the basic structure basic? In C. Sypnowich (Ed.) *The egalitarian conscience: Essays in honour of GA Cohen: Essays in Honour of GA Cohen,* 102–129. Oxford University Press.
Schouten, G. (2018). Political liberalism and autonomy education: Are citizenship-based arguments enough? *Philosophical Studies, 175*(5), 1071–1093.
Scott, P. (2019). Martin Trow's elite-mass-universal triptych: Conceptualising higher education development. *Higher Education Quarterly, 73*(4), 496–506.
Sen, A. (2006). What do we want from a theory of justice? *The Journal of Philosophy, 103*(5), 215–238.
Simmons, A. J. (1979). The principle of fair play. *Philosophy and Public Affairs,* 8(4): 307–337.
Simmons, A. J. (2001). *Justification and legitimacy: Essays on rights and obligations.* Cambridge University Press.
Simmons, A. J. (2010). Ideal and nonideal theory. *Philosophy & Public Affairs, 38*(1), 5–36.
Stiglitz, J. E. (1999). Knowledge as a global public good. In Grunberg, I., Kaul, I., and Stern, M. A. (Eds.). (1999). *Global public goods: international cooperation in the 21st century.* Oxford University Press. 308–325.
Strauss, L. (1949). Political philosophy and history. *Journal of the History of Ideas, 10*(1), 30–50.
Swift, A. (2003). *How not to be a hypocrite: School choice for the morally perplexed parent.* Routledge.
Swift, A. (2004). The morality of school choice. *Theory and Research in Education, 2*(1), 7–21.
Syme, T. (2018). The pervasive structure of society. *Philosophy & Social Criticism, 44*(8), 888–924.
Szablewicz, J. J., & Gibbs, A. (1987). Colleges' increasing exposure to liability: The new in loco parentis. *Journal of Law & Education, 16,* 453–465.

Tanchuk, N., Kruse, M., and McDonough, K. (2018). Indigenous Course Requirements: A Liberal-Democratic Justification. *Philosophical Inquiry in Education*, 25(2), 134–153.

Temkin, L. (2002). Equality, priority, and the levelling down objection. In Clayton, M. and Williams, A. (Eds). *The Ideal of Equality*, 126–161. Basingstoke.

Trow, M. (1973). *Problems in the transition from elite to mass higher education*. Carnegie Commission on Higher Education.

Trow, M. (1976). Elite higher education: An endangered species? *Minerva*, 14 (Autumn 3), 355–376.

Trow, M. (1989). The Robbins trap: British attitudes and the limits of expansion. *Higher Education Quarterly*, 43(1), 55–75.

Trow, M. (2000). From mass higher education to universal access: The American advantage. *Minerva*, 37 (Spring), 1–26.

Trow, M. (2007). Reflections on the transition from elite to mass to universal access: Forms and phases of higher education in modern societies since WWII. In J. F. Forrest & P. Altbach (Eds.), *International handbook on higher education* (pp. 243–280). Springer.

Valentini, L. (2009). On the apparent paradox of ideal theory. *Journal of Political Philosophy*, 17(3), 332–355.

Valentini, L. (2012). Ideal vs. non-ideal theory: A conceptual map. *Philosophy Compass*, 7(9), 654–664.

Wall, S. (1998). *Liberalism, perfectionism and restraint*. Cambridge University Press.

Wall, S. (2006). Rawls and the status of political liberty. *Pacific Philosophical Quarterly*, 87(2), 245–270.

White, J. (1990). *Education and the good life: Beyond the national curriculum*. Kogan Page.

White, J. (1997). Philosophy and the aims of higher education. *Studies in Higher Education*, 22(1), 7–17.

White, J. (2016). Justifying private schools. *Journal of Philosophy of Education*, 50(4), 496–510.

White, M. (2016). *Towards a political theory of the university: Public reason, democracy and higher education*. Routledge.

Index

For the benefit of digital users, indexed terms that span two pages (e.g., 52–53) may, on occasion, appear on only one of those pages.

Arneson, R. J., 207–9
autonomy. *See* autonomy-supporting conception of higher education; personal autonomy
autonomy-supporting conception of higher education
   distributive fairness conditions and, 172–75, 197
   fixed values of the university and, 111–14, 126
   institutions of higher education and, 92, 94, 102–3, 106
   internal aspects of autonomy and, 85
   liberalism and, 94, 110, 121, 188
   liberty-maximizing justice and, 107, 125, 153
   political conception of the person, 121
   public funding for higher education and, 157–58, 174, 176–78, 185
   resource allocations and, 207–11, 218
   rights-based conception of education and, 86, 89, 91, 108, 110–11, 122, 125, 157–58
   social forms and practices and, 110, 170
   socioeconomic equality and, 101–2
   student debt and, 167–70, 182

basic education. *See* compulsory basic education
basic structure of society
   controlling influence institutions and, 104–5, 107–8, 109
   distributive justice and, 105
   the family and, 99
   higher education institutions and, 12, 30, 94–103, 107–11, 115, 119–20, 125, 155, 192–93
   justice-maximizing authority and, 98–99
   liberalism and, 101
   liberty-maximizing justice and, 11–12, 104–5, 120–21
   personal autonomy and, 95, 100–1, 103, 106, 109
   pervasive influence institutions and, 103–4
   Rawls on, 28–29, 95, 99, 103–4
   socioeconomic equality and, 101–2
Bou-Habib, Paul, 159–60, 162
Brighouse, Harry, 158–60, 162
British Sea Power (band), v

Canada, 30, 88–89
civic education
   civic vocation argument and, 58–67
   compulsory basic education and, 42–51, 54–56, 62, 66–67

civic education (*cont.*)
  convergence thesis and, 45–47, 52–53, 58–59, 66–68
  divergent views regarding the good life and, 46–47, 53–54, 60–61, 62–63
  higher education and, 42–43, 49–68
  indoctrination objection and, 46–47, 53, 56, 68
  liberalism and, 43–47, 51–52, 67
  personal autonomy and, 42–47, 52–53, 56–59, 62, 64, 66–68, 182
  political stability and, 42–43, 44–51, 53, 56, 58, 67–68
  professional ethics education and, 60–62
  public funding for education and, 48–50
  as a public good, 44–45, 49
  tolerance and, 44–45
  voluntary nature of higher education and, 25–26
Claassen, Rutger, 161, 227n.11
compulsory basic education
  civic education and, 42–51, 54–56, 62, 66–67
  distributive fairness and, 31–32
  as a fundamental right, 1, 15, 18, 70–71
  higher education compared to, 18–27
  justice-maximizing authority and, 98–99
  liberalism and, 15, 21–22, 28–29, 30–32, 75, 128
  normative weight problem and, 8–9
  paternalism and, 9
  personal autonomy and, 28, 42, 43–44, 47–49, 57, 69, 74–75, 77, 86, 87, 128–29
  public funding for, 15, 18
  societal benefits from, 19
  as "special" good, 20–21, 28, 31–32
  state interventionism and, 28
  sunset clause regarding, 129–31, 142–43
  taxation supporting, 161
  universal access to, 3, 20–21
consumer sovereignty
  consumer protections and, 23–24
  contemporary higher education systems and, 10–11, 22–24, 31–32, 34
  individual dimension of higher education and, 26–27
  personal autonomy and, 23, 79
  state's limited role in higher education and, 23–24
contemporary higher education system
  consumer sovereignty and, 10–11, 22–24, 31–32, 34
  distributive fairness and, 10–11, 23–25, 31, 34
  privilege-based conception of, 18
  state's limited intervention in, 28
  status and selectivity in, 13–14

Daniels, Norman, 77–79
debt financing for higher education. *See* student debt
discretionary public goods, 161–63
distributive fairness
  compulsory basic education and, 31–32
  contemporary higher education systems and, 10–11, 23–25, 31, 34
  distributive consequences of higher education and, 26–27, 32–33, 188
  full public funding for higher education and, 12–13, 155, 164–67, 172–75, 185, 198

public funding for higher
education and, 5, 20–21, 33, 36–37, 159–60, 161, 165, 176
rights-based conception of higher
education and, 12–13, 191–92, 198
socioeconomic opportunities
from education and, 24–25, 33, 36–37, 38–39, 173–74

elite conception of higher education, 6, 193–94, 197–205
epistemic authority, 135

fair play principle, 50–51, 179–81
false consciousness, 10
the family, 99–100, 104
Ferdman, Avigail, 104
full public funding for higher
education
adequate options condition and, 164, 175, 183
alternative repayment scheme
objection to, 171, 176–79
distributive fairness conditions
and, 12–13, 155, 164–67, 172–75, 185, 198
fair play principle and, 179–81
liberty-maximizing justice
and, 171–85
majoritarian democracy as
potential means of achieving, 73
obligations to society for
beneficiaries of, 181–83
overshooting objection to, 171, 179–85
rights-based conception of higher
education and, 12–13, 158, 179, 198
students from wealthy families'
educational choices and, 184–85
unequal liberty objection to, 171, 172–76

Gledhill, James, 213–14
the good life
civic education and diverging
views regarding, 46–47, 53–54, 60–61, 62–63
labor market participation and, 116, 190–91
liberalism and, 11, 134–35
liberty-maximizing justice and, 11–12, 92, 105–6, 107, 210
personal autonomy and, 81, 83–84, 86, 89, 96, 105–6, 142–45, 147, 152
political conception of the person
and, 72
political stability and, 44–45
rights-based conception of higher
education and, 10, 88–89, 166, 173–75, 185
taxation and, 105
Gourevitch, Alex, 169

Habermas, Jürgen, 73, 92
Hart, H. L. A., 180–81
health care
economic security and, 88–89
equality of opportunity
and, 77–78
as presumptive public good, 161
Rawls's "basic structure of society"
and, 104
as a right, 70–71
societal benefit from, 20, 156
as "special" good, 20
taxation and, 161
utilitarian arguments
regarding, 215–16
Hodgson, Louis-Phillipe, 104–5
Huemer, Michael, 61, 225n.19

ideal theory conception of education, 13, 211–17
income inequality, 7–8, 16–17

the Internet as educational resource,
    92, 94, 114–15, 118
justice-maximizing authority, 98–
    100, 102, 104–5

Keller, Simon, 206
Klosko, George, 51, 73, 92, 162–63
Kotzee, Ben, 199, 202–3

liberalism
  anti-perfectionist liberalism and,
      131–36, 152
  autonomy-supporting conception
      of higher education and, 94,
      110, 121, 188
  basic structure of society and, 101
  civic education and, 43–47, 51–
      52, 67
  compulsory basic education
      and, 15, 21–22, 28–29, 30–32,
      75, 128
  directive educational authority
      and, 127–28, 132–33, 135–37
  distributive justice and, 53
  epistemic authority and, 135
  the family and, 99–100
  the good life and, 11, 134–35
  instrumental justification
      of educational authority
      and, 133–34
  literacy and, 21–22
  perfectionist liberalism and, 136–
      38, 152
  personal autonomy and, 28, 42,
      43–44, 46, 61, 69, 74–75, 76–77,
      94, 127–28, 131–38, 146, 152
  rights-based conception of
      higher education and, 8, 10–11,
      70, 75, 125–26, 185–86, 187,
      190, 195
  socioeconomic equality and,
      94, 101

liberty-maximizing authority
  directive educational authority
      and, 127–31, 135–36, 141
  distributive justice in higher
      education and, 131
  fixed values of normative
      institutions and, 111
  higher education and, 125–
      31, 142–52
  personal autonomy and, 148–49
  sunset clause regarding
      compulsory basic education
      and, 129–31, 142–43
  universities and, 113
liberty-maximizing conception of
    higher education
  distributive justice and, 153
  personal autonomy and,
      112, 212–13
  public funding for higher
      education and, 120–21, 153,
      155, 163–71
  student debt and, 120–21
liberty-maximizing justice
  basic structure of society and, 11–
      12, 104–5, 120–21
  equality and, 105, 108–9
  full public funding for higher
      education and, 171–85
  the good life and, 11–12, 92, 105–
      6, 107, 210
  personal autonomy and, 106–7
  public funding for higher
      education and, 165–66, 171
  rights-based conception of higher
      education and, 122, 125, 126–
      27, 149–50, 169–70, 187
  social forms and practices and, 120
  student debt and, 169–70
  universities and, 12, 106–7, 113
libraries as educational resource, 89–
    90, 92, 94, 114–15, 118, 161–62
loans. *See* student debt

mass conception of higher
  education, 6, 193-94
Mill, John Stuart, v
Miller, Seumas, 92-93, 100, 107
moral reasons for pursuing higher
  education, 34-39

normal justification thesis of
  authority, 139-42
normative institutions, 92-93,
  100, 107
normative stage theory of higher
  education, 192-205
Nussbaum, Martha, 41-42

O'Brien, David, 95-96, 97-102, 111

personal autonomy
  basic structure of society and, 95,
    100-1, 103, 106, 109
  civic education and, 42-47, 52-53,
    56-59, 62, 64, 66-68, 182
  compulsory basic education and,
    28, 42, 43-44, 47-49, 57, 69,
    74-75, 77, 86, 87, 128-29
  consumer sovereignty and,
    23, 79
  economic security and, 88-89
  environmental conditions of, 80-
    85, 89, 91
  the good life and, 81, 83-84, 86,
    89, 96, 105-6, 142-45, 147, 152
  independence condition and,
    143-48, 151-52
  instilling focus of education and,
    83-84, 87, 89
  internal conditions of, 75-77, 79,
    82-83, 84-85, 89
  liberalism and, 28, 42, 43-44, 46,
    61, 69, 74-75, 76-77, 94, 127-
    28, 131-38, 146, 152
  liberty-maximizing authority
    and, 148-49

  liberty-maximizing conception
    of higher education and,
    112, 212-13
  liberty-maximizing justice
    and, 106-7
  limits of one's own reason
    and, 143-44
  personal autonomy and, 11, 81-
    82, 91
  practical authority and, 145-46
  public funding for higher
    education and, 43-44, 181
  rights-based conception of higher
    education and, 11, 42, 68, 69,
    76-79, 83, 87-88, 89, 91-92,
    93-96, 100-2, 108, 109-10, 131,
    149-50, 165-66, 167-68, 191-
    93, 195-97, 199, 206-7, 209-10,
    212, 217
  self-determination and, 82-
    83, 87
  social forms and practices and,
    80-81, 85-86, 106, 109, 146-47
  supporting focus of education
    and, 83-84, 85-86, 87, 89
  value condition and, 143-46
  well-being and, 143-45
political conception of the person,
  72, 73-74, 91, 121
political stability
  civic education and, 42-43, 44-51,
    53, 56, 58, 67-68
  equality and, 53
  fair play principle and, 50-51
  the good life and, 44-45
  higher education and, 42, 49, 66-
    67, 70-71
  liberal democracy and, 42
  as a public good, 49-51, 70-71
pre-emption thesis of
  authority, 138-39
presumptive public goods, 51, 73,
  92, 161-64

public funding for higher education.
  See also full public funding for higher education
 autonomy-supporting conception of higher education and, 157–58, 174, 176–78, 185
 democratic society benefits argument regarding, 160–61
 distributive fairness and, 5, 20–21, 33, 36–37, 159–60, 161, 165, 176
 liberty-maximizing conception of higher education and, 120–21, 153, 155, 163–71
 liberty-maximizing justice and, 165–66, 171
 means testing and, 158–59, 165, 166–67
 personal autonomy and, 43–44, 181
 privilege-based conception of higher education and, 15–16, 49, 70
 public goods emerging from higher education and, 70–71, 163–64
 return on investment and, 120–21
 socioeconomic argument for, 158–64
 taxation and, 156, 162–63
 unequal benefits problem and, 161, 176
public goods
 civic education and, 44–45, 49
 contemporary higher education system and, 16
 discretionary forms of, 161–63
 higher education's contribution to, 70–71, 189
 knowledge and, 94, 134–35
 presumptive public goods and, 51, 73, 92, 161–64
 subsides to support undersupplied forms of, 134, 189

Rawls, John
 on the "basic structure" of society, 28–29, 95, 99, 103–4
 on liberalism and civic education, 43–44
 on pervasive influence institutions, 103–4
 on primary goods, 73, 92, 163
Raz, Joseph
 perfectionist account of authority by, 137–43
 on personal autonomy and flourishing, 11, 195
 on personal autonomy as project, 79–80
 on self-determined goals, 117
rights-based conception of higher education
 autodidact's objection to, 114–15, 118–19
 autonomy-supporting conception of higher education and, 86, 89, 91, 108, 110–11, 122, 125, 157–58
 distributive fairness and, 12–13, 191–92, 198
 diversity condition and, 12–13, 165, 198
 elite selectivity in admissions and, 200–4
 expensive taste objection to, 13, 120–21, 205–11
 full public funding of higher education and, 12–13, 158, 179, 198
 the good life, 10, 88–89, 166, 173–75, 185
 ideal theory conception of higher education and, 13, 211–17
 institutions of higher education and, 91–92, 93–94, 127
 justification of educational values of higher education and, 21–22

liberalism and, 8, 10–11, 70, 75,
    125–26, 185–86, 187, 190, 195
liberty-maximizing justice and,
    122, 125, 126–27, 149–50, 169–
    70, 187
non-exclusivity condition
    and, 155, 164–65, 174–75,
    183, 194–95
normative weight problem
    and, 8–9
openness condition and, 12–13,
    197–200
paternalistic aims problem and,
    9–10, 11
personal autonomy and, 11, 42, 68,
    69, 76–79, 83, 87–88, 89, 91–92,
    93–96, 100–2, 108, 109–10, 131,
    149–50, 165–66, 167–68, 191–
    93, 195–97, 199, 206–7, 209–10,
    212, 217
political conception of the person
    and, 72, 73–74, 91
readiness to learn condition and,
    1, 164, 199, 202–3
Robbins Report and, 6–7
socioeconomic equality
    and, 101–2
socioeconomic opportunity and,
    88–89, 96, 110
sufficientarian selectivity in
    admissions and, 199–200, 201–5
Robbins Report, 6–7

Schouten, Gina, 28, 48
social forms and practices
    autonomy-supporting education
        and, 110, 170
    elite institutions and, 200–1
    the good life and, 117, 150
    knowledge and, 94
    liberalism and, 86, 136
    most demanding versions
        of, 115–16

personal autonomy and, 80–81,
    85–86, 106, 109, 146–47
self-determination and, 146–47
social forms thesis and, 136
state-controlled education
    and, 122–23
supporting function of education
    and, 84
at universities, 100, 113, 115–
    16, 153
student debt
    alternative repayment schemes
        and, 171, 176–79
    autonomy-supporting conception
        of higher education and, 167–
        70, 182
    bankruptcy protection and, 15–16
    distributive fairness and, 168–69
    forgiveness of, 2–3
    income-contingent loans and,
        171, 176–79
    liberty-maximizing conception of
        higher education, 120–21
    liberty-maximizing justice
        and, 169–70
    macroeconomic impact of, 71–72
    means-tested public provisions
        and, 158–59
    privilege-based conception of
        higher education, 15–16, 33
    upward social mobility and, 169

taxation
    compulsory basic education
        and, 161
    the good life and, 105
    health care and, 161
    privilege-based conception of
        higher education and, 15–16
    public funding for higher
        education and, 156, 162–63
    rights-based conception of higher
        education and, 2–3

transcendental institutionalism, 213–14
Trow, Martin
　elite conception of higher education and, 193–94, 197–205
　mass conception of higher education and, 193–94
　Robbins Report and, 6
　stage theory of higher education and, 13, 187

United Kingdom, 6, 30, 83, 176, 197
universal higher education, 193–97
universities
　admissions policies at, 100, 199–205
　autonomy-promoting education and, 102–3
　as autonomy-supporting institutions, 113
　autonomy-supporting knowledge and, 114–21
　basic structure of society and, 97–103
　as controlling influence institutions, 107
　distributive justice and, 98
　fixed values of, 102–3, 111–14, 126
　justice-maximizing authority and, 98–100, 102
　liberty-maximizing authority and, 113
　liberty-maximizing justice and, 12, 106–7, 113
　social forms and practices at, 100, 113, 115–16, 153
　upward social mobility, 4, 16, 33, 38–39, 101–2, 109–10, 156, 167–68, 169

vocational education, 95–96, 101–2, 190–91

Wall, Steven, 80–81
White, John, 202–4